HITTING
THE HEADLINES
IN EUROPE

HITTING THE HEADLINES IN EUROPE

A Country-by-Country Guide
to Effective Media Relations

Cathie Burton Alun Drake

the Institute *of* Public Relations

**KOGAN
PAGE**

London and Sterling, VA

Publisher's note

Every possible effort has been made to ensure that the information contained in this book is accurate at the time of going to press, and the publishers and authors cannot accept responsibility for any errors or omissions, however caused. No responsibility for loss or damage occasioned to any person acting, or refraining from action, as a result of the material in this publication can be accepted by the editor, the publisher or any of the authors.

First published in Great Britain and the United States in 2004 by Kogan Page Limited

120 Pentonville Road
London N1 9JN
United Kingdom
www.kogan-page.co.uk

22883 Quicksilver Drive
Sterling VA 20166–2012
USA

© Cathie Burton and Alun Drake, 2004

ISBN 0 7494 4226 3

British Library Cataloguing-in-Publication Data

A CIP record for this book is available from the British Library.

Library of Congress Cataloging-in-Publication Data

Burton Cathie, 1960-
  Hitting the headlines in Europe : a country-by-country guide to effective media relations / Cathie Burton and Alun Drake.
      p. cm
   Includes index.
   ISBN 0-7494-4226-3
   1. Public relations--Cross-cultural studies. 2. Public relations--Europe I.
Drake, Alun. II. Title.
HM1221.B87 2004
659.2'094--dc22

                    2004006457

Typeset by Saxon Graphics Ltd, Derby
Printed and bound in Great Britain by Creative Print and Design (Wales), Ebbw Vale

Contents

Appendices

About the authors

Cathie Burton worked as a journalist for regional and national newspapers and radio stations before moving to France where she freelanced for Reuters and Agence France Presse. She then ran the press office at Wolverhampton Council for four years before becoming the spokesperson for the European Parliamentary Labour Party in Brussels and Strasbourg. Since 1994 she has worked in the Spokesperson's service of the Council of Europe, concentrating on the countries of central and eastern Europe and the Balkans.

Alun Drake began his journalistic career with the BBC, working in radio as a reporter at local, regional and national level, and in TV as a scriptwriter for the Nine O'Clock News and other flagship news programmes. After a short spell freelancing as a radio and TV reporter in London, he moved to Central Television in Birmingham as a reporter. Since 1996 he has been at the Council of Europe in Strasbourg, first as head of its TV, Radio and Photo service, and currently as broadcast press officer.

Although drawing extensively on the authors' recent professional experiences, this book is a private project, and any views expressed in it are those of the authors, and not of the Council of Europe.

About the Institute of Public Relations and the consultant editor

THE INSTITUTE OF PUBLIC RELATIONS

The Institute of Public Relations (IPR) has over 7,500 members, involved in all aspects of the public relations industry. It is the largest professional body of its type in Europe, with rigorous qualifications for membership (based on educational qualifications and/or multi-disciplinary experience) ensuring that standards are high and maintained. IPR runs several PR courses as well as Developing Excellence, a continuous professional development scheme. This is the only life-long learning scheme specifically designed for PR practitioners in the United Kingdom. Further information on the IPR can be obtained from the IPR Web site at www.ipr.org.uk

THE CONSULTANT EDITOR

Anne Gregory is Director of the Centre for Public Relations at Leeds Metropolitan University and the UK's only full-time Professor of Public Relations. Originally a broadcast journalist, Anne spent 10 years in public relations practice at senior levels both in-house and in consultancy before moving on to an academic career. Anne is President of the Institute of Public Relations and was created a Fellow in 1999. She initiated and edits the Institute's *Public Relations in Practice* series of books and is managing editor of the Journal of Communication Management.

Anne is actively involved in PR practice, being a non-Executive Director of South West Yorkshire NHS Mental Health Trust with special responsibility for finance and communication. She is also a practicing public relations consultant and trainer.

Foreword

Just about any general discussion on public relations these days will include certain key themes: globalization, 24/7, the impact of the Internet and the changing nature of the media.

Of course all these things are interrelated. Public relations is increasingly practiced in a global setting that requires a 24 hours a day, seven days a week service; where technology is used as a matter of course and where media relation still accounts for about 70 per cent of the business.

Given the scope of the public relations media remit alone, it's a massive relief when someone can provide the detailed knowledge needed to do the job professionally.

That's exactly what *Hitting the Headlines in Europe* does. Cathie Burton and Alun Drake share their extensive knowledge of media relations in Europe, drawn from many years experience working at the heart of the European Union and in the print and broadcast media.

This very practical guide gives an overview of what the European Union is and how it operates. It goes on to describe the media landscape, outlining the main media outlets and their requirements. It also gives an insight into some of the main European media trends. Against this background, the authors provide practical advice on how to set up a European press office, going into detail on very practical issues such as translation and interpreting. The written word, television and radio are comprehensively dealt with.

A key element of this book is the detailed country by country guide on the media. 43 such profiles make up a mini encyclopaedia of invaluable knowledge. From Andorra through to the United Kingdom the authors provide a brief history and current status report on each country's media, then describe the main press and broadcast organizations with hints about how to work with them.

This book will be of benefit to those already working in Europe, expanding their repertoire of knowledge about the accession nations and those countries on the fringes of the EU. For those who are just dipping their toes into the European water, it will prove a comprehensive reference guide, providing all that detailed information that is so time consuming and difficult to obtain.

By writing this book the authors have done a major service to the public relations industry, and many a practitioner will be grateful that they've committed their knowledge to paper.

Anne Gregory
Consultant Editor

Preface

When an American reporter asked the great British adventurer George Leigh Mallory why he wanted to climb Mount Everest, he replied 'Because it's there.' By contrast, our reply to the question 'Why did you write this book?' would be 'Because it's not there!' Despite hours of searching the Internet we have failed to find any title that comes close to covering the same ground as this book. While other aspects of media relations get comprehensive treatment, the European dimension is notable only by its complete absence. We find this curious, because communicating with journalists and other publics across cultural and linguistic barriers is a specialist skill (beyond the core competences of the PR professional), and one which is in increasing demand as Europe becomes ever more integrated on the economic and political fronts.

Even writing a basic press release requires a different approach when the intended recipients are from a range of diverse countries. News conferences need to have interpretation and press packs in several languages. Web sites and databases likewise have to be planned in a quite different way, as do products such as video news releases. In such a complex environment, there are pitfalls to be avoided and innovative strategies to be adopted, and linguistic skills will only get you part of the way. Drawing on our combined experience of working for an organization with 45 member countries, we have tried to outline the basic issues, the problems that may arise, and some suggestions on how to solve them. In the second part of the book, we provide media profiles of the 43 largest European countries, information that is a vital ingredient in a successful communication strategy.

We have written this book with multiple audiences in mind. It will obviously benefit those already working on the European media scene, either in the private sector, for a European institution or for a pressure group or charity. Similarly, those about to take up such a job, particularly non-Europeans, or Europeans who have only previously worked in their native countries, will also find it useful. Finally, although it is not intended as an academic work, students of public relations, particularly those intending to apply for jobs in the European sector, will learn more about the daily challenges of this fascinating branch of the public relations profession.

Acknowledgements

A book of this scope would have been impossible to write without the help of many colleagues, friends and other contacts who gave us precious advice and guidance. This was particularly important for the country profiles, where expertise from natives of the countries concerned was indispensable.

For the general chapters, we would like to thank Amanda Alexander of World Television, Tim Arnold of Arnold Broadcast, Piotr Azia of the European Broadcasting Union, Diederik Bangert of the European Commission's Europe by Satellite, Fiona Bartosch of Medialink, Niall Campbell of APTN, Tony Charlesworth, media consultant, Susanna Flood of CNN, Alan Hardy of PR Newswire, Helen Kearns of the European Parliamentary Labour Party, Nic Jakob of the European News Exchange, Geoff Meade of the Press Association, Gregory Pasche of Reuters, Julie Redman of Arnold Strategy, Alastair Wanklyn of Feature Story News and Sonia Winter of Radio Free Europe/Radio Liberty. More valuable professional input came from our friends John Boileau, Chris Burns, Jim Gibbons, Geoff Goff, Liz Hannam, Bridget O'Loughlin, Iain Pattison, Anja Rakhimpour and Ernst Übelacker. There was useful general feedback from Peter Howard, Hannah Jansen, Richard Thayer and Jayne Yeo. Robert Szymanski advised us on the work of professional interpreters.

For the country profiles, we were helped by colleagues at the Council of Europe and other international organizations, and by journalists and others living in the countries concerned. Our thanks go to Thorsten Afflerbach, Rosita Agnew, Arif Aliyev, Mida Babiliene, Sergei Bazarya, Stefano Bertozzi, Tatiana Bilankov, Dragan Bisenic, Toni Bissoni, Ansis Bogustovs, Ulrich Bohner, Laura Boian, Sergio Cantone, Anna Chelpanova, Eugene Cibotaru, Raquel Cordoba, Sarmīte Danne, Auron Dodi, Can Fisek, Letitia Fitzpatrick, Alessandro Fracassetti, Christine Gaffner, Henriette Girard, Daniel Gomes, Veronica Gomes, Andrew Grice, Matjaz Gruden, Robert Hajsel, Hartmut Haussman, Marina Irkho,

Andrew Jack, George Jashi, Ülla Jürviste, Kayhan Karaca, Anna Kehl, Ruth Kinet, Jan Kleijssen, Peter von Kohl, Alla Kotcherejkina, HansPeter Kleiner, Tibor Gergely Kovacs, Natalya Krasnoboka, Petr Kriz, Emil Krsteski, Zhanna Litvina, Angus Macdonald, Hanna Machinska, Arne Madsen, Dmitri Marchenkov, Ruben Markosyan, Atanas Matev, Ellen Mickiewicz, Goran Mihajlovski, Razvan Mitroi, Ólöf Ólafsðottir, Marta Onorato, Sarah Painter, Oleksander Pavlichenko, Anna Pelegri, Suzana Volf Pendic, Philippe Potentini, Marija Prokopcik, Aiste Ramanauskaite, Danguole Rokuiziene, Nora Rumbolt, Wolfgang Rössle, Kari Salo, Zoran Sekulic, Margherita Sforza, Ayten Shirinova, Guðrun Helga Sigurðardottir, Willy Soltvedt, Geo Stenius, David Stern, Lisa Kristin Strindberg, Pia-Mari Suomela, Svetoslav Terziev, Pall Thorhallsson, Valentina Tolic, Nikolai Topornin, Anna Trigona, Ivi-Triin Odrats, Tomas Venckevicius, Josef Vessely, Tetyana Vysotska, Susanna Wersall and Peteris Zilgalvis.

The lists of contact information at the back of the book were compiled and checked with the help of Athina Mariakaki and Marina Prokofjeva.

Finally, we would like to thank Council of Europe Secretary General Walter Schwimmer for giving us permission to write this book and our boss Renate Zikmund, at the Press and Spokesperson Division of the Council of Europe, for her support.

Part 1

Working with Europe's media

1

What do we mean by Europe?

Europe is a confusing place... and not just for the rest of the world. For years, the continent has grown; communities have sprung up, developed their own traditions and languages, been overthrown and repressed, and then reasserted themselves; minor kings have become major emperors and empires have toppled and become republics; borders have moved, then changed and then switched back again.

Europe defies analysis. Where is it, after all? Japanese tourists walking up the side of the Jungfrau would describe themselves as being in Europe – but the Swiss hiker next to them would refuse any connection with Europe's main institution, the European Union. A surfer on a Spanish beach looks over the Atlantic and thinks about the American surfing the Californian waves on the other side of the world – yet their continents reach out to each other across the Bering Sea. Can Turkey really be described as European if only 3 per cent of its land mass is on the European continent? What about the former republics of the Soviet Union – Turkmenistan, Kazakhstan, Uzbekistan? And how on earth can Greenland – floating off the coast of Canada – be considered as part of Europe, even if it is Danish?

Institutional Europe is even more confusing. What's the difference between the Court of Human Rights and the Court of Justice? The International Criminal Court and The Hague Tribunal? When is the Council of Europe not the Council of Europe but the European Council? No wonder the switchboards of the different institutions spend 50 per cent of their time redirecting calls from Brussels, to Strasbourg, to Vienna, to Geneva.

And non-Europeans can be reassured – even the Europeans are totally confused. You only need to survey newspaper stories for a month to see that at least a quarter of the stories about Europe are inaccurate – and the rate can rise even higher in countries outside the European Union. The problem is not just one of ignorance – it is also one of language and identity.

One of the most commonly made errors is to confuse the Strasbourg-based Council of Europe with the Brussels-based European Union. The two institutions are completely separate, although they share common values and were born out of the same idealism to rid Europe of its bellicose past and work together to find political solutions to the continent's problems. The first source of confusion is the name – the Council of Europe translates as 'Europarat' in German with near variations in other Scandinavian and Slavic languages. This retranslates into English as the European Council. This, unfortunately, is the English term for the Council of Ministers of the European Union (officially called the Council of the European Union). The EU has a court, the EU Court of Justice; the Council of Europe has a court, the European Court of Human Rights. Then there is the European Parliament... of the European Union, and the Parliamentary Assembly... of the Council of Europe, both of which meet in Strasbourg.

The immediate response of a PR professional would be to give each institution a distinct identity, with its own logo and mission statement. Sadly, the moment for this has passed. The oldest of the European institutions, the Council of Europe, developed its own flag with 12 gold stars on a blue background, and chose its own anthem, Beethoven's *Ode to Joy*. When an infant European Union asked to have joint use of the flag and the anthem, the Council gladly agreed, little realizing that in future the two symbols would become identified in people's minds with the ever-expanding sister organization.

'Europe' grows day by day. And as the institutions spawn more and more committees and conventions and councils, more and more non-governmental organizations (NGOs), lobbyists and voluntary groups form to push their own points of view. So check, check and double-check your information before contacting each organization. It is notoriously easy to get confused. The following guide is aimed at helping you find your way through the maze.

A BRIEF HISTORY

The idea of 'Europe' as a political entity really began to take form after the Second World War. Up until the turn of the century, the nation was sovereign, and state interests provided the dynamic for action abroad. The First World War, along with the Russian revolution, shifted the landscape, putting an end to a system of royal alliances and giving growing democracies a common enemy in the 'Soviet menace'. The League of Nations was a first, idealistic, attempt to create an anti-war alliance. It failed.

At the end of the Second World War, Europe was in tatters, its people dispossessed and its economy in ruins. A new word had entered the vocabulary – 'holocaust'. The politicians were searching for a new way – their Big Political Idea was to create organizations that would find political solutions. More cynically, intra-state institutions would bind Germany and its potentially impressive industrial power to its neighbours. And then, of course, there was the Soviet Union: a club of the West looked like a good insurance policy.

Today's Britons might find it hard to believe, but it was Winston Churchill who led the way. At a conference organized by the European movement in The Hague in 1946, he told other European leaders that Europe needed: 'A remedy which as if by miracle, would transform the whole scene and in a few years make all Europe... free and happy... We must build a kind of United States of Europe.'

The seeds of that 'United States of Europe' were planted with the Council of Europe. Launched by 10 countries in 1949 at St James's Palace, London, it exists today as an organization of 45 members, with its headquarters in Strasbourg, France.

Meeting in Strasbourg for the first time in August 1949, the Assembly of the Council of Europe was the first real pan-European body, but was not enough for the hard-line integrationists, who saw it as a talking shop without powers.

Federalist movements favoured the immediate creation of an integrated European authority with its own parliament, its own government and a written constitution. This proved difficult. It still does. Others favoured a piecemeal approach and among them was the French Foreign Minister, Robert Schuman. His ideas were mirrored (and given more substance) by the French think-tank set up in the rue Martignac in Paris under the civil servant Jean Monnet. But it was the French press who must take at least part of the credit for the next stage. At the tail end of the 1940s, leader writers put forward various notions for uniting the coal and/or steel industries of Europe. The most comprehensive and best thought out was an article in *Le Monde* on 24 September 1949, written by Jacques Gascuel. A Frenchman most people have forgotten gets the credit for dreaming up what would become the European Union.

Schuman had already been sounding out the Germans about the idea of pooling steel production to prevent harmful competition... and then there was the looming menace of the Cold War. The year 1950 was a bleak time and the world seemed to be teetering on the brink. It would, as we now know, continue to teeter in this way until 1989. Germany was seen as a prime area of conflict between the superpowers, and Monnet decided that one way to remove the threat to peace would be to solve the problem of German stability. What he had to do was help French industry overcome its fear of German domination while helping German industry climb out from under the discrimination the country was still suffering after the Second World War. The answer was to create a Common Market, with a 'supra-national authority'.

The European Coal and Steel Community (ECSC) was created by the Treaty of Paris in 1952. The High Authority, to be based in Luxembourg, would oversee the workings of this common market in coal and steel – the two industries Monnet identified as the 'engines of war'. The ECSC was the forerunner of the European Economic Community, which was created five years later with the Treaty of Rome, just as the High Authority was the forerunner of the European Commission.

The Treaty of Rome was the beginning of a real common market, but was flawed. In an attempt to make it something for everyone, it turned out to be a compromise, just one of many that lay ahead.

The EEC's early (and understandable) obsession with ensuring Europe wouldn't starve again led to the Common Agricultural Policy, which encouraged industrial farming. Oddly, this worked in direct contradiction to France's Code Napoleon laws which create smaller and smaller farms by sharing property out among children. Many are now too small to be self-sufficient, requiring ever-greater subsidies to keep going; not the intention of the CAP's creators, and the source of a political conflict that continues and worsens.

Britain, Ireland and Denmark joined the organization in 1973, which changed the tone somewhat; Ireland was suffering from a backward economy and Britain and Denmark were quick to establish their reputation as the continent's most vitriolic Eurosceptics. Greece joined in 1981, followed by Spain and Portugal in 1986.

A new treaty, agreed at Maastricht in the Netherlands in 1991 and brought into being in 1993, extended the organization's remit and set the newly named 'European Union' on the path towards a single currency. Britain, of course, wasn't happy, and Prime Minister John Major was proud of his opt-out on monetary union. But once you start having opt-outs, unity – the very thing Maastricht was supposed to guarantee – goes out of the window. Some would argue that not only has it gone out of the window, but out of the garden and possibly out of the known universe. The whole process became terribly complicated, with bureaucrats using their own bizarre argot to communicate in a way that deliberately excluded outsiders. By 1995, when the next stage of enlargement took place, the EU was pretty unpopular in a lot of places. Austria, Finland and Sweden voted to join (Sweden only just) but Norway said no. Europhiles can take some satisfaction from the fact that prices in Norway have sky-rocketed since they plumped for splendid isolation while the cost of living in Sweden has fallen, so that Norwegians now routinely cross the frontier into their EU neighbour to do their shopping.

Because Maastricht was such a fudge, some parts of the Treaty didn't make sense while others turned out to conflict with clauses in the Treaties of Paris and Rome. So they had another try, this time in Amsterdam. The new treaty did simplify things, but then came the Nice summit in December 2000. Designed to put in place the extra reforms needed to permit enlargement, it ended up so arcane that the then leader of the Socialist Group in the European Parliament, Enrique Baron, said that the formula for taking decisions was now so complicated that nothing could be agreed without a slide rule.

The Byzantine ramblings of the treaty did not stop the next wave of countries preparing themselves for membership, and 10 new countries joined the EU in 2004. Nor has it stopped the impetus for growth, and at the time of writing Europe's leaders are working on the first-ever EU constitution.

In the meantime, the fall of the Berlin wall has given a new lease of life to the Council of Europe. The Council, with its emphasis on human rights and democracy, and its opt-in, opt-out system of conventions, led the way on social integration in the late 1940s and 50s, but as the EU began its rise, the Council found itself trailing behind.

That all changed in the late 1980s. In July 1989 Mikhail Gorbachev spoke for the first time to a meeting of Western European politicians at the Council's Parliamentary Assembly – telling them it was time 'to consign to oblivion the postulates of the Cold War'. Just a few months later, amazed television viewers throughout the world watched as the cameras recorded the toppling of the Berlin wall – the last communist symbol.

The Council was the obvious place for the newly democratized countries, but debate was needed. Some countries were wary about lowering standards, but in the end their reticence was not enough to stop a swathe of new membership applications – the idea being that democracy was much more likely to plant its roots deeply if countries were part of the Council's system.

The results of this have been manifold – and although there are still problems to face in Europe, it is clear that the influence of the Council has been very helpful, and not only in grooming the communist countries for membership of the EU. One great strength is that it acts as a forum for the people of Europe, and a meeting place between east and west. It has helped to forge alliances between people who have historically opposed each other, and many a future prime minister from a central or eastern country has worked his apprenticeship in the Parliamentary Assembly. If nothing else, the Council's Court of Human Rights is now in a position to change the legal landscape for the better throughout the whole of the continent – improving the lives of the estimated 800 million Europeans who live there.

TODAY'S KEY PLAYERS

Cataloguing all the organizations that work in Europe is a very difficult task. Our list of key players purposely notes only the main institutions – but there are many more, from Europol in The Hague to the European Free Trade Association. Both the EU and the Council of Europe have off-shoots that we do not cover here. There are also a huge number of non-governmental organizations working on European turf.

Fortunately, all the main organizations have Web sites, and it is not too difficult to find information. For a press officer branching out into Europe, it is essential to research the scene beforehand to avoid any possible mix-up.

The Council of Europe

The Council covers nearly all continental Europe, with the two exceptions of Monaco (on its way to becoming a member) and Belarus (still labouring under the dictatorship of Lukashenko).

The Council of Europe works in a different way from the European Union. It describes itself as an intergovernmental organization which aims to protect human rights, pluralist democracy and the rule of law. It operates a system of conventions – international treaties which allow different countries to harmonize their approach. The conventions – over 180 – cover a myriad of subjects, but mainly steer clear of economic matters and defence. Countries can opt in or out and there is no pressure for every country to follow the same path, except in the case of the touchstone – the European Human Rights Convention. This is the basic bill of rights for all Europe's citizens, and each new member of the Council has to prove their commitment by signing and ratifying it.

Countries' respect for the Human Rights Convention is monitored by the European Court of Human Rights. The Court came into being in the 1950s and was hugely experimental at the time, since it was the first attempt to create a legal system that overrode national law. Its judgments are binding, and a country is obliged to change its laws or practices if the court hands down a judgment against it. So successful has the system proved that it has led to major changes in the law of European countries – outlawing corporal punishment in English schools, for example, and challenging state monopolies in Austrian television.

The Council's executive body is the Committee of Ministers – foreign ministers from the 45 member states that meet in session twice a year. The day-to-day work is done in the meantime by their ambassadors appointed to Strasbourg. The democratic body is the Parliamentary Assembly, which meets four times a year, and is made up of MPs from the national parliaments, gathered together in delegations which reflect the make-up of their national parliaments. There is also a Congress of Local Authorities, which acts as a forum for the mayors and councillors of Europe's local and regional authorities.

The biggest source of headlines at the Council of Europe is the European Court of Human Rights. The Court works throughout the year and hands down judgments in national cases very regularly. Because the court only deals with cases that have already passed through the national courts, journalists are always likely to know a lot about a case before it comes to Strasbourg.

The court draws so much media attention that it is always a good idea to look at how to campaign around key cases. Many of the individual cases are supported by campaigning organizations such as Liberty (cases on the rights of gays in the military and the homosexual age of consent were brought with the backing of the UK-based gay campaigning group Stonewall), and you may find that a case at Strasbourg is a good opportunity to launch your own press campaign, if you have a similar issue. Issues that have come up over the past few years have caused a huge amount of ripples in the press, even when there was only a hint of a judgment from Strasbourg. Think, for instance, about the issue of smacking children, or euthanasia.

The vast majority of court cases are open to the press and the public. The major cases are filmed by the Council of Europe's audiovisual services and cassettes are available free of charge. There is a small press team at the court who can track down useful information, and the Court's Web site (www.echr.coe.int) is a useful tool for checking the date of judgments and information from previous cases.

The Council of Europe is also an excellent source for expertise about human rights issues. The organization has campaigned since the 1970s to abolish the death penalty in Europe. At the time of writing it had succeeded in making Europe a death-penalty-free zone and has now turned its attention to the United States and Japan, both observer members. It has also recently launched an initiative to legally ban the death penalty in wartime.

Where the Council has added value is in bringing together the whole of Europe to tackle current problems. Bioethics is one of the major topics it has pursued over the past few years, and it is has brought in the world's first convention to outlaw cyber-crime, which includes the USA amongst its signatories.

The Council of Europe operates a comprehensive Web site (www.coe.int), and its Spokespersons' service includes six press officers of different nationalities, each covering a different region of Europe. There is also a small press team in the Parliamentary Assembly. The Council offers a number of audiovisual services free to journalists – including camera teams, stock shots and video news releases. The Spokesperson's Service (+33 3 88 41 25 60; pressunit@coe.int) deals with general enquiries.

The European Union

Compared to the European Union, the Council of Europe is a very modest affair. The EU is impossible to tackle as a unit in press terms, and its entire communications staff is equal to the total staff of the Council.

The Council of Ministers

The executive body of the EU, the Council of Ministers is the only EU institution which represents the member states' national governments. It has the power, along with the European Parliament, to make EU laws and decide the budget.

The Council is responsible for the common foreign and security policy. It also coordinates cooperation on police and judicial questions. It votes according to a peculiar weighted system that depends on the matter under discussion. For some sensitive issues, for example taxation, the council must vote unanimously but other decisions require a simple majority or a qualified majority.

The make-up of the Council depends on the subject in hand – agriculture ministers get together to discuss foot and mouth disease, finance ministers the euro. Meetings are generally held in Brussels, but can take place elsewhere.

Summits could be described as super councils. There is generally a summit meeting during each six-month presidency – and as the presidency rotates amongst the member states, it is held in a different country each time. The summits used to be considered super news fiestas for journalists, but many of them became jaded by the difficulties of getting stories. Coverage of summits is mainly characterized by the journalists interviewing each other in a desperate attempt to fill time whilst they wait for the politicians to come out of their talks. Fortunately, many of the correspondents sent to cover these meetings are specialists – they need to be to understand the many complex issues.

The Council of Ministers operates a Web site at http://ue.eu.int. The pressroom is clearly marked at the top, and contact numbers are given – but the complex nature of the press office reflects the complex nature of the institution. Press releases and background briefings range from the short and snappy to the long and, frankly, ponderous. There is also a gallery of downloadable photographs of the great and the good.

European Commission

The Commission is the EU's civil service, made up of commissioners and a subsidiary staff of about 27,000, making it the biggest of the European institutions. Its main job is to initiate new policy measures – proposing new legislation to the Council of Ministers and the European Parliament after consultation with interest groups and experts. Once legislation is passed, the Commission is responsible for carrying it out.

The commissioners come from all member states, but have to promise to follow the interests of the EU, not their own country. Each has responsibility for a policy area and is accountable to the European Parliament, which is the only body with the power to sack them.

The Commission is based in Brussels, and is a hub for journalists, who gather in the coffee bar before and after the Commission's daily briefings – a very good time to catch them. The main weekly press conference is held every Wednesday, a major date in the diary for the Brussels correspondents.

The Commission's Web site at Europa.eu.int is huge, but well presented, with themes files and useful links. The press room is a rich resource, with the daily briefing Midday Express giving the day's highlights – although not always in a way designed to please the busy journalist. One fun and useful part of the site is the myth-busting section Get Your Facts Straight, aiming to put people right on such thorny topics as whether Europe is going to ban the bulldog or force farmers to give their pigs toys to play with.

European Parliament

The European Parliament is the democratic voice of the EU in that it is the only body directly elected, with Europe's citizens going to the polls to choose their Euro MP every five years. It meets mainly in a very distinct rhythm – three weeks in Brussels, divided between two weeks of committee meetings and one week of political group meetings, in advance of the monthly one-week plenary session in Strasbourg.

The Parliament has significant powers to decide, together with the Council of Ministers, on legislation and on the EU budget, and acts as a democratic watchdog over the European Commission, with the power to sack commissioners. It still has no power over sensitive issues such as taxation.

The Parliament is a treasure trove for stories. There are a huge number of press officers working both for the parliament itself, and for political groups and individual Euro MPs – the most difficult thing is finding the appropriate person. The Web site – www.europarl.eu.int – is huge and complex. The Parliament's press officers work according to subject area, and there is a list on the site. There is also a link through to the political groups, so it is easy to get different sides of the argument. The parliament offers wide-ranging facilities to journalists covering the sessions, and the audiovisual section is a broadcaster's dream – providing camera crews, editing suites and pre-packaged material, as well as archive material.

The European Court of Justice

The Luxembourg-based court of the European Union, often confused with the Court of Human Rights, is the judicial power of the EU. Its job is to ensure that each country is carrying out Euro law. This means its main decisions will touch on issues such as freedom of movement of goods and services, employment, the environment and consumer protection. Sometimes cases brought to Luxembourg could equally well have been taken to the Court of Human Rights, adding to the general confusion. Mostly, however, the ECJ is more likely to be dealing with market matters.

Like the Court of Human Rights, you are most likely to be dealing with the ECJ if you have followed a case brought by an individual, or are involved in issue-based campaigning. You can pick up information on their Web site, europa.eu.int/cj. Press officers are divided up linguistically, and there are press releases – often incredibly dry – in all the EU languages.

Other organizations

The OSCE

The Organization for Security and Cooperation in Europe (OSCE) is the largest regional security organization in the world, with 55 members from Europe, Central Asia and North America. It has operated as a sort of European fire brigade since the early 1990s, stepping into hotspots to help with conflict prevention, crisis management and post-conflict rehabilitation.

The OSCE headquarters are in Vienna, Austria. It employs about 4,000 staff in more than 20 missions and field activities located in South-East Europe, the Caucasus, Eastern Europe and Central Asia.

The great advantage of the OSCE is that it works on the ground, and so gets to know the local situation incredibly well. American membership means it has the clout of the US dollar, and its press operations are always very slick, with former journalists running most of the press centres in the different hotspots. Sadly the OSCE has suffered something of a cash crisis, and some of its work has had to be scaled down.

Its main Web site is at www.osce.org – but the best resources of all are to be found on the individual Web sites for each mission, which you can find by clicking on the link to field activities. The material on them is journalistic and accessible and you will always find pictures that really tell the human story.

2

The European media landscape

Europe's media landscape has grown and evolved in parallel to the continent itself. The story has its very humble beginnings in the Roman era, when daily news was spread to the citizens with the help of paper and glue. Multiple copies of what we would now call flyers were pasted on city walls to keep passers-by abreast of the latest victories, murders, political scandals and earthquakes. It was the Romans who gave us the earliest example of a newspaper – the *Acta Diurna* – which was published by the Senate.

Medieval Europe spread its news and gossip using a strong oral tradition; even bible stories reached an illiterate public via frescos painted on church walls. News travelled in a similar way – not by the printed word, but by story telling and song – even into the 20th century the epic Titanic tale was carried in folk songs with lyrics even more lurid than the worst contemporary tabloid efforts.

The continent had to wait until the 15th century before the newspaper appeared in its current form. Before that, courtiers and merchants got their diet of news thanks to the talents of scribes, who for a few pennies would scribble down a report that would then do the rounds until it fell to bits in the reader's hands. Venice, Nuremburg, Augsburg, Amsterdam, Cologne, Frankfurt, Paris and London were the centres of the trade, and visitors to Vienna can still see some examples in the city museum.

Historians date the production of the first European newspaper to 1457, when a news-sheet was published in the German city of Nuremberg.

Britain's first newspaper – the *Weekly News* – was published in London in 1622, and a whole rash of papers followed, many of which can still be seen in the British Museum in London. The ruling class feared the power of the printed word on the masses, and laws were passed banning the presses everywhere apart from in the university cities of Oxford and Cambridge, and in London itself. It was hard to keep the new medium under control, however, and papers began to spring up in the provincial capitals. Some of the oldest regional newspapers are still going strong – for example, the *Belfast News Letter* (founded 1737), the *Aberdeen Press and Journal* (1746), the *Yorkshire Post* (1754) and the *Glasgow Herald* (1783). Britain's most famous national newspaper – *The Times* – began life in 1785 under the title the *Daily Universal Register*, changing to the name that has stayed with it in 1788.

The newspaper became the main medium of communication for Europeans, with news agencies entering the scene in the mid-19th century as technology advanced. Today's Europe is a spider's web with national news competing with foreign stories, aiming at an audience that is a lot more worldly wise and sophisticated than ever before.

Each country of Europe has developed a subtly different kind of media. Culture, lifestyle, history and demography all play a part in influencing how readership preferences and journalism styles evolve – creating a sort of kaleidoscope throughout the continent. In fact, the idea of a 'European media landscape' is in itself a misnomer: nothing much links the sensationalism of Albania to a British broadsheet or a long French analytical feature.

Another stumbling block is language. The deep-seated belief amongst some English speakers that everyone else in the modern world has a good grasp of the English language does not stand up to scrutiny when you start to explore the media of Europe. According to statistics collected for the European Year of Languages in 2001, only 31 per cent of Europeans can communicate in English as a second language. The BBC's languages section of the main Web site puts the number of native English speakers at 60 million, compared to 62 million French speakers and 121 million German speakers. Russian is in fact the most spoken language in Europe, with 288 million native speakers. Thanks to Soviet imperialism, Russian is also the most spoken second language, but the shadow of communism looms large for some people in the countries of the former Soviet bloc who refuse to speak the language, despite absolute fluency.

Fortunately for the monolinguistic British, there are plenty of Europe-wide media broadcasting in English, and many of the Web sites of the main papers and news agencies provide comprehensive news coverage in English. English language newspapers are published in most of Europe's capitals, targeted either at business or at the expat community.

The linguistic barrier is not the only reason why attempts to launch a pan-European newspaper have failed. *The European*, originally the brainchild of media baron Robert Maxwell, aimed to give a globally 'Euro' view of the news. Originally welcomed as an innovative attempt to exploit a newsbeat that was being ignored, it failed to gain the required market share. It deliberately avoided pitching its wares to the obvious audience – the Eurocrats – but failed to provide enough story material that would appeal across the board. Bought up by the Barclay brothers, and relaunched in new formats and under new editors, it nonetheless sank without trace at the end of 1998, having clocked up huge debts.

The publications that have been successful have been aimed at a very specialized market. Brussels is the base for most of these, and they are specifically aimed at the movers and shakers working around the European Union. The first on the scene was the *European Voice*. Challenged in the courts by *The European* when it first appeared, it has changed in style from a news magazine aimed generally at the English-speaking expats of Brussels, trading in news, gossip and good humour, to a more hard-nosed publication read not only by the politicians but also by members of a business community attempting to grasp the implications of the latest EU directive. Some of the English-based newspapers such as *The Guardian*, *The Times* and *The Daily Telegraph* do print European editions, but these are mainly slimmed-down versions of the daily edition. The daily *European Guardian*, published in Frankfurt, uses the main news stories from Britain, but has proved a source of frustration to its Brussels-based journalists who have often looked in vain for copy they have filed on Europe only to find that it never made the European edition.

EUROPE-WIDE PRINT MEDIA

The *Financial Times*

A number of English language productions can lay a fair claim to the title of pan-European publications. A good rule of thumb is whether they are offered as reading material on international flights or provided in hotels used by the business community. On this basis, a number of papers are truly international – and the first amongst these is the *Financial Times*.

The *FT* was founded in 1888 as 'the friend of the Honest Financier and the Respectable Broker' and switched to the famous pink paper a few years later in 1893. It started to publish its European edition in 1979 in Frankfurt and today prints in 21 cities worldwide, with a daily circulation of just under half a million and an estimated readership of over one million. It is not connected to the national daily *The Times*, which is owned by Rupert Murdoch's News International. The *FT* is part of the Pearson group, which also publishes the German version of the *Financial Times*, the Spanish *Expansion*, and the French *Les Echos*. It keeps a very neutral editorial line. In fact, its readership profile is surprisingly young (25–35 according to the market research firm Claritas), and in the last two British elections it has advised its readers to vote for the Labour party.

Today it is the paper of choice for students, politicians and anyone wanting straight facts in a down-to-earth manner. It is particularly useful for its features sections, and has a very comprehensive range of articles on different countries of Europe, either general or theme-based.

The *FT* has offices and correspondents in the main media centres of the world. If you are working from the UK, it is usually best to contact their London office, but European stories are often handled from Brussels.

The *International Herald Tribune*

Where the *FT* is the paper for business, the *International Herald Tribune* provides a platform for the politicians. Advertising itself as 'the world's daily newspaper', it is *the* publication most likely to be offered to first-class passengers on international flights. It pitches itself to opinion formers and decision makers, making it an ideal place for campaigners to get a voice. Fortunately, it is open to articles from non-journalists, so long as the contributors are well known in their own field and the piece is written in an appropriate style.

The *IHT* has its own independent editorial outfit, but also takes copy from its sister paper the New York Times. The 'Trib' has an office in London, but mainly handles European stories through its Paris office.

The Economist

By far the most authoritative publication for Europe's opinion formers is the weekly *The Economist*. A magazine printed on glossy paper, it nonetheless insists on calling itself a newspaper, partly in loyalty to its history, partly to reflect the way it handles news. It appears on a Friday, and is published in six countries simultaneously, with editions reaching some of the furthest-flung parts of Europe. Although its advertising changes to suit those different market profiles, the editorial content is almost always the same, except for a few extra pages on British news in the UK edition.

The Economist began life in 1843 as a protest magazine against the Corn Laws, introduced by the British government in order to protect farmers' incomes by restricting the import of corn, thereby keeping corn prices high and making bread more expensive. Its first editor and founder was a Scot, James Wilson, a hat-maker in the Scottish town of Hawick who believed in free trade and internationalism. His philosophy has been passed down through generations of editors, making today's *Economist* somewhat of a maverick. A supporter of the right in the shape of Ronald Reagan and Margaret Thatcher, it has a surprisingly radical line on social issues and backed a ban on the death penalty from very early on in its history.

The Economist is almost unique amongst papers in that it does not publish individual by-lines and eschews the cult of the personality that has tempted other papers to employ star columnists. All the editorial content is delivered anonymously, and journalists' contributions – always researched in depth and containing the maximum of facts and figures – are rewritten in plain, conversational language with a hint of irony. You can't place a signed article in *The Economist*, and you can't pitch a story in the same way as you would for a daily newspaper. Where *The Economist* does excel is in using its knowledge base of contacts to research its stories. So if you are working for a campaigning group, or trying to lobby on a newsworthy issue, it would be well worth your while to get to know an *Economist* correspondent.

Le Monde/Courrier International

The French-speaking world also offers a selection of publications that can be considered world class. France's most famous newspaper *Le Monde* is still the newspaper of reference for the world of international politics and diplomacy, containing as it does a huge wealth of analytical comment on world events. It is available in 120 countries and has an estimated readership of two million. Its sister paper – the monthly *Le Monde Diplomatique* – is a rich source of information for international players. The *Le Monde* stable of newspapers includes the *Courrier International*, which gives a weekly digest in French of all the world's leading newspapers, often on a theme.

EUROPE'S NEWS AGENCIES

Reuters

The most famous name in the news agency business, Reuters was set up in 1851 by a German immigrant to Britain. Paul Julius Reuters started off his financial information business by sending carrier pigeons between Aachen and Brussels with the latest stock market figures strapped to their legs, but business really began to take off when he started to use the new underground cable technology to transmit financial information from London to Paris.

Financial news remained the mainstay of the agency, and today over 90 per cent of its revenue comes from its financial services. But it has also built a reputation for fast and accurate reporting. Today, most of the world's news travels on the Reuters wire, and almost all media outlets in Europe are subscribers. Reuters is the biggest news agency in the world – it has 2,400 editorial staff in 197 bureaux worldwide. Its main offices are in London, but regional stories are probably best given to the journalists on the ground.

For someone seeking to sell a story to the press across Europe, the local Reuters office is absolutely the first port of call. The best way to make contact is to call the bureau and explain your story, offering written material and potential interviewees if possible. If you can get Reuters to write about your story, you are more than halfway home – a Reuters story will travel the world, and you should be ready for the wave of interest from newspapers, radio and television that follows in its wake.

Agence France Presse

The French news agency Agence France Presse, or AFP, claims to be the oldest in the world. It began its life as the Agence Havas in 1835, and now has over 2,000 staff. It operates 16 main bureaux and 16 secondary bureaux in Europe and publishes not only in French, but also in Arabic, German, Spanish, Portuguese, Russian and English.

It is always worth contacting the local AFP correspondent. Many media outlets throughout Europe receive the AFP service in English, and its reputation for accuracy means that stories are very likely to be picked up. Another advantage is that the French approach to news is often very different from the Anglo-Saxon model, and the softer sort of news story is likely to appeal to the AFP market. Most AFP correspondents outside France speak fluent English, and staff in the regional offices are often recruited from the local population.

Associated Press

This American-based agency is strongly represented in Europe and worth adding to any contacts book. It has journalists based in 242 bureaux worldwide and sends out news in English, German, French, Dutch and Spanish. AP has offices in most of the European capitals, but the Paris office is the most likely first stop.

Tanjug

Tanjug, the former state agency of Yugoslavia, has known tough times since the break-up of the communist state. It soldiers on, nonetheless, and wins its place amongst the pan-European agencies for its comprehensive coverage of South East Europe.

If you have a story for this region, it is worth remembering that all the individual national news agencies tend to cover stories affecting their near neighbours. Tanjug offers a little more – it covers all the countries of South East Europe and still continues to place journalists in most of the capitals, despite financial problems. It also runs one of the main press centres in Belgrade.

ITAR TASS

The TASS news agency was famously the 'information telegraph agency' of the Soviet Union. It was renamed in 1992 and became the biggest Russian news agency worldwide. It operates 65 foreign bureaux and works with local stringers to get fast and accurate information from the different regions of Europe. History may have tainted it with the shadow of communism, but it has also given a practical legacy of a solid distribution system and a network throughout the Russian-speaking world. TASS correspondents tend to speak the language of the country in which they are based, but are more often than not fluent in English.

INTERNATIONAL TELEVISION NEWS CHANNELS

In a sense, almost every channel is now international, since thanks to digital satellite technology they can now be seen anywhere in Europe. For example, a Polish family living in England can watch national, and perhaps even regional, TV from Poland, providing they have the right satellite system. Indeed there are certain national TV channels that are *only* available on satellite. Sky News in the UK is popular with British people living in Cyprus, France, Spain and elsewhere, since its British-focused news and sport content allows them to stay in touch with events back home. However, for the purposes of this book, we will concentrate on the relatively few channels that set out to appeal to an international audience. They are all available only through satellite or cable, though much of their output can also be viewed on their Internet sites. Many of the truly international channels are available in hotel rooms and on long-haul flights.

BBC World

Based in London, BBC World broadcasts in English to a global audience. Unlike its domestic equivalent, it is allowed to carry advertising. Many of its programmes are also shown on News 24, the rolling news channel serving a UK audience. One of the best programmes to get onto is *Hard Talk*, a current affairs interview slot which subjects politicians and other public figures to 30 minutes of rigorous cross-examination that is not recommended for the faint-hearted or those without excellent English. The programme is repeated several times, so the resulting publicity can be substantial.

Cable News Network

CNN's European headquarters and largest bureau outside the US is in London. With more than 150 staff, it produces over 50 hours of programming a week. It has a reputation for being watched by world leaders and opinion formers, and is therefore an important and prestigious channel of communication. Many guests make their appearances from one of CNN's studios, which in Europe are to be found in Belgrade, Berlin, Brussels, Frankfurt, Istanbul, London, Madrid, Moscow, Paris and Rome. Although best known for its English-language service, CNN is also available in German, Italian, Spanish and Turkish.

Deutsche Welle Television (DW-TV)

DW-TV, the German world service broadcaster, is a rarity – an international information channel owned by a non-English-speaking nation. Based in Berlin, DW-TV broadcasts news and current affairs via satellite 24 hours a day, and claims to have a potential global reach of 137 million households. Broadcasts, which are aimed at providing viewers with news and information from Germany and Europe, alternate every hour between German and English. In Europe, and in North, Central and Latin America, 22 hours of German and English broadcasts are supplemented by two hours in Spanish. DW-TV offers news every hour on the hour, followed by documentaries and magazine programmes, including a weekly business briefing called *Made In Germany*. DW-TV also provides a three-hour Arabic language programme on Nile Sat, while in Afghanistan it transmits news and documentaries in Dari and Pashto.

Euronews

Based in the French city of Lyon, Euronews is a unique channel. Since it started broadcasting in 1993, not a single newsreader's face has appeared on screen. Instead, information is presented in the form of a voiceover, using video pictures, maps and other graphics to tell the story. Another major difference is that the channel broadcasts in seven languages simultaneously – English, French, German, Italian, Spanish, Portuguese and Russian. This means that viewers in, say, Russia, will get the news in their own language, which is not yet the case with CNN, BBC World or DW-TV. This presents a huge translation challenge to the Euronews team, which sometimes results in the occasional mistake, but which most of the time works surprisingly well. Euronews is currently the only international news channel to offer such a comprehensive commitment to simultaneous multilingual broadcasting.

As you might expect from its name, Euronews concentrates much more on European news than any of its rivals, though it also gives comprehensive coverage to global events. Euronews is available to 146 million homes in 78 countries in Europe, the Middle East, Africa, and North and Latin America. It is owned by a consortium of European public television channels.

ARTE

Since it was set up by France and Germany in 1992, ARTE has become a symbol for high quality cultural television, with a reputation for innovative programming. Based in Strasbourg, the channel broadcasts simultaneously in French and German, and is seen in 70 million European households. Most of its viewers live in France and Germany, but it is also watched in Austria, Belgium and Switzerland, and in non-French and non-German-speaking countries and regions such as Spain, Scandinavia and much of Central and Eastern Europe. Like Euronews, ARTE puts a big emphasis on European issues in its news and current affairs programming, while funding European films and drama productions. It identifies itself strongly with issues such as human rights, cultural diversity and tolerance, and this is often reflected in its output. For example, it devoted one theme evening to 'The Death Penalty'. These priorities make it receptive to programme ideas or news stories from organizations dealing with human rights, culture and the European project.

CNBC Europe

An offshoot of the American network NBC, CNBC Europe specializes in round-the-clock business and financial news. Based in London, the channel reaches an audience of 5 million viewers per month, many of them high earners. Screened in more than 1,400 banks and financial trading centres in Europe, it is also available in hundreds of top hotels and 75 million homes. Given its specialist brief, CNBC Europe is always on the lookout for good corporate news stories, and carries out more than 100 interviews a month with top executives. The channel draws on the news resources of Dow Jones and NBC in 25 European cities, and has its own correspondents and market reporters in Brussels, Frankfurt, Milan and Paris.

French TV international

The government in Paris has long harboured the desire for a French international news channel to compete with the likes of CNN, BBC World and Deutsche Welle. This project finally looks like coming to fruition, with the planned launch towards the end of 2004 of French TV International. This 24-hour news channel will aim to give a French perspective on international events, and to provide in-depth coverage of news from 'the Hexagon' (the informal term the French use to describe their country). Provisionally called CFII (Chaîne Française d'Information Internationale), it will be editorially independent of the French government, and will broadcast in French, English and Arabic to Europe, the Middle East and Africa.

JOURNALISTS' EUROPE

For a journalist, a foreign placement can be the passport to a successful career – and the 'foreign correspondent' tag is the ambition of many a trainee. The classical image of the foreign correspondent has changed a lot in recent times – they no longer go into battle armed with a notebook and only a smattering of the local lingo, nor do they have the struggles of former years to keep in touch with a far distant news desk. The Internet and satellite technology have opened up the furthest corners of the world to exploration by journalists, and mean that news desks can stay in almost constant contact.

European history in the late 20th century has greatly changed the picture for working journalists. The old media centres – London, Paris, and Moscow – are still the first on the list for international media bureaux. The fall of communism has, of course, changed the scene drastically in Central and Eastern Europe and meant that reporters are much freer than before to report. New media centres have grown – especially in Brussels, which is now the most prominent.

Europe has changed for the foreign correspondent in more dramatic ways – the Balkans conflict claimed the lives of many journalists who got too close to the fighting, while the troubles in Chechnya caused problems at the other end of the spectrum, as the Russian authorities successfully restricted press coverage of the story, by arguing that the situation was too dangerous for correspondents to be allowed freedom of movement in the republic. Campaigning organizations such as the Paris-based Reporters sans Frontieres (Reporters without Borders) and international organizations, including the European Union and the Council of Europe, have tried to protect journalists' interests. At the same time, journalists have also created their own defence mechanisms – the main one being the Brussels-based International Federation of Journalists (IFJ). Representing around 500,000 members in 100 countries, it gathers together the main journalists' trade unions of each country. Journalists who are union members in their own country can obtain an international press card, which can come in handy for access and accreditation. A campaigning organization, the IFJ is also an excellent resource for journalists. It publishes booklets on safety in war zones (for instance – never wear combat gear and make sure the car you are travelling in is obviously non-military), on human rights and on a host of other current topics.

MEDIA CENTRES

Targeting your story is one of the best things you can do to ensure success. For this, you need some understanding of the main media centres in

Europe – and if you are planning to get your story covered in specific European countries you should read the relevant country profiles in the second section of the book.

Brussels

Brussels is the key city for Europe's media, and any press work should start there.

There are around 1,000 foreign journalists living and working in Brussels. They come from all over the world, but the majority are from European countries. Most of them are either staff of national newspapers, stringers (freelancers) on a retainer to a particular media outlet, or independent freelancers hoping to find a niche.

British readers will be used to the 'Eurosceptic' nature of the media in the UK and the vocal opinions of those opposed to Britain being swamped by the continent. The attitude of the British press towards Europe reflects the opinions of the media owners. Much of this antipathy was engendered in the 1980s and 90s, when *The Daily Telegraph* and *The Guardian* had star correspondents covering Brussels, who cannily and often playfully used the system, taking up and running with stories from their different political perspectives. A clever tactic, for example, was to arrive at the Commission press conference with a rumour (standardizing the size of coffins throughout Europe, for example). When asked for confirmation, the official would stutter some sort of denial. This then became 'Europe denies standard size coffins shock' – giving the impression that the project was firmly on the cards. One of the authors was present at the birth of the prawn cocktail flavour crisp story, which emerged at a dispensing machine around which several British journalists were huddled as they waited for a press conference to begin. The bored hacks began to wonder if there were any plans to ban the additives in the crisps. The resulting headlines on the theme of 'Europe to ban prawn cocktail crisps' ran for weeks! Other journalists in Brussels found these tactics hard to counter, since the news desk back in the UK had only the initial story to go on, and would ask them to follow it up.

Journalists were also influenced by the politics of the time – an anti-European Labour party employed communications professionals who targeted the more absurd aspects of life in Brussels while courting the press. This was the origin of the 'wine lakes' and 'butter mountains' that came to signify the waste inherent in 'Europe'.

This spinning of stories became such a problem for the EU that two different British governments – Conservative and Labour – both ran public campaigns to explode the myths. The Commission now has a dedicated spot on its Web site called Get Your Facts Straight, which deals with such thorny issues as the (mythical) EU ban on British bulldogs and the (mythical) distribution to EU officials of six Viagra tablets monthly!

Some elements of the British press may still be spiritually in those times, but Brussels has moved on. The atmosphere there now is businesslike and the journalists have much more on their plates than before, and consequently little time to pursue other agendas.

It is important to work out the ways that media outlets operate in Brussels – sometimes all European stories are channelled through Brussels, and other times you will need to call the news desk in the country concerned, who will then feed the story back to the Brussels correspondent if they feel it has merit. Occasionally stories that you give to the Brussels correspondent might get bounced back to the national desks.

The British media are well represented in the Belgian capital. The BBC and Reuters both have permanent offices, with a large number of journalists, and there is a long-serving correspondent from the Press Association. Other newspapers tend to rotate their correspondents. There are a few stalwarts who have covered Brussels for years, made their homes in the outskirts of the city and brought up their children to be citizens of Europe.

Life is not particularly easy for the Brussels press corps. They are expected to cover everything 'European' and they have to be very selective. On any given day there will be a handful of press conferences to cover, stories to follow up with contacts and, possibly, the classic foreign desk beat of colour stories on Belgium and neighbouring countries. Any 'nearby' disaster – even if 'nearby' means hundreds of miles away – will be given to the Brussels correspondents.

With such busy schedules, you need to think very carefully about your strategy if you are going to succeed in getting them to sit up and take notice. In general, mid-morning is the best time to catch them. By that time they have usually caught up with the domestic news schedules in their own country (British journalists will, for example, have listened to the *Today* programme on BBC Radio 4). They will have called their news desks with story ideas, and will most likely be working on newsgathering.

The best place to meet journalists is at the daily press briefing held at midday at the European Commission. The Wednesday event is more formal, with journalists crowding in to hear the latest statements from EU commissioners. Many journalists have their offices at the International Press Centre on the Boulevard Charlemagne – also the home of the International Federation of Journalists. And then of course there are the drinking dens and favourite haunts, which change according to fashion but always include the pubs around the European institutions.

Be very careful if you are organizing press events in Brussels, and always make sure you avoid that lunchtime slot – the Commission briefing is the most important of the day for journalists. You should also check that there are no other major events that will keep them occupied. An obvious time to avoid is the one week of the month when they are in Strasbourg to cover the peripatetic European Parliament. The same is true of European summit meetings, which generally take place at least once every six months in the country holding the rotating presidency. Generally though, these extravaganzas are so high profile that it would be difficult for you to make this mistake.

You also need to keep a careful eye on what else is happening in Brussels at the time. Not only do you have to contend with the European institutions, you will also need to keep an eye out for NATO briefings. Never forget that you are not the only person trying to get their message across in Brussels – you will be fighting with many other campaign groups, lobbyists, celebrities and people with an axe to grind.

It is very difficult to get around this completely, but forward planning does make a difference. Keep an eye on the Brussels papers for a guide to events in the city. If you are running a long-term campaign, you could also consider subscribing to a future events news planning service, which would generally give you good advance information, although they are not always foolproof.

Your lifeline here is the specialized media. The *FT* is always the paper of record for the 'Eurocrats' but there are a number of other good publications that can be useful both for forward planning purposes and as part of your media campaign. *European Voice* is the best known of these. Pitched at politicians and people working in the institutions, it is widely read and a good resource for lobbyists, as well as an influential place to plant your story. Publication is on Thursday, so copy needs to be in by Wednesday at the latest. If you want your story to have impact during a Strasbourg session of the parliament, you should be looking at getting it covered in the *European Voice* the week before parliament sits.

EU Reporter is a free newspaper read by the movers and shakers of Brussels, and written in a less institutional style than the *European Voice*. There is also *E-sharp*, a glossy magazine that aims to show the 'faces behind Brussels', and a satirical publication called *The Sprout*. It is also worth remembering the Brussels English language magazine, *The Bulletin*, read by English expats mainly for its events pages. Web sites are also a very useful resource – try EurActiv or Euobserver.

Direct contact with journalists is of course the best method of getting the media to take notice, but in the complex world of European politics it is always helpful to have a few allies. Euro MPs can be very useful combatants on your behalf. First and most obviously, they have a vote, and not only in the parliament itself, but in their political groups. They are also able to persuade colleagues from other countries and could potentially swing a whole block of votes in your favour.

Secondly, they are good mouthpieces for your cause. They will already have their own press contacts, and most of the political groups have a press officer who can help you to shape your tactics. The added value for them is that they will get publicity for themselves at the same time as they act as advocates for you. The way to get their attention is to think of a simple message which they will be able to use themselves, and which will fire the imagination of the voters in their constituencies.

Most Euro MPs have offices in their home country, and in Brussels and Strasbourg. Every month they work for three weeks in Brussels and for one week in Strasbourg. It is easy to find their numbers on the Internet, but if you are in doubt you could contact the national offices in each member country of the European Parliament.

You may simply want to contact your local Euro MP, but you may also wish to work through the political parties, or even target an MEP who works on a specific committee. For example, if you are concerned about food safety, you might want to approach one of the Euro MPs serving on the Environment, Public Health and Consumer Policy Committee. The key figure at any point is someone known in Euro jargon as the 'rapporteur' – the person who drafts the report and presents it both in the committee sessions and in the plenary session. If you are serious about affecting impending legislation, you need to find some way of influencing the rapporteur at an early stage. Political groups also appoint 'shadow rapporteurs' who follow the issue through committee, and they too can be good allies.

Euro MPs are very busy people, and you will need to be careful in the way you approach them. You will need to make your case clearly and concisely, possibly in a short letter or e-mail. Timing is of the essence, and the sooner you get into the system, the more potential influence you will have. You need to know when your subject is coming up at committee, and watch the rather complicated process of debate and amendment to see how it changes over the course of its progress through the parliament.

Another tactic to get your issue into the public eye is to bring a case to the Petitions Committee of the European Parliament. You will need to follow a certain procedure to do this, and your Euro MP will advise you on this. The Petitions Committee is a good platform for stories, and journalists keep an eye on it for more colourful items.

Some of the best stories come from ordinary people who reach the end of the line in their own country and turn to Brussels instead. They may be individuals, groups of people with a similar interest, professional bodies or campaign groups. If you belong to this category, never underestimate the power of your Euro MP.

London

The British capital has always been a key posting for foreign correspondents. It has one of the largest concentrations of foreign media in the whole of Europe and is a major communications hub. Thanks to the so-called 'special relationship', it also has the peculiarity of linking the European scene with the Anglo-Saxon world across the Atlantic.

London is the press venue of choice not only for international politicians, but also for stars of sport and entertainment. There are a vast number of venues for press conferences throughout the capital, and it is important to keep track of events. The *UK Press Gazette* is particularly useful for this – it is published weekly and includes an events diary for the week. It also always carries a list of useful contacts. The online version is even fuller than the printed version – but is by subscription only.

The Foreign Press Association (FPA) in Carlton House Terrace, London, is the umbrella organization for foreign journalists, offering support, social events, and a good venue for press briefings in the capital. It has 700 members, representing around 1,000 media from some 70 countries, and claims to be the oldest press club in the world.

The FPA is an important port of call for politicians and many a keynote speech has been delivered there. As a meeting point for the foreign press, the FPA is an excellent place to network and make contact, and advertises itself to outside groups as a means of contacting the foreign press.

Many media guides include details of the foreign press in London. One of the best is the *Waymaker Editors Media Directory*, available by subscription, which gives a comprehensive list that is updated regularly. The Foreign and Commonwealth Office, which accredits overseas correspondents in London, also keeps track of comings and goings within the foreign press corps. Contact the London Correspondents' Service of the FCO for details.

Paris

Of the older classical postings, Paris was next to London in importance, and has recently upped its appeal to the foreign media by constructing a new press centre at the headquarters of Radio France. The centre is run by the French Foreign Ministry in partnership with different media organizations.

Paris claims the largest number of accredited journalists – with 1,300 listed by the Foreign Affairs Ministry at the last count. Its Association of Foreign Journalists – founded during the Second World War and now to be found at the Rue des Francs Bourgeois in central Paris – claims a total of 500 members representing 450 media in 70 different countries. The association offers a paid-for list of the foreign press.

The best source of information on the foreign media in France is the French Foreign Ministry, which lists the different journalists in its annual reference book, the *Média SIG*. It is available online at www.premier-ministre.gouv.fr.

Strasbourg

A city of about 250,000 inhabitants in the Alsace region of north-eastern France, Strasbourg is associated in most people's minds with television images of the European Parliament in session. However, it is in fact the seat of a number of quite different bodies, including the Court of Human Rights, the Council of Europe, the European Science Foundation and the International Human Rights Institute. It is also the main base of Eurocorps, the embryonic European army made up of soldiers from Belgium, France, Germany, Luxembourg and Spain.

There is a small permanent press corps – Agence France Presse, Deutsche Presse Agentur and Reuters all have offices. In addition, there are some journalists from Eastern Europe, attracted to the city by their country's membership of the Council of Europe. Strasbourg is also home to ARTE, the innovative Franco-German cultural TV channel.

The ranks of the press corps swell every so often with the arrival of a travelling circus of political events. These include the sessions of the EU Parliament, and the Assembly and Committee of Ministers' sessions of the Council of Europe, along with the occasional summit.

Every three weeks, the European Parliament moves around 280 miles from Brussels to Strasbourg. These 'plenary' sessions of the Parliament – as they are called – can be a very useful time for presswork, but you will need to plan well in advance.

Despite its claim to be the capital of Europe, Strasbourg is not easy to get to. The airport does offer some direct flights to places such as Istanbul, Lisbon and London, but generally most destinations are reached via Frankfurt, a two-hour airport bus ride from Strasbourg, or via Paris by a connecting flight. The city is on the motorway network and fairly easy to get to by car, but there is as yet no High Speed Train connection, so the Channel Tunnel link from Britain is not a great deal of help. To get from Strasbourg to Paris by train takes a minimum of four hours, and to Brussels the journey is one hour longer.

It is a good idea to organize your hotel well in advance. Sessions of the European Parliament fill the hotels up – usually well in advance, and it can sometimes be the case that the town is also hosting other conferences, or even sessions at the Council of Europe. If you have your own transport, it can sometimes be easier and cheaper to find accommodation in the German villages across the nearby border.

During the Parliamentary sessions, the European Parliament runs a pressroom with workstations, a press conference room, and facilities for TV and radio. Journalists working permanently in Brussels have the right to a permanent accreditation, but there is also a system for ad hoc visits.

This system is only open to journalists with a press card, and you will need some sort of 'sponsorship' if you want to get into the premises. The best way is to work with your Euro MP (see above), who will be able to get your access card sorted out, and who also has the right to a certain number of facilities for free.

Plenary session weeks are usually extremely busy for the journalists, and you should look carefully at the agenda to work out which would be the best time to try to speak to them. The agendas are available online beforehand, and the Parliament press services also produce daily events diaries, session news and briefing notes, available in all the official languages of the European Union.

The Parliament has a centralized press service, including a specialized and well-equipped radio and TV service. There are also press officers for each of the political groups, and usually a press officer for each of the national political groups.

The European Parliament appears on the Strasbourg scene for 12 weeks of the year, but the Council of Europe and the Court of Human Rights are permanent features in the city.

The Council press service runs a pressroom with around 100 workstations for big events. It also offers camera crews and editing suites to journalists free of charge, although any satellite links have to be paid for by the television company concerned. There are also radio studios and a photographic service, available on a similar basis.

The same facilities can be used by journalists covering the Court of Human Rights.

Geneva

Geneva is the home to a multitude of international organizations – including the United Nations (UNICEF, the UNHCR and the World Health Organization are based there – along with many of the other UN offshoots), the World Trade Association and the Red Cross. This inevitably attracts a large number of foreign correspondents, as well as a regular population of visiting journalists.

The main organizations have their own press services, and many of them have comprehensive online press facilities. There are of course many venues for press conferences, and it is a particularly good centre for networking with like-minded organizations – perhaps persuading one of them to act as host for your event.

The Geneva Press Club is a relatively recent innovation. Set up in 1997, it now counts 400 journalists amongst its members. It is based at the villa La Pastorale on the Route de Ferney and has a Web site at www.pressclub.ch.

3

The European press office

There are many reasons to 'go European'. In a global world, it no longer makes too much sense to limit your campaigning, and there are many eager eyes and ears on the continent that will be ready to see and hear your message. The important thing is to use the right tactics to reach them.

Journalists may have their different styles, but no matter whether they are in Walsall, UK, or Warsaw, Poland, they want the same thing – a good story. This chapter, and the following chapter on press releases, will help you to work out how to get that story to them.

Extending your operations to Europe also means extending your basic techniques – and of course extending your contacts. You need to make sure you are targeting the right audience, and deciding the best way to get your material to them. You will also need to develop new strategies to talk to a multilingual audience.

All of this can be a long slow process, and the way you develop it will depend on the nature of your work. But in the end a good story, well told and pitched to the right person, will ensure you coverage.

THE LOCAL ANGLE

Basically, everything boils down to the 'local angle'. If you have a 'European' story which you want to place in national and regional media your biggest obstacle will be to persuade the news desk that your story is relevant to them. Domestic stories swamp the national press, and any local story needs to mean something to the people in that town or city.

Some of the best 'European' stories are by pressure groups that have been able to take the core out of a complicated Euro-story and bring it to life. A fine example of this was the way that the motorcycle lobby mobilized when the European Commission was considering rules to limit big bikes in the interest of safety. Clad in their leather, astride their Triumphs and Harleys, the bikers took off from Leeds and Leicester and London, and drove down to Brussels, organizing their fraternity to lobby against the changes. And their main weapon was the media. Their campaign was a success because they targeted each town and city separately, finding, for instance, bikers from Birmingham for Central Television and Midlands Today. They made sure their story was visual – with huge cavalcades of shiny 1,000 cc bikes. And they got their point over by training their members in media skills so they came over as articulate and determined.

So the lesson is, make your story mean something for the locals. Most people are immediately turned off by complicated facts and figures, or what they see as 'Brussels bureaucratese'. But if a policy will have an impact on their family, prevent them from carrying out a favourite hobby or put up the price of beer, they will soon stop and think twice.

NATIONAL HEADLINES

Journalists on the nationals are – with rare and noble exceptions – generally horribly ignorant about Europe, and you can't be certain that they know more than you do. Don't assume anything when you are briefing and make sure your written material has a 'back to basics' section (possibly a note at the end). A good journalist will get their facts straight, but if you have your doubts, double-check politely but firmly. And remember the sub-editors – many a respected journalist has had their story ruined by a dodgy headline. One particular sticking point is the difference in the European institutions – dealt with in an earlier chapter. Be particularly careful if you are handling a story that deals with a case at the Court of Human Rights – sub-editors are notoriously prone to shorten it to 'EU Court', despite the fact that the Human Rights Court is nothing to do with the European Union.

If you work in a specialized area, such as human rights, it could be well worth your while to cultivate appropriate journalists on the main newspapers. Putting in the hours to brief journalists on your mission will give you a much easier 'in' when you have a specific story. The specialized press corps is usually much more informed, and you may become an important contact to them – one that they ring for general comments as well as for specific stories.

Specialists are also more likely to spend time on research and on building their own contacts – so it is a good idea to spend some time meeting and greeting – perhaps inviting them for a lunch, or for a 'getting to know you' meeting.

Networking is the strategy 'par excellence' to ensure optimum coverage for events. Contact books are not just for journalists – it works both ways, and a well-placed call is often more successful than dispatching thousands of press releases.

It is worth getting a working relationship with the main media in the different countries you want to target, and the national media profiles in the second part of this book give an 'at a glance' idea of where you should be looking.

YOUR AUDIENCE – CHOOSING THE RIGHT STYLE

In an ideal world, your contact base will be wide-ranging and varied. You'll have, for instance, the numbers of the news editor of your regional paper, a specialist on a national broadsheet and the presenter on your local radio station. Equipped with such a broad range of contacts, you can put much more thought into strategy when you come to launch your story. Some subjects cry out for a popular tabloid treatment. Other times you may want to avoid tabloid attention and give your story its first airing in a more serious broadsheet. You may wish to try a trickle approach – releasing your story first to, say, a radio talk programme, so that people become gradually aware of the issue.

THE PERFECT TOOLKIT – DESIGNING A DATABASE

Fostering contacts is the key to getting your story. But your efforts will come to naught if you don't have the right tools for the job – and it is here that you can count on modern technology to help you out. It takes effort to maintain a contacts base at the best of times, but when your clientele stretches from Newcastle to Nicosia you need discipline to quell the impression that you are fighting a many-headed hydra.

There really is nothing to replace personal, face-to-face contact, but without an expenses budget and the means to pay airfares, it is hard to make this work effectively across international borders. A well-designed and up-to-date database is going to save you mountains of effort, and maximize even the smallest amount of work.

But first you need the information to fill your database. Never underestimate the power of card swapping – not just for the Japanese, but as a great way of collecting people's names. If you are the sort of person who finds it difficult to fit names to faces after the event, make a note of anything that strikes you about the person's physical appearance – the crazier the better – but don't note their clothing, unless you're certain they will never change their clothes! Make sure the details get into the database as soon as possible – you don't want that key contact to disappear into the next laundry.

There are plenty of media guides on the market, and online, but the paper versions quickly get out of date, and the online versions can be prohibitively expensive. It is possible to find Europe-wide guides, and there are a few international organizations such as the Council of Europe and the OSCE that keep databases, and may be willing to share information with you. It is worth investing some time in collecting media guides from countries you will be targeting. Many foreign ministries keep guides – in France, for example, the *Média SIG* is published every year by the government information service, and brings together over 7,000 names from both the domestic French press and foreign correspondents based in France and the information services of different government departments and embassies. Most countries provide this sort of service, and the government information services are generally online (although not always in English).

But the media world is fast-paced – and you cannot always rely on paper guides to be 100 per cent accurate. There is really no easy and foolproof way of tracking down contacts and keeping up with them, and a lot of it is just making sure that you take the time to research, ring, and keep the contact up. One shortcut is to subscribe to industry publications, such as the *UK Press Gazette* in the UK, or equivalents in other countries. They generally give information on the main changes in the media and can be a great help, not only to see where journalists are swapping jobs or specializations, but also to get an idea of market trends.

Not so long ago, press officers would have to rely on postal services or personal contacts to pass on written material. Then came the age of the fax machine – remembered fondly for the hours spent feeding in pieces of paper. Fax machines (now happily programmable) are still a staple, but electronic communication is now the rule – and essential for anyone working across time zones.

E-mail is a boon for communicators – it gets you straight to the person you want to target, and gives you the potential to work in real time. But there are many possible stumbling blocks – not least that your mail is likely to end up going into the bin along with the Spam e-mails. The only answer to this is to try to keep personal contact with the journalists you are mailing, firstly so that they will recognize anything coming from you, and secondly so that you are certain they are using their e-mail and your information is not getting lost in a traffic jam somewhere along the information superhighway. At any rate, a conscientious press officer will always follow up mails with a call.

The technical possibilities for computerizing your communications are manifold, and you should be able to find a package to suit your needs and your budget. Before parting with your hard-earned cash, though, make sure you are investing in a product that is right for you. If you do not have the necessary technical expertise in the team around you, you should make sure you are getting good advice. You don't necessarily need the latest, most powerful package on the market. Your equipment has to meet your needs and your budget.

Most office packages have a database, with Microsoft Access predominating. These are generally perfectly adequate to keep anything from 10 to 10,000 names, and can be designed to allow a flexible system. Think logically about what you want before you begin work on the database. Do you want to be able to send to regional groups separately? Do you want a flexible system that allows you to 'pick and mix' your targeted journalists according to themes, or geography? Will you need to use the database for traditional mail shots, or e-mail and faxing? How much detail will you need? What can you do without? Be sure of your needs before you start and you will save a lot of grief afterwards.

Take the case of a press officer for a campaigning group on human rights issues, based in Manchester, but wanting to send information to the whole of Western Europe. Some of the stories are aimed only at the British press – indeed some are only for the regions. But sometimes she will want to target continental Europe. Her ideal database will allow her to pick out individual journalists, to make selections according to where journalists are based, and to pick and choose different names.

If your work involves a number of different issues, the system can be designed in an even more sophisticated way, knitting in fields for themes such as green issues, animal rights, human rights etc. The database will then allow you, for example, to pinpoint the names of UK journalists interested in green issues, and working in Brussels. This is especially useful if you are likely to be travelling and organizing press events in different countries.

The database currently used by the authors was designed in Microsoft Access and has contact details for nearly 8,000 different journalists and 5,000 different media. It covers 62 countries – from Armenia to Uzbekistan, passing by Japan and the Vatican, and can categorize journalists into 41 different areas of interest.

You should think of your database as living and changing. The media world changes almost every day, and you need a system that will cope with this. Your software needs to be flexible, and you need to be diligent about fostering your contacts and changing your database when they change. Don't expect them to get in touch with you!

And a few final points – some of them common sense, but none the less worth remembering:

- Spellings – be careful with name spellings. This might be obvious in an English-speaking context, but if you are dealing with Russians or Bulgarians, for example, you need to be aware that their names may have different spellings when transliterated from Cyrillic. You also need to decide what to do about accents. To ensure your database is workable, everyone must use the same system of spelling. You can decide on your own system, but basically everyone using the database has to know the spelling rules and stick to them. If you are using one of the Latin languages, such as French, you will need to decide whether to include the accents. Germanic languages – such as German itself, Danish and Norwegian, use umlauts and accents such as å and Ä which can be rendered into English spelling with the addition of an e (for instance, Rössle becomes Roessle).
- E-mail addresses – if you are sending out by e-mail, you need to make sure that the message will reach the news desk even if your particular contact is away from the office. You do not want your story to get lost while it waits for someone to come back from their holidays. Always double up with a news desk address if the message is not purely personal.
- Faxes – e-mail is already predominant worldwide, but you might find that you need to use faxes. Make sure your fax is going to reach the right person – you may even try to find out where the fax is physically located, so that you are sure your material will reach the right place at the right time.

DISTRIBUTION

E-mail has made distribution of press material a lot easier, and many PC packages allow multiple e-mailing without additional software. But you may want to look at a specially designed distribution system for your own purposes, especially if many of your clients insist on using faxes.

There are various ways of dealing with this. There are many independent agencies on the market, and you could hire one of these – they will receive your press release and then take over the job of distribution. This can, however, be expensive.

Another option is to hire the equipment to allow you to send out material yourself. This is something offered by the main telecom firms, and you will need to compare prices carefully to get a fair deal. Privatization in the telecom market means there are plenty of options and, of course, Internet technology means that you could find a firm in Birmingham, Bombay or Berlin to do the work for you.

THE SPOKEN WORD

You have your press release, you have your targeted journalists and you've set up your interviews. Now to meet the press face to face....

But before we start – a word of warning. Beginners in the media game tend to think that they *have* to hold a press conference, but this is often not the case. Most media professionals try to avoid them, and in big media centres like London and Brussels it is very hard to find a time when journalists will be able and willing to attend. If you must organize a 'presser', make sure that you fit in with the rhythm of the place you are in – check beforehand when the best time will be, and make sure there are no other major meetings, summits – or indeed other press conferences – planned that could rob you of an audience (see the section on media centres for some useful information on timetabling).

On the whole, journalists prefer informal briefings, and many are keen to have exclusive interviews rather than potentially waste their time in packed press conferences. But there are some circumstances when a formal press conference does the trick – and some places in the world where journalists expect it.

Press conferences work best:

- during a large conference or summit;
- if you have a panel of experts rather than one interviewee;
- if you have a mixed language audience and need interpretation;
- if you are limited for time.

Press conferences can range from one person with a standing microphone to a purpose-built room with full interpretation facilities. Your choice may depend on a number of things – including of course the cost – but you should never underestimate the need to make sure the technical side of things is completely watertight: nothing will give a poorer impression than a badly run presser.

THE STANDING MIKE

The standing microphone is an excellent solution for top-level political visits where you can expect journalists to 'doorstep'. It is an especially good way to keep control and avoid a chaotic scrum. It comes into its own if you are shepherding a politician or expert on a visit to a foreign country. A good formula is to set up press briefings after meetings, allowing journalists shots of your star at the presidential building, for example, and then getting his or her comments after the meeting. Journalists in Eastern Europe are especially fond of this. It is also often used at summits and conferences where time for press conferences is reduced to the minimum.

You must make sure you have an adequate microphone, and that the timing is precise enough to avoid journalists getting impatient. Also, be sure everyone will understand you, and if not, arrange interpretation.

THE INFORMAL PRESS BRIEFING

If you have a loose, informal group of people and a good interviewee, the simplest solution is to get them together around a friendly cup of coffee. This can work well for soft subjects, but is also a good way of diffusing tension and putting journalists at ease if you have a tricky subject to handle. Informal press briefings also work well if you have three or four people on your press conference panel – especially if you have a small and comfortable room, and you don't need interpretation.

THE PRESS CONFERENCE

The traditional press conference puts your star on the platform, with a theatre-type set-up. As press officer, you are most likely moderating, and taking the questions. The advantages are that it gives all the journalists a chance to put questions, and it gives you the chance to pass on your information in a packaged manner. The disadvantage – for you and for journalists – is that none of the information will be exclusive, meaning you might run the risk of over-exposing your story and not getting the coverage you want.

THE WORKS

The 'showcase' press conference usually involves a president, a prime minister or a media star, backed with a designer set, a video wall, interpretation, lights, cameras and action. If you are involved in something of this splendour, you probably do not need our help!

ORGANIZING PRESS CONFERENCES

The success or failure of your press conference can depend on a number of things. Timing is essential, and you have to make sure that you hold it as early in the day as possible if you are going to meet newspaper deadlines and catch the news bulletins. You also need to choose a place that is convenient and easy to get to: your own premises, if you are lucky enough to have a suitable room, otherwise a local community hall, theatre or cinema will do the trick (in Kosovo we used the local ABC cinema between showings of *Tomb Raider*). You have to decide how much you can afford to pay, and perhaps negotiate some sort of deal for hiring the room. If you are short of money, you could try to get a sponsorship deal with a sympathetic local company, or if you are holding press conferences in Brussels, Strasbourg or Westminster, enlist the help of your local MP or Euro MP.

It is notoriously hard to guess attendances at press conferences, but you should make sure you have enough places for journalists, and arrange the seating so that TV crews do not block the view for others. You can do this by using an aisle arrangement, a semi-circle with space at the sides, or a podium at the back that raises cameras above the heads of the audience.

If your interviewees are not well known, it is a good idea to put a clearly visible nameplate in front of them with the exact spelling of their name and their title. You may need to organize interpretation: for this you will not only need your interpreters but will also need to make sure you have the necessary technical equipment, along with a technician to push the buttons.

It is a good idea to get a colleague to list the names and media of the journalists, and note down their telephone numbers, e-mails etc for future contact.

STORMING THE TOWER OF BABEL: TRANSLATING AND INTERPRETING

If you want to talk to Europe, you need to speak its language. And that takes more than an A level and a holiday phrasebook.

There is no way around it: if you want to communicate in another language, you need people who know the language fluently and who also have the skills to help you.

Translators, who work with the written word, need to know the language fluently, and how to write in press style. Tips on how to deal with translators are dealt with in Chapter 4.

Interpreters, who work with the spoken word, need to be able to switch instantly from one language to another, something that even people brought up bilingually are not always able to do.

These skills come with a price tag, but even if you have minimal funding, there are ways to avoid the pitfalls and get your message across.

Interpretation

Interpreters translate the spoken word. It is a very technical skill, which takes years of university study.

Your main difficulty in choosing an interpreter will be to judge how professional they are. If you don't know the language, you won't be able to gauge this, but you can lessen the odds by choosing from professional guides and using word of mouth.

Interpreters often advertise in the local yellow pages. But sadly, it is too easy for under-skilled people to sell their wares, and poor interpretation could send you horribly off-message. It might be worth checking their references from previous clients before you start. Ask about their training and experience – this will also give you important clues. They should have completed a course in one of the recognized interpreting schools. Look for consistency in the work they have done – if they have worked regularly for a particular outfit, this could be a guide to their trustworthiness.

Another rough guide is the interpreters' professional association, the International Association of Conference Interpreters (AIIC), but again, this is not foolproof. You can visit their Web site at www.aiic.net. The Association has more than 2,400 members based in 77 countries. The *AIIC Yearbook*, which is published annually, contains their names, addresses and language combinations.

How interpreters work

There are three main techniques in interpreting. *Whispered interpretation* is quite literally what it says, the interpreter sitting behind someone and translating for them individually. This works only for small groups, and would rarely be used for press events. *Consecutive interpretation* means that the speaker pauses to allow the interpreter to put their words into the other language. *Simultaneous interpretation* means the interpreters speak at the same time as the speaker. It involves specialist equipment – sound-proof interpretation booths, microphones and headsets for the audience.

Interpreters can be fluent in one or more languages besides their mother tongue. These languages are known as *active* when they are able to speak them fluently and *passive* when they can understand enough to translate into one of their active languages.

Interpreters generally work in pairs, but consecutive interpreters can sometimes translate both into and out of a language, in, for instance, a question and answer session.

How much it costs

A good interpreter will expect to get around €600 for a day's work, but there are no standard rates. Generally, you have to pay higher rates to get decent work, although that doesn't always follow. And beware the black market. It is possible to find freelances who charge less, but there is absolutely no guarantee of quality.

Simultaneous interpretation is very costly. You will need to cover the interpreters' wages, the proper technical equipment (an adequately sized room, soundproofed booths, microphones, ear sets, relays), and an experienced technician to twiddle the buttons. This would generally be outside the budget of charities or voluntary groups.

But if you are a poverty-stricken but worthy organization, do not despair. There are interpreting schools in many big cities, with students eager to put their skills to the test. They may not match the experience of a fully fledged interpreter, but they will be enthusiastic. The main interpreting schools in Britain can be found in London (University of Westminster) and Edinburgh (Heriot Watt).

Another practical ruse if you are planning an event in Brussels or Strasbourg is to get backing from your local Euro MP (for the European Parliament) or from your MP (for the Council of Europe or the OSCE Parliamentary Assembly). These organizations allow their members to use the facilities without cost – including both interpretation and conference rooms.

Working with interpreters

Once you have found your interpreter and decided how you want to handle the conference (consecutive or simultaneous), you will need to put in some work. Your interpreter(s) will appreciate a briefing beforehand. You need to make sure they are familiar with your organization, and with any specialist vocabulary you might use. They would appreciate a bit of information about the person they will interpret – do they speak fast, or with a regional accent, for example? It is essential to give them written material (although there is nothing worse than a pre-prepared speech, so this should be avoided!).

If you are planning simultaneous interpretation, you need to make sure all the technical equipment is in place and functional before the conference begins. It's a good idea to do a dry run, with the interpreter on hand, before the actual event. Make contingency plans in case the equipment breaks down. It happens, and you do not want to be stuck with a room full of eager journalists who can't communicate with you.

Speak to the people who will be on the platform and explain that they will be interpreted. They should speak as naturally as possible and need to avoid overusing acronyms, or peculiar technical words.

If you are working with *consecutive interpretation* don't forget to pause for your interpreter! You shouldn't give them too much to translate at once, but by the same token, you need to avoid breaking every few words – which can be very annoying for the audience.

You need to provide a wandering microphone for journalists' questions (and someone to wander with it, of course). You need to make clear when you move to questions that the journalists will have to speak clearly. There needs to be a pause of a few seconds in order to allow the interpreters to switch from the speaker to the person taking the questions.

It is only fair to set a time limit on a press conference when interpreters are involved. At the end of your conference, don't forget to thank them. If they've done a good job, nobody will have noticed them!

Pitfalls and problems

Some of the pitfalls are obvious – a missed negative could completely change your message. The only way to deal with this is to monitor the cuttings afterwards, and if there has been a mistake, start the rescue operation immediately by picking up the phone to the main media (starting with agencies, which should have someone who speaks English).

When you have a controversial story, you need to be especially aware of the restrictions of interpreting, and explain clearly to journalists that these are purely practical. They might think your attempts to make the conference run smoothly come from censorship rather than organizational concerns!

In some parts of the world, political correctness is all-important. Linguistic sensitivities can overshadow your message and give you big headaches. For instance, be aware of the difficulties of using only French in Belgium. If you are planning action in some of the Balkan states, the wrong choice of language could get you or your interpreter on a hit list. In these circumstances, it is sometimes better to stick to English.

THE FRUITS OF YOUR LABOURS

Every media professional agrees on the importance of monitoring the media. It gives you the chance to see which stories are the top-runners of the moment, and plan your launch accordingly. And more obviously, you need to see the results of your work, and see how you can follow up.

If you are giving an interview to the print media, it is perfectly acceptable to ask them to send you cuttings afterwards (although many journalists would baulk at the idea of giving you sight of their copy before publication – you can always politely ask if you feel it to be necessary).

Television and radio stations will sometimes agree to give you a cassette of the report, but remember to specify which format of tape you want. The chances are you will want a simple VHS copy rather than the most commonly used professional standard, Betacam SP.

It is, however, a frustration of many press officers working with a wide European audience that they sometimes only see the results of their work if a friend is taking a plane trip to the country where the item appeared. In the past the only solution was to ask the journalist to send copies, but now universal access to the Internet has made this a lot easier. Many of the main media outlets in different countries have an English language site, and if you work consistently with any region it is well worth keeping them among your 'favourites'. For example, Tanjug, the former state agency in Yugoslavia, has changed radically since the Velvet Revolution of October 2000 and has an efficient English service which covers the whole of the Balkans. Other agencies such as Agence France Presse and the Deutsche Presse Agentur also have English language sites, but they are only free at a very basic level. Otherwise you will find yourself paying to subscribe to their professional wire services.

There are special agencies which offer to do the job for you, but at a price, and it normally means paying quite a lot of money for their services. They will rapidly notify you of media coverage, and might be worth considering for a one-off important story. However, it is hard to be sure of the extent of their monitoring.

4

Press releases etc

Every day, Europeans exchange millions of messages in dozens of languages across the continent. Anyone with a story they want to sell has to find a way to grab attention – first the attention of journalists, and then the attention of their readers, viewers or listeners.

The tried and trusted techniques of public relations can only get you so far in a multilingual, multicultural context. Some huge obstacles face anyone trying to spread their story wider than the English-speaking world – gaps of knowledge, limited access to the journalists you want to target, inability to communicate in their mother tongue, and a misunderstanding of the way journalists pick up the news in different countries. Many a PR person has come unstuck outside a national context, not because they were unprofessional or failed to follow the tried and trusted techniques – but because even the most tried and trusted techniques can lead you down the wrong path if you are missing some essential part of the picture.

One of the trickiest areas for the novice in Europe is the business of written material. A news release, a press pack, Web site material or posters are the first things to leap into your mind when you are planning your campaign on home turf. The first thing that leaps to mind when you branch out into Europe is… how do I communicate?

THE BASICS

No matter how much you use your imagination, you cannot escape the need to give decent written material to journalists if you want to get a good result. The best starting point is to develop your campaign exactly as you would for a single country market, but keeping it as simple as possible. Make clarity and plain English your goal.

THE NEWS RELEASE

In the old days of PR, the news release was the essential tool for anyone trying to get a story noticed. Strangers to the world of press and public relations work still tend to think of it as 'what the press office does', much to the frustration of their communications staff who have spent the last week face to face with key contacts explaining the issues in depth. In fact, some politicians seem to think that the work begins and ends with the press release. Many a hapless politician has instructed his or her staff to 'put out a line' on something they know will never get coverage.

These problems – inherent to the profession of PR – pale into insignificance when you are working in a European context. Selling your demanding politician is going to be even harder when the people you are selling to do not even know his or her name. Sometimes you may even be faced with the reverse problem – many people who have made a name for themselves on the European scene are unknowns in the Anglo-Saxon world. You need to be quite clear about this – and never make assumptions.

'Going European' means you have to think even more carefully about how you use press releases. You are going to have to get round a number of problems – and the obvious one, the challenge of producing something in other languages, may not be the biggest. How do you get the release to your clients? Who, in fact, are they? How do you find their fax and e-mail numbers? How well do communications work in the country you are trying to contact? What are the libel laws? Nonetheless, most journalists *will* ask you for a release, so you need to produce something that will work.

Most people who have tried their hand at PR – even on the most basic level – have given some thought as to how to get their message over on paper. The basic rules still apply... your text is going to be fighting for attention with a thousand other things, and it needs to get the essentials over at a glance.

A good trick to prepare yourself for the task in hand is to get inside the head of a journalist. Imagine the demands on a Brussels-based journalist from the UK, for example. Like all correspondents, she or he needs to check the news diary with London in the morning, then there is a huge amount of conflicting appointments – meetings at the European Parliament, NATO briefings, the daily press conference at the European Commission, not to mention the latest antics of the Belgian government and any disasters or demonstrations in and around a hundred-mile radius. Journalists in Moscow, Madrid, Belgrade and Berlin have very similar pressures – you need to give them something very easily digestible if they are going to take any notice.

Remind yourself of what a journalist wants – who, why, what, when, where. You need to get these facts over as quickly and concisely as possible. Harold Evans, the former editor of *The Sunday Times*, gives a good tip in his book *Essential English* – to imagine yourself writing a telegram when you're penniless. How do you make it as short as you can and still keep in all the essentials?

Although news angles change from country to country, and you will need to think about this (see below), journalists worldwide are still most interested in stories about people. Keep to the human angle. Even if your story is very technical, try to think about how it will affect people's lives, and tackle it from this angle. Another good trick is to think about how you would tell your friends about what you're doing – you would be very unlikely to use any kind of jargon.

All these rules are true of any kind of press release, but when writing for Europe you need to keep things as simple and tight as possible – not only to make sure your message gets over clearly, but to avoid a huge amount of work for yourself if you do decide to get a translation.

Use English that is plain and simple. It is exceptionally important to avoid ALL jargon and acronyms. Native speakers can often misunderstand jargon – but a non-native speaker is going to be completely flummoxed. Acronyms – even famous ones – don't always translate in the same way, and can lead to much puzzlement. And don't use words like 'flummoxed' and 'puzzlement'! Even the most fluent speaker of English as a foreign language will have difficulty understanding what you mean.

Be very careful, as well, with the way you use language. In an English-speaking context, you probably advise people to speak and write conversationally and try to do so yourself. It makes you clear to ordinary people and helps you get your message over. When you are working with non-English speakers this rule needs delicate handling. Words like 'road rage', 'opt-out', 'come clean', 'no show', 'dodgy' will not be understood. English is a wonderful language and we can invent and adapt it very quickly, but most European English speakers won't have the access to the everyday press and television programmes that will get them used to that sort of language, and they simply won't follow.

Europeans are also likely to be lost if you refer to British habits or British stars. Continental Europeans could probably handle the idea of cups of tea and the royal family, but anything beyond that needs to be carefully filtered. Stars who are well known in Britain will leave your average German or Russian cold, although sometimes reputations can cross the English Channel – the Albanians, for example, apparently have a great fondness for the British slapstick comedian Norman Wisdom.

Finalize your press release carefully. Take care with headlines!! The British habit of finding a snappy, witty headline might not go down too well in continental Europe. You need to have an incredibly good grasp of English to understand the average British newspaper headline, and even highly experienced interpreters have trouble trying to decipher the tabloids. Opt for something straightforward and informative.

It is a good idea to put any dates and venues in larger type, and set them apart from the rest of the text. Don't risk having an empty press conference room because the person reading your release had difficulty understanding.

Finally, make sure you make the contact number very clear. Think, first of all, about whom you want as a contact. Don't necessarily opt for the person in your team who has the best linguistic skills if they are not the person best able to brief a journalist on the story. Give telephone numbers complete with the international code of the country you are in so that someone outside the country is not confused, and let them know *where* you are, just in case they have to track down the code themselves.

Always give an e-mail and a Web site address, if you have one. It would not be an exaggeration to say that e-mail has revolutionized communication in Europe. Not only can you work across time zones without difficulty, but you can also circumvent some of the problems caused by the rather sub-standard telecommunications networks. Quite frankly, in some parts of Europe telephones just don't work, and e-mail represents your best hope of getting in touch with the media.

PRESS PACKS AND BACKGROUND BRIEFING PAPERS

The business of producing press packs and background documents is not always a favourite activity, and many of the ex-journalists working in the PR world eschew the method in favour of plain, simple, face-to-face briefing. Press packs can be very useful – especially at press conferences or other events where a huge amount of information needs to be digested in a small amount of time. They can, however, be quite expensive and cumbersome to produce unless you have the luxury of a large amount of money at your disposal.

Even if you do not usually resort to colourful background documents, you are likely to find them useful when you start your European campaign. Journalists in the Anglo-Saxon world tend to take them with a pinch of salt, and are not terribly impressed by a glossy production. Other nationalities react in different ways. In France, even the simplest, most humble, PR campaign would not be complete without a beautifully produced 'dossier'. Journalists in the countries formerly belonging to the Soviet bloc are also used to a lot of written material.

Briefings can form a bridge between your world and the foreign journalist. They give you a space to explain some issues that might not be easily understood by a foreign audience. They can be the place to put the biography of a VIP who is a stranger to the European scene. You can include previous press cuttings or 'advocacy statements' that help you to sell yourself to a media who may not necessarily know your status.

You do not need a lot of money to produce a useful press pack. Your first step is to put yourself in the shoes of the journalist. What background information do you think they will need? How ignorant are they likely to be about your organization or company? Do you need to add CVs and pictures of the people you are putting on the platform?

When you have decided the content, you need to apply the same rules to the writing process as you did to writing your news release. You need to be plain, clear and simple. Include images and diagrams if necessary. If you are explaining historical background, you might think about adding a timeline diagram.

If you have statistics, include them. Journalists adore anything that compares the countries of Europe; they can make stories around simple demographic statistics, for instance, if they have the right material. Check the proofs carefully to make sure the figures are accurate!

If you are able to provide research to back up your story, do so, and source it. Avoid long, turgid articles, however: try setting out your argument in bullet point style.

Busy journalists need all the help they can get if they are going to make the most of your material. A tip to make life simpler for them is to design each page with contact details in a prominent place, say the header or footer – it saves them having to look through the whole pack if they feel the need to call you. Again, make sure you put the appropriate name, and include international dialling codes, an e-mail address and a Web site, if you have one.

How press packs are received depends a lot on the journalistic culture in the country you are targeting. You need to do some research on the sort of work that is being produced for that market to get an idea of what succeeds.

NEWS ANGLES

If you are going to pitch your story successfully to different European media, you are going to have to put much more research than you normally would into finding the right angle. News sense is pretty much the same the world over. Most journalists worldwide would admit that 'dog bites man' is not news, but 'man bites dog' might just be unusual enough to merit a word or two. The appreciation of news priorities, however, changes from country to country.

The second half of this book describes the different countries of Europe in greater depth, and gives some idea of the way the journalistic style differs from place to place. In general, you can always bet that a journalist will go for his or her 'local angle' and it is well worth putting in the time to discover what that might be. Gather information, network and find out how the country you are targeting is affected by the particular issue you are involved with, and change your sales technique accordingly. For example, a story about asylum seekers, or human traffickers, might use examples from Moldova, Russia or Romania, or might talk about how the problem is manifesting itself in Amsterdam, Marseille or Manchester.

A certain amount of research, and some surfing on different Web sites over a period of time will help to give you an idea of the sort of news angles that are likely to come up in different countries, although this can be a hard task if you do not understand the language. One of the best ways is to befriend or recruit 'correspondents' in different countries who can keep an eye on the news for you and report back on what is taking up the attention of the news pages. A Bucharest-based contact could, for instance, pick up on the fact that a bill on homosexual rights was going through their parliament, or that plans were afoot to get rid of the stray dog population in the city. The violent death of a famous French movie star in a foreign city will draw the French media's attention away from the national scene and focus them on international issues such as extradition.

Searching for the appropriate news angle is admittedly not always easy, but if you can hit on a topic which strikes a chord with the local press, it will always put you well ahead of the game.

DANGEROUS LANGUAGE – THE PERILS AND PITFALLS OF TRANSLATION

The blood, sweat and tears spent on your English texts could go to waste if your audience doesn't understand a word of English. If you add up all the different recognized languages spoken in Europe, you come to at least 37. Admittedly, you are unlikely to have to put out a press release in the Karaim language, spoken by a Lithuanian minority, or the Ghalghaaj language of Ingushetia. But at some point you are likely to come up against a need to express yourself in French, German or even Russian.

Translation is a major business. Some organizations – such as the Council of Europe – use only two official languages in their day-to-day work, expanding it to a handful of others for major meetings. They restrict the amount of languages they offer for purely budgetary reasons – it costs an enormous amount of money to pay for professional interpreters and translators. The Council of Europe expects its staff to be bilingual in French and English, and asks individual governments to pay the cost of translating into or out of their own language. The United Nations uses six languages – English, French, Spanish, Arabic, Russian and Chinese.

The main organization to take a political stand on languages is the European Union. The European Union works in all the languages of its member countries – and every written word has to be translated and every spoken word interpreted into each one. The practice dates back to the very beginning of European unification in 1958, when a special resolution was passed guaranteeing the citizens of Europe access to information in their own mother tongue. The principle is at the heart of the EU to this day, and any new country has its language or languages added to the list. There are at present 1,170 translators working for the European Commission, translating over a million pages a year. The translators run an excellent plain English site, and their booklet can be found at http://europa.eu.int/comm/translation/en/ftfog/.

The skills of a translator should never be underestimated. Translation is a minefield, for the unwary and the experienced alike. A badly translated text can at best raise a giggle, at worst end up by causing a major massacre. The world of diplomacy is strewn with near catastrophes where a 'not' was missed out, or where a fairly bland text was rendered in a way likely to cause insult. The world of commerce has not escaped either – many are the international companies who have been forced to withdraw their products because of an ill-advised translation. (There are hundreds of examples of these on the Internet – try searching for the phrase 'translation mistakes' and enjoy the results.)

All this we offer as a major warning – never attempt your own translations unless you have a fluent command of the language you are translating into, and then get a mother-tongue speaker to reread your text, and if your text is for journalists, try to make sure that person is used to press style!

A WORD ON WEB-BASED TRANSLATORS

For years, desperate monolinguists have tried to find the philosopher's stone of communication by inventing a mechanical translation system. Up until now, no one has discovered a foolproof method. Although Internet-based translators such as Babelfish and Google may seem useful tools, they are reliable at only a very basic level – and even then you have to take care. Try checking this out by using them to translate a simple phrase, then retranslate it back into the original language – chances are you will get something unexpected.

FINDING GOOD TRANSLATORS

If you consider that translating and interpretation swallow up more than half the EU administrative budget, it is not so hard to understand why it is an expensive business to find good translators. The best are highly skilled and well paid, and mostly work for international organizations or multi-national firms. The worst are cowboys, who try to make a living from a few years abroad or a language degree taken in earlier years and forgotten about until the bills need to be paid.

Fortunately for the press officer branching out into continental Europe, the UK has a rich supply of well-trained translators. Many universities teach both interpreting and translating skills (see also the chapter on the European Press Office), and they will happily give you contact lists for ex-students and bona fide qualified people. Particularly renowned translation schools are the Heriot Watt University in Edinburgh and the universities at Bath and Bristol.

Another excellent means of finding a translator is through the Institute of Linguists. Set up in 1910, it is one of the main professional bodies for people working with languages and is the examining body for recognized translation qualifications. The Institute operates a 'Find-a-Linguist' service on its Web page (www.iol.org.uk), which allows you to find a translator in the language you want, and even allows for specialities. Sadly, it offers only a limited range of languages.

Another possible source for translation is to contact the embassies or consulates of different countries, which should be able to put you in contact with specialists working in their own mother tongue.

When you have found your translator, it is a good idea to sit down with him or her and brief on what you need. You should think about explaining what sort of audience you are hoping for, and perhaps outline some of the background elements.

Different styles are important in pitching the news to journalists – but style is a major factor in translation too. Literal translation is not always the right way to do things – you need to make sure that your translator has thought about the cultural context and used images that mean something to the language group you are addressing. If you have used vivid images from daily life, they will have to be as vivid to people in another country. A good translator will know how to use alternative references to paint the picture you want.

Lastly, make sure that you leave a contact number so the translator can call you with any queries.

CHECKING YOUR TRANSLATION

If you have found the right translator, and your original text is plainly written, then you shouldn't have too much trouble getting a decent text. You may have to be wary if your translator is more used to bureaucratic or technical language – ideally you should try to double-check the finished product with another mother-tongue speaker, and in an ideal world you would also run it past a journalist for style.

This is not the easiest thing to do if you are not internationally based, but there are a number of points you can look out for:

■ Figures and numbers – do you need to change the way they are written? English uses different punctuation from other languages for numbers, and you may need to double-check this.
■ Place names and proper names – place names and people's names may be spelt differently. This is especially important if you are dealing with a number of different language versions, or if you are using names that were originally Cyrillic. Chernobyl in English is Tchernobyl in German. Yeltsin in English is Eltsine in French.
■ Politics – if you are working in the 'hotspots' of this world, you need to be aware of the way that politics influences language. Be very careful, for example, if you use the term Kosovar Albanians. This is the spelling of choice for the people of Kosovo who wish to have an independent state. International organizations stick to the generally more accepted Kosovo Albanians.
■ Press style – English style will always use a precise set of formulas for such things as people's names, jobs and quotations. This may differ in the other language. In English, our first reference would be something like 'Prime Minister Tony Blair', and subsequently 'Mr Blair'. This becomes much longer in French, and in German and Russian journalists tend to refer to the people they are writing about using their surname only.

A WORD ABOUT LIBEL

A visit to the Web pages of organizations such as Amnesty International or Reporters without Borders will attest to the fact that you need to have at least a nodding acquaintance with the law in different countries before you embark on anything contentious.

European law is different from the law of England and Scotland. Libel and slander are civil offences under English Common Law, and this stems from a tradition that recognizes the need for debate as the 'life blood of democracy'. In general, British people believe that it is part of a politician's job to be scrutinized. In contrast, the law of most other European countries is based on the Napoleonic code. Originating in a France fresh from the revolution, this made it an offence to insult a public officer, and has left a legacy of criminal defamation in most of Europe.

Countries such as Romania and Serbia used this to restrain and censor journalists, and public officials in the new regimes in various Eastern European countries have kept the law on the statute books and proved trigger-happy against their own journalists. Be warned, and if you have any doubts about your material, get in touch with a lawyer in the country, or contact one of the main campaigning organizations for advice.

5

Television in Europe

GETTING YOUR STORY ONTO TV

In terms of the number of people receiving information, television is by far the most important medium in Europe. While the UK's biggest-selling daily paper, the *Sun*, has a circulation of around 3.5 million, the BBC's early evening news programme attracts an audience nearly twice that size. In Russia, where the removal of communist subsidies has sent newspaper prices rocketing, the effect is even more pronounced. One of the country's biggest-selling daily papers – *MK* – has a circulation of over 2 million, whereas *Vremya*, the main evening news show on the Channel One Russia (formerly called ORT), regularly reaches around 45 million viewers. Clearly, with such enormous potential, you cannot afford to ignore television. Yet this most popular of media can often seem distant and daunting when it comes to promoting your organization. However, with the right approach and a modest financial outlay, you can succeed in placing your story with national TV channels watched by significant percentages of the population, and even with international networks with global audiences.

KNOW YOUR MARKET

There are more than 1,000 national and international TV stations in Europe. Contacting them individually would be a logistical, not to mention a linguistic, nightmare. Fortunately this is not necessary, because there are a handful of key organizations that between them supply television news to every major channel on the continent.

Most TV pictures from abroad are shot either by a commercial news agency such as Reuters Television or Associated Press Television News (APTN), or by a national channel in the country concerned. They are then passed on to what is effectively a publicly owned TV news agency called the European Broadcasting Union. If you can succeed in feeding your material to these primary sources of news pictures, your distribution worries will be over. Think of it like a major hub airport such as Heathrow or Frankfurt. Passengers arriving from North America or the Far East use the hub to fly on to hundreds of other European destinations. In the same way, your television pictures could end up in hundreds of national newsrooms if you can either persuade or pay the hub organizations to feed them into their systems. Of course, being in the system is no guarantee that your pictures will be used, but it does mean that news organizations have them at their disposal, which is already a big step forward.

When targeting regional stations, however, you will need to adopt a different approach, since most of them are not subscribers to foreign news agencies such as Reuters and APTN. By definition, their news perspective is local. Central News in Birmingham, for example, is interested in what happens in the West Midlands region, although sometimes these stories will have a foreign angle – for example, when Rover was taken over by BMW of Germany. If your story fits a regional news agenda, it is better to make direct contact with the stations involved. An example of how this works in practice is provided by Arnold Broadcast, a consultancy based near Heathrow Airport. When promoting a cooperation agreement between the Port of London and the port of Algeciras in Spain, they contacted the London correspondent of Spanish TV, who put them in touch with the regional TV company concerned. Pictures of the event were sent over by satellite, and the story made the lead item on the Spanish regional news. Arnold Broadcast director Julie Redman says: 'The journalists were delighted with our material, which was of course provided free of charge. It contained Spanish language interviews with the key players in London, plus great pictures of the river Thames.'

'HUB' ORGANIZATIONS

European Broadcasting Union (EBU)

Based in the Swiss city of Geneva, the EBU is the largest professional association of national broadcasters in the world, and by far the most important means of distributing television news in Europe. Nearly all the main publicly licensed TV channels in Europe are members of the EBU network. Interestingly, the European broadcasting area includes North Africa and the Middle East, which explains why, for example, the Jordan Radio and

Television Corporation is an active EBU member. Indeed, the EBU has global reach, through its links with other broadcasting unions and the Eurovision Content Service, a subscription service aimed at TV stations in Asia and the Americas. Significantly, the world's two biggest privately owned television news agencies, Reuters and APTN, contribute to the EBU news exchanges, though they are not themselves EBU members.

Each year more than 30,000 news items pass through the system – a threefold increase in the past 15 years. It works like this: if Tony Blair is giving a news conference in London, the BBC or ITN will offer their pictures to the EBU in Geneva, who will take the event live, and also run a short edited highlights sequence later. This saves other EBU members the effort and expense of sending their own camera crews to cover the event. The same day, EBU members in other countries will be offering their top stories to the EBU news exchange, and a duty news editor in Geneva will be able to request items which are not offered, but which are nevertheless of interest to the members. The whole system is based on a simple cooperative principle: member broadcasters contribute their material for free, and in return they receive free material from the other members. Everyone benefits from this system of sharing pictures and saving money.

Each day there are about 10 universal Eurovision news exchanges, in which the leading news and sport stories of the day will be transmitted to all EBU members. A Eurovision news editor will decide the content, based on what stories are in demand that day. Only those most relevant to a wider European audience will be accepted for the main exchanges. Stories with a more limited geographic appeal (eg only of interest to Romanian and Hungarian TV) will be distributed in regional news exchanges.

As well as acting as a clearinghouse for top news stories, the EBU also organizes news coverage of major political and sporting events both in Europe and around the world. Again, the idea is to pool the resources of European broadcasters in order to save time and money.

Certain non-broadcasting organizations – for example, the Strasbourg-based Council of Europe, which televises proceedings at the European Court of Human Rights – are able to contribute pictures to the EBU network. This worked particularly well in the case of Diane Pretty, the British woman who asked the Court to recognize the principle of assisted suicide, so that her husband could legally help her to die. Pictures shot by the Council's audiovisual team were edited and sent on to the EBU in Geneva, who transmitted them all over Europe, for use in news bulletins in nearly every country.

European News Exchange (ENEX)

Based in Luxembourg, the European News Exchange operates on a smaller scale than the EBU, but the central idea is the same: reducing costs by sharing pictures among its members. There are 30 of these, all of them privately owned TV channels in Europe, Israel, Japan and the USA. New partnerships are expected soon in Africa, India and China.

Nearly 5,000 news items pass through the ENEX system every year, not including picture sharing at a regional level (eg between Norway and Sweden) or between correspondents from member organizations working together in the field. ENEX also organizes pooled news coverage of major events, such as the war in Iraq and the Moscow theatre siege, as well as summit meetings of European and world leaders.

As a relative newcomer to the video news pictures distribution game, ENEX is keen to develop its links with international organizations and NGOs, with a view to expanding its supply of newsworthy video pictures.

Reuters Television

In 1851, what would eventually become one of the world's most famous news agencies was founded in London by the German Paul Julius Reuter. His modest business has grown into a leading source of foreign and financial news, with 197 text bureaux in 94 countries. Of these, 84 have dedicated television staff.

The television side of the business started in 1957 with the creation of Visnews, which was jointly owned by Reuters and the British Commonwealth's government TV channels. In 1994 Reuters took over Visnews and renamed it Reuters Television. Visnews/Reuters has maintained its position as the world's leading television news agency, supplying an average of 70 stories a day to its clients, of whom more than 200 are in Europe. Its only rival is APTN (see below).

For corporate clients, the Reuters World News Service is a good way of distributing video news releases (VNRs) to professional users (see below for a full explanation of VNRs). This satellite circuit carries all Reuters daily video news to subscriber stations worldwide. However, not all VNRs are acceptable – the requirement is that the corporate material should be 'newsworthy' and not merely promotional. It is important to remember that even if your VNR is carried by Reuters or APTN there is no guarantee that it will be used by those TV stations that receive it – putting a product in the shop window is not the same as selling it. However, its chances of being used are much greater if a reputable news wholesaler such as Reuters or APTN is involved in the distribution.

Associated Press Television News (APTN)

Based in London, APTN was formed in 1998 from a merger between Associated Press Television (APTV) and Worldwide Television News (WTN). The main competitor to Reuters as a supplier of agency television news pictures, APTN distributes its product to hundreds of TV stations across Europe. It has 83 bureaux in 67 countries.

For corporate customers, APTN offers a range of services. These include satellite media tours (where an interviewee sits in a TV studio and does a series of appearances via satellite on TV stations across Europe, or indeed around the world) and video news releases (a press release in video form).

Europe by Satellite (EbS)

Based in the Belgian capital Brussels, Europe by Satellite is the European Union's own TV news agency. Run by the Audiovisual Service of the European Commission, it is aimed primarily at television journalists rather than the general public. Instead of showing programmes, the channel transmits a mixture of live coverage of EU-related events (eg news conferences, summit meetings, sessions of the European Parliament, deliberations of the Council of Ministers etc), plus TV news summaries and related thematic library pictures (called stock shots) on a wide range of EU subjects. Video stock shots are designed to give TV journalists all the pictures they need to illustrate a given subject. They are often transmitted to coincide with specific EU meetings and events. So, for example, if an upcoming meeting is about air travel in Europe, the video dossier might show pictures of airports, planes landing and taking off, airport security checks etc.

EbS is the only professional TV service in the world that provides live coverage of news events in up to 24 languages. It also offers news coverage of events involving the EU. For example, a referendum on EU membership in a certain country would be filmed and a selection of pictures of people voting would be edited together and transmitted on EbS within hours of the event, with the aim of being used in news bulletins that same day.

Television channels interested in covering EU issues and events will record the agency's output when it interests them, and either retransmit it live (eg for sessions of the European Parliament), or use the recorded pictures in their news output. All pictures are free of charges and rights if they are used for information programmes. There is also no charge for receiving the channel, which can indeed be watched by any member of the public with the right satellite equipment.

EbS's satellite transmissions are also offered live on the EbS Web site, in all available languages, and for one week after transmission as 'video on demand'. Anyone anywhere in the world can therefore follow EU news online whenever they like. The same Web site offers permanently updated transmission schedules and other news services (http://europa.eu.int/comm/ebs).

Unless your story concerns the EU or the EU integration process, it is highly unlikely that you will succeed in placing your pictures on EbS, given its well-defined remit.

THE TOOLS OF THE TRADE

As in all press and public relations work, when it comes to grabbing the media's attention, there is no substitute for having an interesting story to tell. Television airtime is the most valuable of all media commodities, and if you are to get your share, the raw material has to be strong. In television terms this means your story must be capable of being explained visually, which in turn means you must have appropriate pictures to illustrate it. The following tried and tested techniques will help you meet these requirements.

Written press releases

If you have a story with strong visual elements, then the traditional written press release can be as good as anything in persuading television journalists to cover it. A TV-friendly press release should point out the visual elements of the story and how they could be covered, including the names and areas of expertise of potential interviewees. If your event is covered by one or more TV channels at their own expense, the advantage for you will be in cost savings (as you do not have to hire your own film crew), while the downside is that the broadcaster will own the copyright to the pictures. This may pose a problem for you later on. For example, if the BBC covers your event the copyright will be its property, and if you want to use the pictures for a future video you will have to pay – often a high price – for the right to use them. If, on the other hand, you cover the event yourself, then the copyright will be yours, and you will be able to reuse the pictures whenever you want at no further cost.

The video news release (VNR)

What is it?

The VNR is the visual equivalent of a press release, in that it contains all the elements (or as many as possible) needed by a television journalist to tell the story in an interesting way. So, for example, if the story were Amnesty International's concern for the human rights of asylum seekers in Europe, the VNR would need to have shots of border crossings and patrols, passport checks, holding centres for asylum seekers etc. An interview with a spokesperson from Amnesty would also be included, focusing on the same points as highlighted in the press release.

Sometimes the journalist will label the donated pictures with a caption (eg 'Council of Europe video'), but often they are used without any such identification of the source. Video pictures supplied to newsrooms with the deliberate aim of gaining publicity for a specific story or organization are known as video news releases, or VNRs.

Why are VNRs popular with both newsrooms and public relations campaigners?

With TV newsrooms facing increasing budget pressures, journalists are more willing than ever to use video pictures supplied by outside organizations. The benefit for the newsroom is that the pictures are free and of high quality, thereby saving them the time, trouble and expense of shooting the same pictures with their own personnel. The benefit for you and your organization is that you get to control the pictures shown on television. If a TV news crew comes to your headquarters, factory etc, they might film something you do not want their viewers to see. However, when the TV crew is working for you it is, literally, a different story. You tell them what to film and whom to interview (and you will choose which part of the interview to use). Even if, by accident, they film something potentially damaging to your reputation, you can edit it out of the final product. The two key words are 'control' and 'convenience' – control of the content for you, and convenience of the content for the TV journalist.

VNR basics

One important thing to bear in mind is that there is no commentary or voiceover on a VNR – it is simply a collection of raw material, which will be edited and voiced by the journalist who uses it. This allows the journalist to put his or her stamp on the material, and produce it in his or her own 'house style'. You can, of course, provide a suggested script, but at the end of the day it is up to the journalist to decide how to use it. The important thing is to provide good quality pictures and interviews, and, in written form, all the information needed to write the commentary. One thing to avoid on VNRs is graphics – maps, tables of statistics, bullet points etc. Not only are they expensive, but also, more to the point, each TV station has its own graphic style, so no one would choose to use yours. Also, place names and other written information will of course differ from one language to another, and you thereby risk alienating journalists whose language is not included.

The VNR should be on a widely used professional TV format – the best option at the moment is Betacam SP. It should be accompanied by a shot-list or dope sheet (a complete list of all the shots and the exact times at which they appear on the tape), together with the names and titles of any interviewees, and a suggested text for the voiceover. Such accompanying written material should, if possible, be available in several languages. You may also want to supply a CD ROM or DVD version of your VNR, so that journalists can view it on their computers. Not all TV journalists have access to expensive Betacam SP players, and foreign correspondents, for example, often work from home, hiring camera crews and edit suites as required.

Generally speaking, a VNR should not last more than 15 minutes – busy TV journalists do not have much more time than that to look at incoming video material. Another advantage of this duration is that it fits onto a small Beta tape, which is easier for a journalist to carry. Another important consideration is that many newsrooms buy satellite time in 15-minute segments. If a broadcaster is paying to receive your VNR by satellite, it will therefore be twice as expensive if the VNR lasts more than 15 minutes, since that would involve a booking of 30 minutes. Remember too that the shorter the VNR, the cheaper it will be to produce and to duplicate. At least two-thirds of the tape should consist of pictures, with the rest given over to interviews. The pictures should come before the interviews.

Watch your language

For a European VNR it is important that, wherever possible, interviews should be done in different languages, so that the VNR will be relevant not only to English-speaking channels, but also to French, German etc. It does not really matter whether the same person does all the interviews in different languages, or whether several different people conduct them. However, it is obviously very useful to have a spokesperson that can speak several European languages, particularly if that person happens to be the head of the organization. Whatever the language, it is a good idea to provide a transcript of the interviews to save the journalist time (as it is quicker to read what someone says than to listen to it).

Distributing a VNR

Timing is vital when dealing with television news, so make sure your VNR is distributed at the right moment. If it arrives weeks in advance, the chances are the tape will be mislaid. On the other hand, if it arrives too late, there will be no time for it to be considered. Most newsrooms hold a weekly planning meeting, and your VNR should arrive in time to be discussed at the planning meeting immediately prior to your event. This means that it should be there on the Monday or Tuesday of the week *before your event*. When contacting news organizations outside the EU, bear in mind that the tape may have to be accompanied by a special customs letter, indicating its nominal value. In our experience, you will have to use a courier service when dealing with countries in the former Soviet bloc, and even then your tape may not arrive on time (or indeed at all). The surest and cheapest solution is to send it with someone visiting the country in question, although this may not, of course, always be possible.

If you are aiming for Europe-wide coverage, then the VNR should be sent not only to the so-called 'hub organizations', but also to the main national newsrooms in your target countries. The quickest way to reach the latter may well be through the foreign correspondents based in your capital city. For example, if you are in London, then you should contact the journalists who work for French and Italian channels etc. These correspondents are constantly searching for good stories to send back home, and if you can convince them that your subject is interesting, they will be your best allies in selling it to their news editors in Paris, Milan and so on.

When sending a VNR, make sure it is addressed to a specific person. Usually this should be the person responsible for forward planning, unless you have a reliable contact in another part of the newsroom. All news organizations rely on a diary of upcoming events, and this is the job of the forward planning team. If they consider your VNR newsworthy, they will include your event in the news diary. A decision on whether to use it will then be taken closer to the time, either at the weekly planning meeting (see above), or on the day of your event, by the duty news editor.

General VNRs

Up to now we have discussed VNRs aimed at promoting a specific event. But it is also useful to have a general VNR (sometimes called a video kit or video dossier) illustrating your organization and its activities. At the Council of Europe, this product includes helicopter shots of the headquarters in Strasbourg, black-and-white archive footage from 1949 when the organization was set up, pictures of the city of Strasbourg etc. The idea is that the tape can be given to journalists to help illustrate any story about the Council. It saves visiting TV crews the time of having to take standard shots of the outside of the building, the centre of town etc. They can instead concentrate on making interviews, pieces-to-camera etc.

Get your VNR archived

Whether your VNR is built around a special event, or is meant to serve as a visual summary of your organization's activities, it is vital that it ends up in the video archive of the television company concerned. This will allow the pictures to be used over and over again for future stories involving your organization. If, on the other hand, it remains in the drawer of a particular journalist, only he or she will know of its existence, and its longer-term publicity value will be much reduced. That's why it is essential that the tape is logged by a librarian and put into the video archive. The tape should be clearly marked with the words 'copyright free', so that producers and reporters understand they can use it free of charge – an important consideration in cash-starved newsrooms. The best way to make sure this happens is to send two copies of the VNR – one to the newsroom and one directly to the video archive. This will of course increase the number of copies you may need. If this is an extra cost you cannot afford, then you should either remind the journalist to send the tape to the archive once he or she has finished with it, or inform the archivist that the journalist has a very useful tape, which they can ask to be sent to them after the transmission date.

One thing to guard against is the use by TV newsrooms of out-of-date VNRs, which they have kept in their archives. For example, in 2001 the European Parliament moved into a new building. However, some television producers continued to use archive footage of the old headquarters, to the frustration of Euro MPs (and their press and PR officers!) who were now working in a brand new parliament building. The solution is to keep a record of who has received VNRs in the past, and to ensure they receive updated versions, with an accompanying letter making it clear that all previous copies should be removed from their archive.

Making the VNR

Unless you are an experienced TV professional you should not attempt to produce a VNR on your own. There are many production companies Europe-wide who specialize in the making and distribution of VNRs, and some of the best of them are based in London (listed in media directories such as *Hollis* and *Contact UK*, and trade journals such as *PR Week*). Before making a decision on which company to go with, ask them to send you a demo tape (also known as a 'show reel') with examples of their previous work. It is always preferable to have personal recommendations from PR professionals in other organizations that have already commissioned VNRs from the company you are considering using.

Satellite media tours

Like so many media ideas, the satellite media tour (SMT) was imported from the United States, where it became a favourite campaigning method of presidential candidates who needed to do a large number of TV interviews in the shortest possible time. From a TV studio in New York or Washington, the candidate's publicity team would book a series of satellite slots with TV stations in different states. The candidate would then come to the studio, and do interviews one after another, often repeating exactly the same message each time, but with local references thrown in where appropriate. The result would be widespread geographical coverage on the same day without the need for the candidate to travel to the regions concerned.

In a European context, obvious differences apply. The number of interviews is limited by the number of languages the interviewee can speak – most TV channels want to hear their own language, and often won't go to the trouble of finding an interpreter to do a voiceover. The other major constraint is cost – satellite connections that cross borders are generally more expensive than those within national frontiers. To keep costs to a minimum, the satellite 'tour' should take place at a major media centre such as London, Paris or Brussels. Doing interviews from other locations such as Geneva, Luxembourg or Strasbourg will inevitably work out to be more expensive. However, if money is no object, then anything is possible from a technical point of view – one SMT even came from a Norwegian fjord! The organizers of that event, London-based Medialink, provide specialist producers to make sure there are no technical problems. According to Medialink's Matt Burgess, 'Broadcasters around the world place their airtime and trust in us during the transmission, so the output has to look and sound perfect.'

Offers to Eurovision and Europe by Satellite

Getting your story distributed by the Eurovision network (EVN) is like winning the lottery, with similar odds against it happening. In general, the EVN news desk only takes items that are very topical and newsworthy. Normally, the contributors to EVN feeds are either TV stations or international organizations. If you are in neither of the above categories, your options are very limited. However, if your news event really is something that TV channels across Europe are likely to want to cover, then you should contact the Eurovision newsroom, preferably by e-mail, several days in advance. If it is of high importance they may even organize their own news coverage, with live cameras, editing and satellite feeds. Much more likely, however, is a polite refusal.

Europe by Satellite, the European Union's satellite channel, is only interested in stories that have a direct EU involvement. Do not waste your time or theirs by contacting them if your story has no EU angle.

Sponsored television

Sponsored television in a news context has nothing in common with the sponsorship of sporting events. The latter involves getting the sponsor's name onto the screen as often as possible, through advertising billboards, players' shirts etc. Sponsorship of news coverage, on the other hand, is altogether subtler, with the sponsor seeking to disguise their involvement as much as possible, because the power of television news lies in the belief that it is independent.

In television, sponsorship can take several forms:

Programme sponsorship

An organization can financially support a single programme, or a series of programmes. For example, Parlemento, a Euronews series that covers events and issues at the European Parliament, is sponsored by the Parliament. European institutions are often asked to support documentaries on worthy subjects such as the fight against trafficking in human beings. When considering sponsorship, you should always check that the production company has firm commitments from broadcasters to screen their programme. All too often, programme makers are forced to seek funding outside the television industry precisely because they have failed to find any professional backers for their project. In this case they will be forced to make the programme first (at the sponsor's expense) and only afterwards try to sell it to the broadcasters.

Many television channels, however, will not accept sponsored programming because it is against their rules. So beware producers seeking sponsorship because they cannot finance their film in any other way. An interesting programme will usually get made without the help of sponsors, and will be sold to TV channels even before it is completed.

Paying for a journalist's travel and living expenses

There is no better way to encourage a journalist to attend your event than by offering him or her a 'freebie'. If you can afford to invite a group of journalists, you can make economies of scale, by block-booking hotel rooms, hiring a coach for transport etc. Some TV channels, which are particularly hard-pressed financially, will even demand that you pay for their camera crew, picture editor and satellite transmission costs. Only you can decide whether such a deal is worthwhile, but bear in mind that compared with the cost of advertising, news sponsorship of this kind is usually very good value for money. Just as important, news coverage of a story carries far more credibility than advertising, because the journalist is seen as independent. In effect, you have bought airtime without the viewer knowing it, and the publicity value of this alone is enormous. Remember, however, that some media forbid their journalists to accept expense payments from outside organizations, and even if there are no such official rules, individual journalists may be reluctant to compromise what they see as their editorial independence by letting you fund them in this way. Even reporters with fewer scruples cannot be relied on to provide favourable coverage, and you should not feel offended if a journalist on a paid invitation writes a negative story – it is still a risk worth taking.

Paying for a production company to make and distribute a TV news report on your behalf

London-based World Television, for example, has a partnership with Reuters Television, which distributes its news reports around the world in various categories of satellite feeds. Reuters World Alert specializes in stories from charities, NGOs and international organizations. Reuters World Health, as the title suggests, focuses on health issues. Reuters World Technology was set up to provide stories on products using new technology, while Reuters World Travel features stories from the global travel industry. Peter Sibley of World Television says:

We plan, shoot and edit the story to professional broadcast standards, alert the target TV stations across Europe and further afield, and then distribute it using the appropriate Reuters satellite feed. One good example was a video news release for a manufacturer of compression stockings for the prevention of deep vein thrombosis. Distribution on Reuters World Health Service ensured that the VNR was received by all Reuters' clients (approximately 380 broadcasters worldwide). The story ran on all UK national television channels, while in the US it was featured in the national news bulletins of all networks and on a huge range of their local affiliate TV stations. British Satellite News carried the story on their feeds to 500 broadcasters in 120 countries, and Euronews ran it on their weekly current affairs programme. This shows how a good story can be used by hundreds of Reuters clients.

An experts directory

Journalists of all kinds often need expert comment and analysis to give depth and authority to their reports. Your organization may have a large pool of technical expertise in its field of activity. One way of making sure that it is *your* colleagues that get called by the journalists, and not those of a rival organization, is to produce a directory of experts.

This is a list of an organization's experts on different subjects, arranged in a way that will be useful to a journalist. Most importantly this means a list of topics that the journalist can understand, though the list may not necessarily coincide with your organizational structure. It is important to simplify what you do into news categories, rather than impose your own categories, which may mean nothing to an outsider. Another important category of classification is language. A German TV journalist will always prefer an expert who speaks German, and so on. Make it clear in your list of experts what languages they can speak. A photo of each expert is a good idea, especially for television journalists, who like to know what a potential interviewee looks like.

You would be well advised to send all your experts on a media-training course, or organize in-house training yourself. This involves explaining how journalists work and what they are looking for from an interview, and preparing your staff for radio and TV performances by means of simulated interviews (usually carried out by a professional journalist). A training programme also gives you the chance to weed out unsuitable experts who would not project a good image of your organization. They may be inarticulate, eccentric-looking or excessively shy. Whatever the reason, don't let them in front of a camera or a microphone if you think they might damage your organization's reputation.

Once you have your group of selected experts ready to meet the journalists, it is time to promote and distribute your directory of experts. The most important place to put it is on your Web site. You should also produce it in booklet or paper form, which you can then send to your target journalists. Whichever way you distribute it, you have to be ready to respond when the journalists start calling. You will need a system that allows a journalist to make contact with your experts 24 hours a day, 7 days a week. Our recommendation is a centralized phone number, preferably in the press office, which has an out-of-hours message with the number of the duty press officer. Never publish home or mobile numbers of experts on your Web site or in the booklet – it may result in nuisance calls from members of the public, or even cases of stalking.

Our favourite experts directory site is the World Bank in Washington. You should also check out those of the University of Cardiff and the University of Warwick.

Corporate videos

A good corporate video can significantly enhance your organization's image. A bad one can do a lot of damage. Getting it right in a European context is much harder than tailoring your film to the needs of just one national audience. Cultural and linguistic differences can invalidate a creative concept that would work perfectly well in a national context. Here are some examples of the kinds of issues you have to bear in mind when commissioning or writing a film for an international audience.

On-screen presenter or unseen voiceover

It is popular to use celebrities to front a company video in order to give it added prestige. However, using a well-known British newsreader to present your video will mean nothing to a German or French audience, who will almost certainly not recognize him or her. There are a few personalities who are well known in several countries – the actor Peter Ustinov is perhaps the best example, appearing frequently on chat shows in both the UK and Germany – but they are very rare, and will almost certainly be very expensive.

There's an even more fundamental reason to avoid using on-screen presenters, of whatever nationality. Quite simply, a presenter can only talk in his or her native language (the number of bilingual TV presenters being so small as to be insignificant). In communication terms, this fact has important consequences. If we take the example of a video that uses a native English-speaking presenter, this means that in the French language version, there are only two realistic options. Either the parts of the video featuring the English presenter will have to be removed, or the French voiceover will have to continue over the pictures of the English presenter. Either way the film will suffer. There is a third option, but we don't really consider this to be realistic. If you have a huge budget and great contacts in the world of European television, you can employ a French presenter for the French version, an Italian for the Italian adaptation etc. Quite apart from the expense, you will also have the headache of finding a different presenter for each language. In our opinion, a far better solution is to dispense with on-screen presenters altogether, in favour of a voiceover which can be easily changed from one language to another. Even this approach, however, has its pitfalls.

Voiceover tips and pitfalls

The most important thing with voiceovers is making sure you get a good performer for each language. This may sound like obvious advice, but all too often people assume that because somebody can speak a certain language they can do a voiceover in it. This is as foolish as thinking that because a person can drive a car they can take part in a Grand Prix. To avoid falling into this common trap, make sure you ask potential voiceover artists to send you a demo tape with several examples of their work. Then get some native speakers to listen to it and give you their opinion. Only in the event of positive feedback should you proceed with a contract for the voiceover. A sub-standard voiceover can ruin a good company video, and make a laughing stock of your organization. So be very careful to employ only experienced voiceover artists. Never employ non-native speakers to do a voiceover, no matter how good their linguistic skills. It may seem like a cost-effective idea to use a British voiceover artist who speaks perfect Russian to do the Russian version as well, but this is a false economy. Even using the same native speaker for different countries that share a common language can lead to disaster. Tony Charlesworth, an experienced VNR and corporate video producer, has a cautionary tale for anyone contemplating breaking this rule: 'We once had an American client who insisted on using an American voiceover artist for the British version of the film. He made the recording in what he imagined was an upper-class English accent. The result was unintentionally hilarious, but completely undermined the credibility of the video for a British audience highly attuned to accent, and in this case, an obviously false accent at that.'

Before you get to the voiceover stage, you'll need to translate the script into the different language versions. You should always make sure that the original script is well written in a simple style that will easily lend itself to being translated into other languages. Puns, idioms and jokes which are too monocultural (eg only British people would understand the references) have no place in a script for a European video. Once you've checked the original script for potential linguistic pitfalls, make sure you get a good translator. Remember that many translators are used to translating into the written word, but not necessarily the spoken one. Your foreign language versions may therefore not sound as elegant on the ear as the original. One way round this problem is not to employ a professional translator at all, but to find a radio or TV journalist who is used to writing for the spoken word. You may even be able to use the same person who does the voiceover. This avoids a common problem that arises at recording sessions, when the voiceover artist asks questions such as 'What does this mean?' or 'What did the translator mean here?' By employing the same person to do both the translation and voiceover stages, you avoid any such misunderstandings. Bear in mind, however, that it is very hard to find someone who can not only translate from one language to another in a spoken rather than written style, but can also deliver a professional voiceover.

Content must reflect geographical diversity

As for the film itself, if it is going to be seen in different parts of Europe, then it should reflect that diversity in its content. This means that images should not be drawn exclusively, or excessively, from one particular country or region of Europe. The producer should make every effort to find video pictures from the four corners of the continent. Italians will not identify with a film that mainly shows people from Nordic countries, and vice versa. If the film is about a subject that has negative connotations, then do not appear to target one particular country (unless, of course, that is the point of the film). For example, if the film is about the Europe-wide problem of corruption, be careful not to show too many images from one country, or you will risk alienating its citizens. Also, bear in mind that people or locations that may be famous in one country may mean absolutely nothing to citizens of another country. If the meaning of the film depends on making such associations, then you will have to rewrite the script.

Multilingual credits

Finally, if your film has a title, or if there are credits at the end, make sure they're translated into the same language as the voiceover. If you don't do this you risk offending the audience, who will get the impression (probably correctly) that you were too lazy to translate the title and credits into their language.

6

Radio – the neglected medium

Radio journalists seem to be the poor relations of the news family. While everyone pays close attention to the requirements of television journalists and their print counterparts, very few communication professionals fully understand the special needs of the radio reporter, and even fewer do anything to satisfy them. Press and video news releases are well-established tools of the trade, but the audio news release is seldom used, and too often is merely the soundtrack from the VNR. Yet radio is a vital medium of communication in Europe, which can sometimes wield an influence far greater than either television or newspapers. The following examples prove the point.

United Kingdom – BBC *Today* programme

In the UK, the *Today* programme on BBC Radio 4 is nothing less than a national institution. Broadcasting from 6.00 am to 9.00 am on weekday mornings, with a shorter programme on Saturdays, it sets the news agenda for the day, as other media feed off its robust live interviews with leading public figures. *Today* has a weekly reach of more than four million people, including many top politicians and business leaders. One of its most loyal listeners is Baroness Thatcher, who once telephoned the programme from the kitchen of 10 Downing Street after hearing an interview with a spokesman for President Gorbachev, who was about to visit Britain. She wanted to comment on what the Russian had said, and was put straight through to one of the presenters, John Humphrys, who duly interviewed her. The programme's reputation grew as a result, because it could demonstrably claim to have the ear of the British prime minister.

Serbia – Radio B92

In a very different context, the radio station B92 has played a key role in the development of democracy and civil society in post-communist Yugoslavia. Founded in 1989 as a temporary student radio station, its mix of alternative music and independent news reporting soon gained immense popularity among a wider audience. B92 took a firm stand against the wars that tore the Balkans apart, and supported and helped organize the mass demonstrations against Slobodan Milosevic. The station led a precarious existence, often broadcasting from secret studios. On several occasions it was closed down by the authorities, but managed to continue operating on the Internet, with a Web site that attracted up to one million hits a day. In the run-up to the presidential election of 1999 it organized two concert tours across Serbia to encourage people to vote in elections that saw the defeat of Milosevic. In recent years the station has been able to shed its semi-illegal status. It remains very popular and has branched into new areas, including television, Internet, music, film and publishing, although radio still remains the backbone of the group's activities.

Russia – Radio 'Echo of Moscow'

Since its creation in 1990, Echo of Moscow has been a symbol of free media in Russia. The station broadcasts to an estimated audience of four million listeners in 67 Russian cities and towns, including many of the country's political and business elite. It has a reputation for attracting visiting world leaders to its studios, high above Moscow's famous Novy Arbat street. US President Bill Clinton and German Chancellor Gerhard Schroeder have both been interviewed there, but the visit of another VIP guest, President Jacques Chirac of France, was cancelled when security police raided the station on the eve of his appearance. In 2001 the continued independence of the station was cast into doubt by the arrival of new owners Gazprom, the gas giant partly owned by the government. Despite the change of ownership, Echo of Moscow seems to have retained its high reputation for objective reporting.

TACKLING THE RADIO MEDIUM

With such influence on key decision makers, radio cannot be ignored. But getting to grips with it can be tricky, particularly on a pan-European level.

With thousands of radio stations to choose from, how do you get your message across to even a fraction of them? Then there's the problem of language. Radio is a speech-based medium, so the number of languages in which you can explain your story limits its appeal. A German journalist will want an interview in German, and if you can't provide one, your story will receive a drastically reduced amount of airtime, if indeed it is covered at all. But despite the challenges, radio is definitely worth the effort.

INTERNATIONAL RADIO

If you have a story with a European news angle, the most likely takers are the international broadcasters. Although nearly every country in Europe has an international voice, invariably funded by the taxpayer, only a handful enjoy a wide reputation and a significant audience. The 'big four' are BBC World Service, Radio France International, Deutsche Welle and Radio Free Europe. International broadcasters usually seek to promote the values and culture of their country of origin, often including language courses in their schedules, although news and current affairs form the mainstay of their programming. Of vital importance, each station broadcasts in many languages, so, for example, even if you speak only English, you can still make contact with the English language service of, say, Radio France International and offer them your story, thereby significantly extending its potential audience beyond the UK and Ireland.

BBC World Service

Set up in 1932, BBC World Service made its reputation during the Second World War, when it maintained a flow of precious information on the course of the conflict to countries occupied by the Germans and the Japanese. It has since consolidated and strengthened its position as the most respected voice in international broadcasting, with a regular audience of 150 million listeners around the globe. Financed separately from domestic BBC services, the World Service broadcasts in 43 languages from its headquarters at Bush House, London. There is a separate Web site for each language, and the Internet is an important means of listening to the station's programmes without having to find the right frequency on a radio receiver. The number of online users has more than doubled to 13 million in just one year, and this service looks set to continue its rapid audience growth.

The English language service includes a daily current affairs programme called *Europe Today*, which covers the continent in the widest sense (not just member countries of the EU). It is a useful outlet for political and cultural stories with a strong European news angle.

Radio France International

Originally established in 1975 to broadcast to French speakers, Radio France International now has a global audience of 45 million people who listen to its 20 language services, of which the French is unsurprisingly the largest. Every day this service runs 58 bulletins of international and French news. RFI is re-broadcast by 723 partner stations worldwide, in 137 countries.

Deutsche Welle

When Deutsche Welle was set up in 1953 it was the international voice of West Germany, and its main target audience were the 17 million East Germans living next door under communism. Since then it has broadened its audience, and DW's radio programmes are now broadcast from Bonn in more than 30 languages, including English, to all regions of the world. Under its charter, DW's task is to convey an accurate and comprehensive picture of political, cultural and economic life in Germany, and to describe and explain German opinions on important international issues. Among the programmes worth targeting on the English language service is *Inside Europe*, which covers a broad range of social, political and economic issues. This slickly produced 60-minute weekly transmission is carried by other radio networks, notably in the USA and Canada, so it is well worth trying to pitch your story to the journalists who put it together, providing of course it fits their format. For scientific, health and technology stories, the *Spectrum* programme is a good potential showcase.

Radio Free Europe/Radio Liberty

As the name suggests, Radio Free Europe/Radio Liberty was a product of the Cold War. In 1949 America decided that countries behind the Iron Curtain needed a source of free and impartial information. RFE/RL used to receive its money from the CIA, but that connection was severed in 1971 and the station is now wholly funded by the American taxpayer through the US Congress. The Polish leader Lech Walesa was among many who credited the station with a major contribution to the collapse of communism. Its main task accomplished, RFE made cutbacks in the 1990s, closing its Hungarian and Polish services and merging Radio Free Europe with its sister station Radio Liberty. But with continuing instability in the Balkans and elsewhere in Central and Eastern Europe, and global uncertainty following 11 September 2001, the station has found a new role, and currently broadcasts in 34 languages, including Arabic, Chechen and Kurdish. Its main aim is to provide impartial news and information, thereby demonstrating the benefits of a free press to audiences living in countries which are still some way from achieving widespread freedom of the media. According to the latest estimates, RFE/RL programmes reach a total of 23 million listeners each week. Like other major players it is gaining a significant new audience on the Internet. After 45 years based in the German city of Munich, RFE/RL decided to move its broadcast centre to Prague and has been headquartered in the Czech capital since 1995.

RADIO NEWS AGENCIES

The problem of language means that audio material cannot be shared between countries to the same extent as video pictures. A German radio station, for example, will not be able to use interviews in English without voicing them over in German, a tedious process requiring a translation from English into German, and then finding someone to do the voiceover. So it is not surprising that the amount of audio material shared across linguistic barriers is minimal. The European Broadcasting Union in Geneva does, however, have a radio service that organizes a daily exchange of news and sport audio material. Every year the EBU Radio Department coordinates the transmission of 440 sports fixtures and 120 major news events. Otherwise there are few radio equivalents of the pan-European 'hub organizations' mentioned in Chapter 5. But on a national level, radio news agencies are important channels for distributing news. In the UK, Independent Radio News (IRN) supplies news to the commercial radio sector, while the BBC has an equivalent service for its local radio stations. On a smaller scale, Feature Story News is an American-owned news agency whose London bureau sends stories from the UK and elsewhere in Europe to English-speaking radio stations around the world. Often the same story will be repackaged and sent to many different outlets in America, the Far East, Australia and South Africa. When targeting a country, or group of countries, be sure to contact their radio news agencies, as well as leading radio stations.

INCREASING YOUR RADIO COVERAGE – TECHNICAL TIPS

It is often said that compared with television, radio is a cheap medium, and you can turn this to your advantage when it comes to boosting the amount of radio airtime devoted to your organization. The following suggestions are not overly expensive, especially if you are lucky enough to have a radio studio already at your headquarters. However, even if you have to set up your radio infrastructure from scratch, the return in publicity terms will repay the financial investment many times over.

Investing in a radio studio

For as little as £10,000 you can set up a basic radio studio with a microphone, headphones, voice level indicator, sound mixer and recording equipment. To provide an effective service for radio journalists, you will not necessarily need broadcast-standard equipment across the board – in many cases domestic or semi-professional CD and MiniDisc equipment will be good enough. Nor will you need spacious or lavish surroundings – there are plenty of studios in the proverbial 'broom cupboard', without any noticeable loss of sound quality. What you will need, however, is the following checklist of facilities that the modern radio journalist has come to expect:

- *ISDN line.* ISDN audio quality is so good it sounds to the listener as though the person being interviewed is in the same room as the journalist asking the questions, even though in reality they will often be hundreds of miles apart. By contrast, phone interviews are often deliberately kept short by radio producers because listeners find it hard to concentrate for more than a few minutes on the metallic sound of a telephone line. The cost of ISDN lines has fallen dramatically in recent years, as they have become increasingly popular with Internet users.
- *Good acoustics.* One thing you should not economize on is the acoustic quality of your studio. Poor quality surroundings, which produce echoes and other distractions, will do nothing to enhance your credibility. Effective soundproofing is essential for the same reason. Nothing is worse than the sound of drilling or hammering in the background when you are listening to someone (and of course it also interferes with the concentration of the person doing the talking). Finally, do make sure you have good quality microphones. They are the most important pieces of equipment in your studio.
- *Recording and copying facilities.* You will almost certainly want to record the interviews you organize, and later on you may want to make copies of them, so you will need recording and copying facilities. You can choose from a wide range of formats, from the basic audiocassette to Digital Audio Tape (DAT) and MiniDisc. You may need to buy several different formats, to cater for different users. For example, audiocassettes are good enough for non-professional purposes (eg for colleagues), but a radio journalist will want a higher standard format such as DAT or MiniDisc.
- *Editing facilities.* The days of splicing reel-to-reel radio tape with a razor blade and putting it back together with sticky tape are long gone. What you need now is computer-based editing, which will allow you to take full advantage of the possibilities offered by the

Internet (see more below in the section on audio files). Any newish PC will do for the hardware, but the software is more specialized. Cool Edit Pro is a user-friendly system widely used at the BBC, though there are plenty of others to choose from, with more coming onto the market every year.

Get a professional opinion on what you need from a technician who regularly works with radio journalists. He or she will also be able to give you a rough idea of the cost involved, and may even have some useful journalistic contacts to get your radio campaign started. You will in any case need a technician to operate the studio, unless it is either so simple you can do it yourself, or you happen to be technically gifted. In most cases you can employ a freelance who will work when required, but if you are lucky enough to receive daily requests for radio interviews, you should consider a full-time technician.

Provide sound files on your Web site

In the bad old days, sending high-quality radio material (often referred to as 'actuality' by radio professionals) from one country to another was both costly and time-consuming. For a start, only radio studios had the kind of enhanced-quality telephone lines that would do the job, so if you were sending material from Vienna to London you would first have to find a studio in Vienna. Then the telephone lines between the two studios would have to be booked, often at considerable expense, because technicians would have to be on hand to play out the material. If for any reason there was a technical hitch, the booking would have to be extended, at additional expense.

Today the procedure is very different. The radio journalist no longer needs to book lines or studio time. He or she can simply transfer the audio material from the digital tape recorder to his or her computer (most likely a laptop, given the mobile nature of the job), do any editing that may be required, and then send it anywhere in the world as an e-mail attachment.

In spite of this technological revolution, very few virtual pressrooms are up to speed when it comes to servicing radio journalists. Most offer only text information and photographs. But for a modest additional outlay you can provide a lot more. Press conferences, for example, can be transmitted live as a Web cast on your site, and can also be made available afterwards, preferably in easily downloadable 3–5-minute chunks. You may choose to highlight the answers you think are important by offering them as separate files, along with a transcript of the content. Basic texts such as your organization's mission statement, constitution or charter can be professionally voiced in several languages and kept in a special section of your site. You may even want to call this resource your 'radio toolbox' in order to attract the attention of radio journalists.

Set up and maintain a sound archive

A sound archive is a precious resource, which not only provides an accurate record of important events, but can also be exploited for publicity purposes. For a radio journalist, a written transcript of a speech is of limited use, but a radio recording of it has much more potential. Very old archive material has added value in radio terms, because its inferior quality sound contrasts with the cleaner-sounding contemporary sources, giving the journalist's report a more varied feel.

If you already have a radio studio, then setting up and maintaining a sound archive is straightforward. Doing it without the technical infrastructure is more difficult, but not impossible. The British Labour politician Tony Benn has maintained a personal sound archive throughout his long career in government and politics, recording and referencing every interview or speech he has ever given.

You will need copying facilities in order to respond to demands from radio producers. The golden rule of archiving is never to lend an original to anyone – always make a copy for them. Similarly, you should always know what they want to use the material for, and be sure that it corresponds with your public relations goals. You may not be willing, for example, to release your chief executive's speech if the request comes from a comedy satire programme with a reputation for lampooning those in authority. In order to protect yourself, you may wish to use a standard archive release form that lays down the conditions of use. These should preclude the passing of your material to a third party (a bona fide radio journalist may have a friend who is a comedy producer!) and should oblige the user of your material to send you a copy of the programme in which it appears.

Be careful to choose the right format for archiving your material. Magnetic tape can deteriorate dramatically, to the point of becoming unusable. Sound stored on computer can be lost if there is a catastrophic failure of the hard disk. One of the safest options currently available is the ordinary audio CD. Not only are they made of sturdy material that does not degrade over time (the modern equivalent of the vinyl disc, which has proved a remarkably durable format), but also if you lose or break one, the rest of your collection is not affected (unlike the computer nightmare scenario where everything is lost when a hard disk fails). For archiving purposes, never economize on quality – always buy the best, or at least the best you can afford.

INCREASING YOUR RADIO COVERAGE – STRATEGY TIPS

Target Europe-specific programmes

Even if you have no special radio facilities, it is still possible to increase your radio coverage. A good place to start is with those magazine programmes devoted specifically to Europe. They are always looking for interesting subjects with a European angle. There are of course plenty of such programmes on the international channels mentioned at the beginning of this chapter, but they can also be found on national radio channels. For example, the BBC's Radio Five Live has a slot called *Euronews* (nothing to do with the TV channel of the same name) which is broadcast every weekday morning.

Draw up a shortlist of the programmes that reach your kind of audience, and make contact with them whenever you have a story likely to be of interest. Listen to the ones that deal with subjects closest to your area of activity, and make a note of the names of the presenters and reporters. You should also study the programme Web site, if there is one, and try to get a feel for the kind of stories they cover.

Contact foreign radio journalists based in your capital city

Whichever country you are in, another option is to approach foreign correspondents of national radio stations based in your capital city. They are always looking for interesting stories to send back home. It helps, of course, if your press release is in their language. Most importantly of all, you should be able to offer interviewees who are either native speakers or fluent in the language concerned.

In most countries you can get an up-to-date list of foreign correspondents from the government, which keeps track of them for diplomatic, tax and media purposes. In the UK it is the London Correspondents' Service at the Foreign Office; in Moscow the Department of Information and Press at the Foreign Ministry should be able to help.

Don't forget local and regional radio

It may seem strange to mention local and regional radio in the context of European news stories, but in fact they can sometimes be the most eager consumers of such events. Take the example of the awarding of a prize for the most interesting museum in Europe. This would be a big story in the city where the museum is based, and the local media would be very likely to give it extensive coverage. Similarly, when someone is appointed to a top Euro job, it makes news wherever he or she comes from. After the initial publicity surrounding the appointment, there will be plenty of takers for stories of the 'day in the life' genre. So do not forget the local and regional angles of your story, whether it is for radio, TV or the press.

Sponsor a radio programme

Quite a few radio stations in Europe accept sponsorship, though most prefer the sponsor to have some link with the content of the programme. For example, a bank or investment trust would be an ideal sponsor for a financial news bulletin, an airline for a travel programme, and so on. Sponsorship can sometimes involve the creation of an entirely new programme with the sole aim of covering the sponsor's activities. This is the case with some European institutions, such as the European Parliament, which pays radio networks in France, Denmark and other countries to make programmes to cover its parliamentary sessions. In such cases sponsors are usually, but not always, entitled to check the programme before it is broadcast. As well as providing publicity, such programmes can be posted on your Web site to add interest, and kept as archive material for future radio and multimedia projects.

Make an audio news release (ANR)

What is an ANR?

An audio news release is the radio equivalent of the video news release or the press release. While words are the raw material for the print journalist, and pictures for his or her television counterpart, the radio reporter needs sounds. That can mean music, speech and background noise often referred to by the professionals as 'actuality' (eg chanting at a demonstration, the roar of the racing cars at a Formula One meeting). A good ANR should cater for these various needs.

ANR content

The first priority is the spoken word, so it should contain interviews with your key spokespersons and/or voiced texts from key documents (always use professionals to do the voices, unless you have someone with a good voice in-house. Using an authentic voice can sometimes sound more convincing than a voiceover professional).

As well as providing a full interview, select several sound bites of about 20 seconds that highlight the main points. Some radio stations are so busy they may not have time to listen to the whole interview, or even more likely, they will not have the airtime to use the whole thing. In this case they will prefer to use a sound bite, so be sure to provide these. Speech elements can be supplemented by other relevant sounds. For example, if the story is about a manufacturing company expanding its workforce, you might consider recording the sound of the factories where the new workers are going to be employed.

If the story is about the European Union or the Council of Europe, two distinct organizations that share a common anthem, Beethoven's *Ode To Joy*, then it makes sense to include this music in the ANR. Always provide radio journalists with options, so they can choose the most appropriate version for their programme format. For example, the Council of Europe offers not only the traditional orchestral version of Beethoven's *Ode*: there are also electric guitar and jazz violin versions, and even one in techno style! Different radio stations have different target audiences, and one aimed at young people will be more likely to take the techno version than its classical counterpart. Another measure of flexibility is length. For example, you might provide versions of 15, 30 and 45 seconds in each style, thereby allowing the journalist to choose the most suitable length for his or her purposes.

But however you use music, be very careful with copyright. Anything by a famous artist, living or dead, could cost a huge amount to use, and although there is a lot of off-the-shelf anonymous 'mood music' which is much cheaper to use, this will still come with a price tag attached. The only sure way to avoid copyright problems is to commission original music with a contract that assigns all conceivable rights to your organization. But this option is also expensive, and takes time (someone has to compose the music, then it has to be performed and then mixed etc). Copyright can be extremely complicated, so if in doubt, get specialist legal advice, or leave out the music altogether.

Transcripts

Wherever possible, you should provide a transcript of the speech content of the ANR. This will help the journalist to rapidly identify the elements that he or she can use. As with the video news release, an ANR aimed at journalists from different countries should offer a wide range of linguistic versions of the key interviews or statements. This means that either the same person who does the interview in English should also be able to repeat the points in other languages, or you use different people for each language.

Format flexibility

Finally, it may be necessary to produce the ANR on several technical formats, because there is a much wider technological variation between different radio stations than between television outlets. Giving a radio journalist an ANR in the wrong format will at the very least lose you good-will, because it will oblige him or her to transfer your material onto a more convenient standard. In the worst case, the radio journalist may be discouraged from using it at all, and simply throw it into the bin. If you want to play it safe, put your ANR on an ordinary CD, because this format is as universal as you can get. But if you want to provide a range of formats, then seek advice from a radio technician.

Organize a radio media tour

While ANRs can be a good method of tempting overworked and financially challenged local radio stations into covering your story, well-funded regional and national programmes are much less likely to take the bait. For them it is crucially important to do their own interview conducted by one of their star presenters. This is when the radio media tour (RMT) can be very effective. RMTs are much simpler than their TV equivalents from a technical point of view, and infinitely cheaper. It involves your spokesperson doing a series of interviews with different radio stations in a short space of time – usually a morning or afternoon – all from the same radio studio. You can either use your own studio, if it is equipped with an appropriate Codec (decoder) and ISDN line, or hire an outside studio. The interviews can be done with radio stations in one country or several countries – there is little difference in cost.

RMTs are usually used only for big events, because most leaders only have a limited time to do media interviews. If you do not have the time to set up the interviews yourself, we recommend contacting a company that specializes in this field. They will be able to advise you on the costs involved, and handle the technical and organizational side of things. Alan Hardy, Head of Broadcast Services at PR Newswire, says no matter where you are on the planet, it is possible to reap the rewards of the RMT:

> We went to San Antonio in Texas to cover a medical conference on a new breakthrough in the fight against breast cancer. I hired a portable ISDN Codec locally in San Antonio, and was able to provide 'down-the-line' radio interviews in studio quality to a range of stations back in Europe. We offered appropriate experts for each country. For example, the German international broadcaster Deutsche Welle did an interview with a German doctor for their science and technology programme. It is vitally important to make sure that the equipment you are using is compatible with the radio stations you want to connect to. Systems can vary and as a result linking between studios can be a problem, especially internationally. But as long as you get it right technically, you can target radio stations anywhere in Europe, from wherever in the world you happen to be.

Part 2

Europe's media: country by country

Introduction

Our aim in this section of the book is to help newcomers by giving a snapshot of the media scene in 43 European countries (with apologies to the micro-states of Europe, such as Andorra, Liechtenstein, Monaco and San Marino, which we have not included in our survey). Every country is different – in style, in professional standards and in the choices people make to receive their everyday news. Neighbouring countries can have completely different approaches to their media – take for instance Romania and Moldova. These varying styles have been shaped by history, politics, economics and social factors such as literacy.

Between us we have worked with journalists from all the countries covered. We have visited many in a professional capacity, and some have become close to our hearts. We have worked with the struggling journalists of the Balkans during the Milosevic era, and seen them emerge from the darkness into a more transparent, democratic age. We have tried to help developing countries to overcome their lack of financial resources to report important stories from abroad. We have also tried to find ways of equipping the poorer television and radio stations in Albania and Macedonia with donations in kind from richer Western news organizations. Our approach to each country comes spiced with a lot of affection and sympathy, and hopefully some understanding and insights. We did not set out with any quota system in mind, but perhaps inevitably we have given more space to the larger countries of Europe, and in particular to the country we know best of all, the United Kingdom.

Wherever possible, we have given approximate circulation figures for newspapers, but these should be treated with caution for at least three reasons. Firstly, by the time this book is published they will already be out of date. Secondly, in some countries there is a tendency to exaggerate circulations in order to make a paper look more successful than it really is. Finally, in other countries the reverse is true – because papers are taxed on the number of copies sold, owners tend to downplay the circulation size in order to pay less tax. Even taking these problems into account, however, we feel it is a useful pointer to the paper's influence.

Precious sources of information were the European Journalism Centre in Maastricht, the Netherlands, with a huge treasure trove of information in their so-called 'toolbox' of country media profiles. The IREX organization provides facts and figures backed up with careful research and scientific methodology. Pressure groups such as the Campaign for Press Freedom, Reporters without Borders, Amnesty International and Freedom House keep a constant and very close check on media freedom throughout the world. Many governments cover the national media on their own Web sites, and the BBC Web site has a range of country profiles that gives a useful quick overview of the media.

We could not have finished this project without the help of many friends – journalists, media experts and colleagues – who took the time to check the accuracy of the information. Their names can be found at the front of the book, and we would like to say a special thank you to them for all their efforts.

Albania

Until 1990, Albania was the land that Europe forgot, where bicycles rather than cars were the preferred mode of transport, and 1960s British slapstick comedian Norman Wisdom was one of the top stars. But the death of dictator Enver Hoxha and the collapse of communism throughout Central and Eastern Europe changed all that forever. After half a century cut off from the rest of the world, Albania has a long road to travel before it catches up with accepted standards – and that also holds true for media matters.

Democracy and freedom of expression have come as a mixed blessing to the people of Albania. In fact, one look at the media scene might be enough to convince an observer that there is too much freedom of expression – or at least too much freedom for journalists to express their stories in any way they happen to fancy. One regular reader of Albanian papers confirmed that the 10 different national papers could easily give 10 completely different versions of the same story.

Part of this is to do with the influence of politics and mafia – part of it is the lack of adequate training for journalists. IREX (the International Research & Exchanges Board), the main US organization specializing in independent media, reported in their Media Sustainability Index that 'the notion of professional standards for journalists in Albania does not have much currency' and that the journalism faculty of Tirana University is 'deplorable'.

Brave attempts are being made to redress the situation. The international community and broadcasters such as the BBC and Deutsche Welle are putting a lot of effort into raising journalistic standards through training programmes – both in the country itself and by hosting trainee journalists in London or Berlin. There are also moves afoot to draw up a training programme for journalists at Tirana University with support from the University of Massachusetts in the USA.

In the meantime, anyone working with the Albanian media has to be aware of its peculiarities. Amongst these is the lack of any respect for confidentiality, a lesson learnt by the staff of one international organization who held back a report from their own colleagues, believing it to be highly confidential, only to find it all over the next day's papers. The media in general also has scant regard for privacy – non-Albanians were shocked to see close-up pictures of a young girl's dead body plastered across the front pages after a ferry accident. Nor are journalists too hot on accuracy. Arban Leskaj, Editor of the *Albanian Daily News*, told the French magazine *Telerama* that: 'Journalists do not investigate, never check any facts and are happy just to write sensational stories.' Of the main national newspapers *Shekulli*, owned by a Tirana businessman, and the Italian-owned *Gazeta Shqiptare* are the most reasonable. Another popular newspaper is *Korrieri*.

Most papers are tied to one political party or the other, but nepotism is at its worst in the audiovisual sector. A very common practice is for budding tycoons to supplement their businesses with a TV channel or a newspaper.

Albanians are obsessed by television. In a country of 3.5 million people there are 80 channels – but almost all have tiny catchment areas, and very few cover the whole of the country. The main television stations licensed to broadcast nationally are TVSH, TV Klan and TV Arberia.

The Albanian love affair with television has its roots in the communist era, when families would realign dodgy antennae to pick up the Italian stations across the Adriatic. This was not necessarily a political action – simply a symptom of the massive curiosity the Albanians had for the world outside their borders. Today the fans of Italian TV are restricted to the seaside towns – the signal no longer reaches into the interior.

The home-grown market is in a state of flux. At the time of writing it was basically controlled by political parties, large industrial groups or powerful individuals (TV Klan, for example, is backed by the Ada Group), but discussions were under way on a frequency map to regulate the situation. In the meantime, the state operator, Albanian Radio and TV (RTSh), operates national radio and TV networks. Faced with domestic crises and uncertainties, many Albanians now consider that their best and most trusted source of accurate information remains the foreign operators – the BBC, Deutsche Welle, Radio France International, Radio Free Europe and the Voice of America, who all broadcast in Albanian.

Armenia

One of the world's most ancient civilizations, Armenia has an extensive Diaspora (some estimates put it as high as 10 million, more than three times the population of Armenia itself), with large communities living in Los Angeles, Moscow and Paris. Famous Armenians include the singer Charles Aznavour, chess champion Gary Kasparov, novelist William Saroyan and composer Aram Khachaturyan. After the collapse of communism, Armenia gained independence and fought a short war with Azerbaijan over the disputed enclave of Nagorno Karabach, officially part of Azerbaijan but with an Armenian majority. This has soured relations with both Azerbaijan and its ally Turkey, who continue to embargo land-locked Armenia, with catastrophic results for living standards. In 1999 Armenia's fledgling democracy suffered a serious blow when Armenian gunmen stormed the country's parliament, killing the prime minister, the speaker, two deputies and three other people.

The US-based human rights NGO Freedom House recently downgraded the status of Armenia's media from 'Partly Free' to 'Not Free'. It deplored the use of criminal libel and state security laws to prosecute journalists as a way of stifling criticism. The NGO also disapproved of a decision to close A1+, an independent TV station that had often been critical of the government.

There are currently more than 30 newspapers in Armenia. Most have links with political parties and institutions, and are generally either pro-government or pro-opposition. Government-supporting papers include *Azg* (Nation), *Hayastani Hanrapetutyun* (Republic of Armenia) and *Hayots Ashkar* (Armenian World), and papers that lean more towards the opposition include *Aravot* (Morning), *Haykakan Zhamanak* (Armenian Times) and *Iravunk* (Right). *Novoe Vremya* (New Times) is published only in Russian. Another Russian language publication, *Golos Armenii* (Voice of Armenia), is more or less neutral politically. For the business community there is the weekly *Delovoy Express* (Business Express).

Newspaper sales are extremely low in Armenia. Not one sells more than 10,000 copies a day, and average sales are around 3,000 to 4,000.

There are more news agencies in Armenia than in either of the other two Caucasian republics. No fewer than eight agencies ply their trade: Armenpress (state owned), Arminfo, Arka, Mediamax, New Image, Photolur, Spiur and Noyan Tapan.

Television is the prime source of news for most Armenians, and watched by 90 per cent of the population. The two main Armenian television channels are the state broadcaster Public Television and Radio of Armenia, and the privately owned Armenia TV. ALM and Prometevs are also popular. Russian TV channels such as ORT and RTR can also be seen throughout the country, and Euronews is re-broadcast on ArmNews TV. Most key decision makers in Armenia get their news from state TV, especially the main bulletin, *Haylur*.

Radio is without doubt the least politicized of the media. A range of FM stations, available in the capital and nearby cities, provide news and information in Armenian, Russian and even French. The most popular are Hai-FM 105.5, Radio Van FM 103, Radio Ardzaganq and Russkoe Radio (broadcast from Moscow in Russian).

Austria

Austria's imperial past as the seat of the sprawling Habsburg empire is often overlooked by the rest of the world in favour of more recent triumphs such as the film *The Sound of Music* and Mozart chocolates. Underneath the surface, though, this Alpine country is a politically fascinating place. The rise of the populist right-wing politician Jörg Haider in the early 1990s gave the European political establishment a lot to chew on, as his neo-Fascist policies made waves throughout the continent. Austria is nothing if not a land of contrast: it is also the land of the Green Party, of anti-globalization protest and ecology movements. The capital, Vienna, is the seat of one of the main international organizations – the Organization for Security and Cooperation in Europe – and one of the four global headquarters of the United Nations.

Daily life for an Austrian would not be complete without a newspaper to go with their coffee and cakes. The Austrians even claim to have founded the oldest newspaper in the world still in print – the *Wiener Zeitung*. Despite its veteran status it has managed to keep up with the times and runs a rich Web site, which includes many facts and figures on the country, with a large amount of information in the English language. Every Tuesday, the *Wiener Zeitung* publishes an English language supplement *The Week in Austria*.

Austrians love tabloid gossip, and some of the home-grown varieties are especially vibrant and colourful in their approach to the news. The biggest seller is the *Neue Kronen Zeitung*, which claims to have 3 million readers. Its main rival, *Kleine Zeitung*, also prefers a tabloid format for the news, but the ultra-tabloid *Täglich Alles* – once the third most popular – closed a few years ago.

There is also a wide range of quality broadsheets that cover the news in a more sober manner – including *Kurier*, *Die Presse* and *Der Standard*. *Die Presse* operates an English Web site at www.diepresse.com.

Austrians also enjoy their news in a glossy, weekly format, and a range of news magazines feed the appetite for political analysis and lifestyle articles, amongst them *Profil*, *News* and *Die Ganze Woche*. There is a healthy regional press, and daily papers like the *Salzburger Nachrichten* and the *Tiroler Tageszeitung* have a faithful following. However, the strong influence of the nationals throws a shadow over the regional scene – *Neue Kronen Zeitung*, for instance, prints regional editions of the main newspaper, creating fierce competition for the local press.

The Austria Presse Agentur (Press Agency) is the national news agency – providing balanced coverage on national and international topics. They have a small amount of information in English on their Web site www.apa.co.at.

The rise of the right wing in Austrian politics has proved a challenge for reporters, and led to some heavy criticism from international watchdog groups. The Council of Europe's Commission Against Racism and Intolerance (ECRI) noted in 2001 that 'some mainstream newspapers regularly report on immigration and asylum issues in a manner that contributes to creating an atmosphere of hostility and rejection towards members of minority groups... The influence that these newspapers exercise on public opinion appears to be very strong.' On a more positive note, many newspapers took a firm stand against Haider, and many journalists fought against political manipulation at the risk of personal attack or lawsuits.

One of the main sources of concern for most media freedom watchdogs is the concentration of ownership in the Austrian media – two groups own most of the newspapers and magazines, and electronic broadcasting is only just opening up to competition. The public broadcaster Österreichischer Rundfunk (ORF) had the distinction of being the last state broadcaster to operate a monopoly in both TV and radio, until a law to free the market came into effect only in January 2002. In June 2003 the first Austrian-wide private TV channel ATV+ started operating, but for the moment ORF still dominates the television and radio scene, running two television and four radio channels. Nonetheless, there are a number of private radio stations, mostly providing chat and music targeted to the different regions.

Cable or satellite is the alternative to this national monopoly, and about 75 per cent of Austrian homes use this, often to watch German stations, some of which tailor their output to the tastes of their nearest neighbour.

Azerbaijan

At the start of the 20th century, Azerbaijan supplied half the world's oil. Although production has greatly declined since this peak, it remains a major earner for the country's economy, and recent discoveries of vast gas deposits in the Caspian Sea have brought Western companies back to the capital Baku to negotiate new contracts. Although the oil and gas bonanzas have not yet brought visible benefits for the ordinary Azerbaijani, the country's long-term economic prospects are the brightest in the region. However, one major concern remains the long running Nagorno Karabach dispute with neighbouring Armenia. The conflict has left 1 million Azerbaijanis homeless as a result of the loss of one-fifth of the country's territory.

The US-based media monitor Freedom House classes the Azerbaijani media as 'Not Free' because it claims there is too much political interference, including the use of libel laws to punish media outlets seen to be critical of the government. There are also reports of physical attacks and other forms of intimidation on journalists who step out of line.

Newspapers have been published in Azerbaijan since 1875 – the first to appear was *Akinchi* (The Ploughman) which lasted less than two years, but despite its short existence it managed to lay the foundations of the country's journalistic traditions. Today more than 800 newspapers are registered but fewer than 150 appear with any regularity.

Regional newspapers are weak, and of the national titles, most have political links, financed either by the government or political parties. Among the government category are *Azerbaijan*, *Bakinskii Rabochi*, *Respublica* and *Khalg Gazeti*. Papers with party political links include *Yeni Azerbaijan* (New Azerbaijan Party), *Azadliq* (Popular Front), *Yeni Musavat* and *Mukhalifat* (Musavat party), *Millet* (National Independence party), *Istiglal* (Social Democratic Party), *Khurriyet* and *Ulus* (Democratic Party of Azerbaijan), *Vatandash Hamrayliyi* (Civil Solidarity Party) and *Politika* (Adalyat Party). The most widely read opposition paper is *Yeni Musavat*.

The remainder of the press is independent or linked with business or industrial interests. Of these the most influential are *Ayna, Ekho, 525th Newspaper* and *Sharg. Ayna* also produces a Russian version called *Zerkalo*.

The main Russian language papers are *Ayna/Zerkalo, Ekho* and *Novoye Vremya*. English language newspapers include *Azernews, Azeri Times, Baku Sun, Baku Times* and *Caspian Business News*.

The leading news agencies are AzerTaj (state-run), Turan News Agency, Azerpress, Olaylar News Agency, Trend Information Agency, AzadInform News Agency and Media Press Agency. As well as Azeri, all of them offer a service in English and Russian.

TV broadcasts started in Azerbaijan in 1956. Today 5 national and 11 regional companies share the market. State television covers the whole country with its two channels. The most important of the remaining broadcasters are ANS (Azerbaijan News Service), Lider TV, Space TV and Azad Azerbaijan TV, which cover about 60–80 per cent of the country. They all have a commitment to provide extensive coverage of news and current affairs. Many Azeri people can speak Turkish, which is very similar to Azeri, and Russian – a legacy of the country's long-standing links with Russia, before, during and after communism. Turkish and Russian TV channels are therefore also popular sources of news and entertainment in Azerbaijan.

There are a number of national radio networks in Azerbaijan, including two state channels run by Azerbaijan Radio. Independent speech-based national stations include ANS-Radio, Azad Azerbaijan Radio, Lider Radio, Space Radio and Antenn 101. The Azeri service of Radio Liberty is also a popular source of information.

Belarus

One of the poorest countries in Europe, Belarus has had an exceptionally raw deal in the past century. During the Second World War it was ravaged by the conflict between Nazi Germany and the Soviet Union – one in four of its population was killed in the fighting. In 1986 a quarter of its territory was polluted by radioactive fallout from the Chernobyl disaster in neighbouring Ukraine. In more recent years the country has been an international outcast thanks to the anti-democratic antics of its eccentric leader, President Alexander Lukashenko, described by human rights groups as the last communist dictator in Europe. State control over the economy has discouraged foreign investment, and living standards have plummeted.

The media scene reflects the political climate, and freedom of the press is under constant attack from the state. Independent media outlets are put under financial and legal pressure (libel is still a criminal as well as a civil offence, and journalists can also be punished for insulting an official). After the 2001 presidential elections, three journalists were sentenced to several years of forced labour for writing critical articles about the president. In the most extreme case of its kind, a cameraman for a Russian television station is still missing, presumed dead, after disappearing on a journey to Minsk airport in 2000.

The majority of media outlets are either directly owned or subsidized by the state. Pro-government papers are charged lower prices for printing and distribution (a high proportion of papers are delivered by the state postal system, or sold at state-owned kiosks. The state also has a monopoly on printing presses). The result is that independent papers cost much more than those that follow the government line. Moreover, access to printing presses and the means of distribution can be denied at any time to papers that annoy the government.

Sovietskaya Belorussiya (Soviet Belarus) is the main mouthpiece for the regime, and has a bigger circulation (330,000) than the 15 leading non-state publications put together. The main independent daily *Narodnaya Volya* (People's Will) sells around 35,000 copies, well ahead of its rivals, the nearest of which is *Belarusskaya Delovaya Gazeta* (Business Paper of Belarus).

Unsurprisingly, in a country that has always maintained close cultural ties with Russia (Belarus means 'White Russia'), Moscow-based publications are very popular, with *Argumenty I Fakty* and *Komsomolskaya Pravda* leading the field. Together with the rest of the Russian press, they carry Belarusian supplements.

Some of the best papers offering considered opinion and analysis, and constructive criticism of the government, are *Belorusskaya Delovaya Gazeta* (Business Paper of Belarus), *Belorusskj Rynok* (Belarusian Market) and *Belorusskaya Gazeta* (Paper of Belarus). Their more measured approach is popular with business people and other movers and shakers of the Belarusian elite.

The leading news agency in Belarus is the state-run Belta. Bela Pan and Interfax-Zapad (modelled on the Russian Interfax agency) are its two private sector rivals.

There are three domestic television channels available nationwide. Two are directly run by the state broadcaster, Belteleradiocompany. The third, ONT, is nominally independent but the state has a controlling shareholding, so it is effectively a third state channel. The First National TV Channel has been around since Soviet times. By contrast, the LAD channel was launched in October 2003, and describes itself as the 'first-ever family channel in Belarus... with programmes devoted to culture, education, upbringing and religion'. The station's homely motto is 'Our creed is sharing kindness with others'. ONT has managed to gain a reputation for more objective news coverage than its rivals. Much of its entertainment programming is bought from Channel One Russia, which is ironic, as the Russian station is no longer available in Belarus since ONT took over its frequency in 2002.

There are 21 regional and local stations, linked in their own network. However, according to an independent survey, most Belarusians prefer to watch one of the two main Russian channels, which between them account for more than 80 per cent of viewers (though Belarusian channels do get large audiences for their news programmes, for the simple reason that Russian newsrooms pay scant attention to what happens in Belarus).

Radio is much more of a home-grown affair, with nearly half of all listeners tuning into the First National Channel, which is run by the state. The rest of the audience is shared between a host of independent stations, including Radio BA (an American-Belarusian joint venture), Radio Rocks, Alpha Radio, Radio Unistar, Nashe Radio and Radius FM. Some Belarusians follow the news on Radio Free Europe/Radio Liberty, the American-funded international broadcaster based in the Czech capital, Prague.

Belgium

The land of beer and chips with mayonnaise is also the home of Tintin, the ace cartoon reporter, and his dog Snowy, who inspired many a youngster to dream of a career in journalism.

As the main seat of the EU institutions, Belgium merits its own section as an international media hub. But it is also one of the most politically interesting of the European countries – and its uniqueness is reflected in the nature of its national media.

Belgium is a federation – and a country of two main linguistic groups. The French and the Flemish (a dialect of Dutch) speakers do not see eye to eye. The two languages are officially recognized, along with German, which is spoken by a small minority. Anyone venturing into Belgian territory has to be aware of the acute sensitivity of the language issue: if you are not prepared to change everything into both French and Flemish, you would be better off sticking to English rather than risking the wrath of one language group or the other.

This linguistic divide also cuts through the media world. Belgians may not be great newspaper readers (it is estimated only 36 per cent buy one on a daily basis), but there is nevertheless a plethora of newspapers. The biggest seller in the Flemish part of the country is *Het Laatste Nieuws*, with its French equivalent *Le Soir* heading the French-speaking league. There is also a newspaper in German – *Grenz-Echo*. Readers seeking financial news look to *De Financieel Economische Tijd* or *L'Echo*.

Of 26 regional newspapers in Belgium, only 10 stand on their own – the other 16 papers are parallel editions of the main papers printed for the regions, and differ only slightly from them.

Belga – the national press agency – began its life in 1920 and today sends out more than 200,000 dispatches in French and Flemish. Its Web site gives information in English, Flemish and French.

Each language group has its own separate broadcasting companies – VTM and VTR for Flanders and RTBF for the French-speaking Walloon region and the capital Brussels. Private radio stations in both languages flourish, and often broadcast to very small communities. Belgium is also the most densely cabled country in the world (over 90 per cent of all households) and is also able to pick up terrestrial broadcasts from neighbouring countries, including Britain.

Bosnia and Herzegovina

Bosnia and Herzegovina's media suffered as much as the rest of the country during the Balkans conflicts. Journalists became one of the weapons of war – with propaganda taking over from professionalism and biased, politicized reporting becoming the norm.

The Dayton agreement in 1995 divided the country into a federation between what are called the two 'entities' of Bosnia and Herzegovina: the Republic of Srpska (mostly Serb) and the Federation of Bosnia-Herzegovina (mainly Moslem and Croat). The country's institutional scene is therefore extremely complex, and can cause headaches to anyone wanting to achieve political correctness.

Thankfully, post-war rebuilding has extended to the media, and a new generation of journalists is beginning to appear. Much of the credit for this has to go to the international organizations and international media such as the BBC and the Independent Media Commission, who have taken up the challenge of retraining the journalists to ensure higher standards in the future. Nonetheless, the people of Bosnia and Herzegovina are still deeply cynical about their media and it is certain that there is still a long way to go before professional standards apply across the board.

The biggest-selling paper is the daily *Dnevni Avaz* (the Daily Voice). Professionally produced, giving reliable information in bite-sized chunks, it is mainly read by the Bosniak (mostly Moslem) population. The most popular paper in Republika Srpska (the Serbian part of Bosnia) is the Belgrade-produced *Blic*, an excellent independent tabloid. *Nezavisne Novine* (Independent Newspaper) is another paper that gives fair and balanced information and is read throughout the country. Newspapers and magazines imported from Croatia are popular amongst the Croatian section of the population.

For the outside world, the most famous paper of all is *Oslobodjenje* (Freedom), the only one that continued production during the war.

Suffering from poor management, *Oslobojenje* is the best for well-researched articles and sharp editorials, but poor organization means it sometimes misses important news stories.

Weeklies are important, with *Slobodna Bosna* (Free Bosnia) generally digging out interesting stories, but sometimes presenting them in a sensationalist manner. *BH Dani*, its main rival, is more serious minded. The biggest seller of all is the *Express*. Claiming a 40,000 circulation, it hardly ever covers politics and concentrates instead on celebrity gossip.

There are a number of news agencies. ONASA was set up in 1994 by the *Oslobodjenje* management in Sarajevo. SRNA covers the Republika Srpska, while FENA is the agency of the other part of the country – the Croat/Moslem dominated Federation of Bosnia-Herzegovina. The SENSE news agency, based in Belgrade and covering the whole of the Balkans, also serves Bosnia and Herzegovina.

Television is much watched in Bosnia, where more than half the population are jobless, and is therefore a worthwhile target for good stories. There is no federation-wide public television station (and only one news programme at 7.30 pm on TV BH1), but there are plans to change this. Meanwhile, only the evening news programme is broadcast to the whole country, with regional opt-outs for the rest of the day. The main private television station – TV Hayatt – has a good reputation and is available on satellite to millions of Bosnian expatriates around the world.

Radio is an important medium throughout the Balkans, and this is equally true in Bosnia and Herzegovina. All the main broadcasters are based in Sarajevo, with strong regional radio.

Bulgaria

The Bulgarian media is in a state of flux and semi-crisis, mainly caused by government and mafia interference.

Even after the fall of communism, newspapers were still linked to political parties or trade unions, but the links gradually broke. One of the main politically backed newspapers, *Demokratjia*, ceased publishing in 2002. *Duma* is the only paper still run by a political party, and even that is in financial crisis.

All print media in Bulgaria are now privately owned. Major private newspapers include the German-owned *24 Chasa* (24 Hours), which has a circulation of 150,000, and *Trud* (Labour), with 200,000. The market is volatile and new publications come on to the market all the time, although Bulgarians are not big newspaper readers, and circulation figures are fewer per head than other countries in the region.

There is a wide and varied range of opinion and colour to be found amongst the newspapers. Tabloids dominate the market but some of them, such as *Sega Daily*, are of very good quality. *Dnevnik* remains the only quality broadsheet. There is a fair amount of self-censorship to fit in with the views of owners, but professional standards are high amongst many journalists.

Journalists complain that the two main newspapers have a monopoly, and that it is exceptionally hard to break into the market because of alleged mafia control of distribution. It is certainly true that anyone wanting to read anything other than the main newspapers has to be an early riser – it is almost impossible to find independent newspapers after nine in the morning.

Bulgaria was one of the last eastern European countries to pass a broadcasting law in 1996, followed by another in 2001. Government interference, especially in broadcasting, is still a hot topic. Journalists from the state radio even went on strike in 2001 to protest against a government-appointed director. There are more than 60 private radio stations and several privately owned regional television stations. In May 2000, Balkan

News Corporation, part of Rupert Murdoch's News Corporation, launched the country's first national commercial channel.

Established in 1898, the Bulgarian News Agency (BTA) is one of the oldest in Eastern Europe and is still the most prestigious and professional agency in the country. It employs several hundred journalists and translators at its headquarters in Sofia, and has an extensive network of correspondents in the country. BTA has recently had to fight its own battle against government control, with journalists striking against the appointment of a new director who they felt was a government placeman. But it has not stopped their expansion and, in a bid to attract the attention of the foreign press stationed in Sofia, BTA recently opened an ultra-modern press centre, complete with a press conference room equipped with interpreting equipment, a work room for journalists and a bar.

Croatia

Croatia, with its incredibly beautiful coastline and rugged interior, was the setting for one of the most ferocious conflicts of the late 20th century. The first Balkan country to descend into outright war, it had a difficult start on its path to democracy. Governed until his death in 1999 by the autocratic Franjo Tudjman, Croatia is now enjoying the benefits of democracy, and its society is changing at a phenomenal pace.

Tudjman's authoritarian nationalist style was reflected in the country's media. His party, the HDZ (Croatian Democratic Union), kept a tight grip on journalists – even to the point of searching their homes – and broadcasting was rigidly government-controlled right up until his death. However, the past few years have seen freedom return to the media world, and journalists are now able to work and report independently. A big problem for journalists has been how to shake off the habit of self-censorship that in former years guaranteed their protection from prosecution. The main threat to media freedom now comes from the concentration of media in fewer hands: the German media conglomerate WAZ now owns the majority of publications and has a major influence on the third TV Channel.

The result of these changes has been a big improvement in the quality of the media in Croatia. The main daily newspapers report more or less accurately, and are receptive to international as well as national stories. The top seller is the *Vecernji List*. Previously allied to the Tudjman regime, it is now owned by the Austrian Styria group and reports the news in a balanced way. The next most popular is *Jutarnji List*. Launched as an opposition paper in 1998 to challenge the *Vecernji List* monopoly, it is a tabloid with a broadsheet mentality that provides excellent analysis and commentary from the left and centre of the political spectrum. Third in the newspaper league is *Slobodna Dalmacija*, the regional paper for the Dalmatian coast. It was Croatia's most important independent newspaper until 1993, when it was taken over by a tycoon from Tudjman's party and dragged to the right. It remained a nationalist newspaper until 2001 when the government replaced the management and steering board. It now reflects a range of views, although it is sometimes accused of toeing a pro-government line. The fourth paper, *Novi List*, is independent financially and politically and owned by its employees. It is devoted to the principle of multicultural-ism and gives excellent political commentaries.

One newspaper now lagging behind in the market is *Vjesnik*. It was the Croatian newspaper of record before the war, and has retained the best quality reporting, although its readership has dwindled. It is fighting hard to shake off the shadow of the Tudjman years, when it was the govern-ment mouthpiece, and now once more offers accurate reporting.

News magazines are very popular in Croatia and the most influential and widest read is *Globus*. It is owned by the same group as the *Jutarnji List* and generally supports the left SDP party. It skilfully blends gossip with commentary and was instrumental in shaping opposition to Tudjman. *Globus* is seen by many as the paper that sets the country's political agenda and is useful if you are looking to 'leak' a story. The other weekly *Nacional* has a lower readership than *Globus*, but is very similar. It is critical of both sides of the political world and can sometimes be sensational to the point of inaccuracy but it is nevertheless often the first to open up debate on important issues.

One of the other interesting weekly papers in the country is the *Feral Tribune*. Originally a satirical supplement of *Slobodna Dalmacija*, the paper which covers the coastline of Croatia, it launched independently after the government took over *Slobodna Dalmacija* in 1992. Left leaning and unafraid of criticizing the authorities (sometimes to the point of sacrificing accuracy for clever satire), the *Feral Tribune* has had to fight tooth and nail to stay alive, sometimes facing financial problems as it struggled to pay fines. *Feral* is often the only media outlet to cover human rights issues, and to give a positive view of minorities and refugees. It enjoys the reputation of having maintained a strong anti-nationalist stance throughout the 1990s.

The main Croatian news agency is HINA. It was formally state-owned, but is now a public institution and has improved dramatically since the war. HINA tends to be a bit undiscriminating in what it publishes (seem-ingly everything sent to it!). It includes English on its Web site, although written in a wooden style designed to irritate the average English mother tongue speaker. Nevertheless, it is the main news provider for most of the dailies. The second agency is privately run and based in Split – the STINA, but it lacks the resources to be a serious competitor to HINA.

The biggest problem for media freedom in Croatia has been the years of monopoly by the state broadcasters, Croatian Radio and Television (HRT). During the Tudjman era, Croatian State Television (HTV) and radio acted as the mouthpiece for his regime – 'the most irritating symbols' according to some observers. It has taken some time for the sector to open up. New, more professional programmes from the private television companies have provided healthy competition, and the quality of television and radio production is on the up. The choice of programming reflects a new atmosphere in the Balkans, and even the stolid state radio managed to broadcast the Serbian Orthodox Christmas service in 2002. Changes to media legislation are expected to change HTV from a state broadcaster to a public broadcaster.

HTV is hugely influential in Croatia, with opinion polls from the past few years suggesting that it shapes 80 per cent of public opinion. Viewers now get more variety and a better production than before, thanks to the challenge posed to the HTV evening news, *Dnevnik*, by the success of news programmes on the local networks. The establishment of the first commercial television, Nova TV, has also given the state company something to think about. There are around 17 other television stations in operation, most of them covering a well-defined geographical area. As the book went to print, the third HTV franchise had been awarded for a 10-year period to a consortium led by the Luxembourg-based RTL. The new channel will be called HRTL and should start transmitting within six months.

As far as radio is concerned, state broadcaster HRT has three different channels aimed at different audiences. HR1 is the news channel – something akin to BBC Radio 4 – with rolling news and current affairs programmes. The second channel is devoted to entertainment and magazine programmes, featuring longer, lighter shows, and more music. The third channel is pitched at the intellectuals with a mix of classical music, radio drama and opera.

Commercial radio has an interesting recent history and has played its part in the development of democracy in Croatia. The main player was Radio 101. Set up in the late 1980s by a branch of the Yugoslavian communist party's youth section, 101 soon became one of the country's most influential and independent media outlets. They came onto the market at a time when Croatian state radio held a monopoly, and began to attract a hip new audience with music, shows and excellent news programmes. One of the top programmes was *Aktulac*, which used music to comment on news stories: at a time when censorship was the rule, the music acted as a coded way of editorializing in a freer manner. Another popular programme was *Scarface*, which was based around a different person each week, giving an in-depth look at their personality and life. During the war, 101 was the best source of radio news, even providing material to the state broadcasters.

The tables turned in the mid-90s, when 101 lost the concession for radio to a ghost company, in a political manoeuvre designed to take them off the air. After the announcement, crowds took to the streets of Croatia to protest and the news desk was swamped with gifts – 101 roses, 101 cakes, 101 tee-shirts. When Tudjman found out about the protests, he ordered the police to go in, but the interior minister refused to act, and became a popular hero. The voice of the people – and international pressure – meant they kept the concession, but some claim the celebrity went to their collective heads, and many people think the previous excellent news coverage is now sacrificed for image.

Two other radio stations that broadcast at national level are Narodni Radio (People's Radio), airing mostly dull middle-of-the-road pop, and Otvoreni (Open) Radio, which broadcasts a more eclectic, trendier mix of music. They have won awards for their news programming, although many of their best journalists have now left.

Cyprus and the Turkish Republic of Northern Cyprus

At the beginning of the 21st century this was the last divided country in Europe, split along the so-called 'green line' since 1974. The southern and more affluent side of the island is Greek-speaking; the north, Turkish. Both sides have a large population of expatriates, including many British and Germans (on both sides of the island), Russians (mainly in the South) and Turkish (in the North). This means that the English language media in particular take on a greater importance than they otherwise would, and both sides of the island have their own English language newspapers.

Newspapers on the island of Cyprus have a long and rich history. The first appeared in 1878, and since then more than 350 newspapers and periodicals have seen the light of day. The small number of people on the island and the consequently limited potential for advertising income means that newspapers have fewer resources to send correspondents abroad. However, the republic of Cyprus (southern, Greek-speaking side) is well served in newspapers, despite its small size. These include the independent morning papers *Phileleftheros* (Liberal) and *Politis* (Citizen) and the right-wing papers *Simerini* (Today) and *Alithia* (Truth), and the newspaper of the communist party *Haravghi* (Dawn). The main weekly paper is *Kypros Simera* (Cyprus Today), with most other weeklies dedicated to sport.

Cyprus could probably win a prize for the large proportion of television stations per head of population. The two main channels are run by the state broadcaster, the Cyprus Broadcasting Company. There are also a number of commercial channels (Mega, Antenna, Sigma and Alpha) as well as eight regional and local stations. Relays from the mainlands of Greece and Turkey are also picked up by residents.

The airwaves are equally swamped with radio stations – the main island-wide broadcasters (including a channel run by the church) compete with British armed forces broadcasters for the attention of Cypriots and expats alike. As a former British colony, English is widely spoken and indeed there are so many British expats in the South that there are two thriving daily newspapers and a weekly. The oldest of these is the *Cyprus Mail*, set up in 1945 and still going strong today.

Cyprus is served by its own news agency, the Cyprus News Agency, which provides news in English, Greek and Turkish.

Given its past history, and its proximity to the Middle East news hotspots, the island has been a classic posting for foreign correspondents. The main international news agencies maintain a presence in the capital Nicosia (Greek-Cypriot), with Reuters, Agence France Presse, the Deutsche Presse Agentur and ITAR/TASS all represented.

The northern part of the island has a large assortment of newspapers in the Turkish language, some of them very tendentious. The dozen or so newspapers produced on the island are matched in popularity by papers imported from mainland Turkey. The top seller is *Kibris Daily*, which has correspondents in various media hubs, including London. The most noteworthy of the Northern Cypriot press is *Afrika*. It expresses a vitriolic anti-government attitude – to the point that its editor Sener Levent and chief reporter Memduh Ener were jailed in 2002 (and later released) for insulting 'presidential authority'.

If you are targeting a story at the Turkish Republic of Northern Cyprus (TRNC) the likelihood is that you will also want to reach the English-speaking community. From retired army officers and civil servants to tourists, there is a wide range of people who mix in different circles. Most of them receive the UK media, and to keep up with events on the island they have their own weekly newspaper, *Cyprus Today*. Very similar to a British evening paper, it gives national and international news from the islander's perspective and covers the events of the British community in Cyprus – from art exhibitions to charity fashion shows and cricket matches.

Czech Republic

Since the Iron Curtain fell, the Czechs have restructured and modernized their country and are part of the new wave of European Union members. After many years of communism, they have been able to grasp the reins of their economy and make the most of a rich cultural past, even electing as their first president the famous playwright Vaclav Havel. Prague, the capital city, has become a destination of choice for discerning travellers, and an important stopping point on the international media circuit.

The communist era was a straitjacket for journalists. Forced to prepare party propaganda in the guise of newspapers and electronic media reports, they breathed a collective sigh of relief when the advent of democracy brought immediate freedom to their world. Journalism received a new lease of life, and reporters were quick to turn their critical attention to big business and the government. Czech journalists have since earned themselves a reputation as 'feisty' (the chosen description of the Committee to Protect Journalists) both at home and abroad. State-owned companies were privatized during the 1990s, and foreign-owned companies, mainly the Germans, Swiss, Austrians and Americans, moved into the market, which mushroomed overnight. The only three remaining state-owned media enterprises are Czech TV, Czech Radio and the Czech News Agency.

There are now over 60 daily newspapers in the Czech Republic, and eight of them are national, with a total daily print run of 1 million. The biggest seller is the right of centre *Mlada fronta Dnes* (the Young Front Today), pursuing the news with a young and fresh approach that nets it around 1.3 million readers every day. The tabloid paper *Blesk* (Flash) was one of the rare new arrivals to maintain its popularity and it now takes 16.3 per cent of the market. Close behind it is *Pravo* (Our Rights), which leans towards the left. The former dissident paper *Lidove Noviny* (the People's Paper) also managed to survive the turbulent transitional period. There is also a successful business paper – *Hospodarske Noviny* (Economic Daily).

The liberalization of the newspaper market was a huge incentive to foreign buyers to move in. The main national papers are now owned by companies from Germany, Switzerland, Austria and the United States. The Passauer Neue Presse based in the Bavarian city of Passau owns all the regional press.

CTK – the Czech News Agency – is a public corporation run along similar lines to the BBC. Its journalists competently cover national and regional stories in both Czech and English. It also operates a number of overseas offices, and has correspondents based in all the major media centres of Europe.

The gust of fresh air that swept through the media world at independence was nowhere more pronounced than in the audiovisual sector. Over the past decade, radio and television stations have sprung up all over the country – Prague itself gained 16 new radio stations. There are now more than 60 radio stations, 7 of them covering the whole country.

The state broadcaster Cesky Rozhlas (Czech radio) holds onto a third of the listening public with its five channels. The most popular of the private stations is Frekvence 1, a sister station to France's Europe 2. Another popular radio – Radio Kiss – has an Irish businessman as its majority shareholder.

Czech viewers have the choice of four nationwide television stations, two of them run by the state broadcaster. Of the commercial companies, Nova TV can claim the distinction of being the first private station to start broadcasting in a former communist country, attracting half the viewing public in a short space of time. Less popular is the alternative commercial channel Prima TV which takes just over 19 per cent of the audience.

TV has been one of the most turbulent media sectors in recent years. All Central and Eastern European countries have seen tensions in the media landscape as old habits of censorship and government control are challenged and discarded. The Czech Republic is no exception. There have been a number of court cases and strikes. The most important of them was in 2000 when the journalists at the state-owned Czech Television occupied their offices in a dispute over the appointment of a director general who was regarded by the protesters as a government crony. They claimed that management practices contravened guarantees of impartiality and minimum interference. Calm was eventually restored, but the issue rumbles on under the surface.

Denmark

As you might expect from the land of the famous storyteller Hans Christian Andersen, the Danes are great consumers of information and the trend is towards a steady increase in media outlets, both traditional and new, nationally and regionally.

The first Danish newspaper appeared in 1634, but it was not until 1849 that the print industry was freed from censorship. Even so, this made Denmark one of the first countries to enshrine press freedom in its constitution. The press followed the economic, social and political developments of the day. As the 20th century dawned, Denmark became politicized, and as more and more people were given the vote, a system of party political papers came into existence. Competition from radio and television led to a shrinking print market later in the century, but newspapers remained a part of every Dane's life, and from 1910 to 1955 every household bought at least one daily paper.

TV, radio and now the Internet have cut into the Danes' appetite for the printed word, but newspapers remain an important part of the media scene, with the three national broadsheets, *Berlingske Tidende, Jyllands-Posten* and *Politiken*, easily retaining both readers and respect for their balanced coverage. The tabloid *EkstraBladet* is also very popular and *Berlingske Tidende* publishes a tabloid called *BT*, along with a weekly newspaper *Weekendavisen*. A few more marginal newspapers have a strong market influence, including *Kristeligt Dagblad*, a Christian newspaper, *Børsen*, giving financial news, and *Information*, which started as an illegal news agency during the Second World War. Regional newspapers are also strong, and each household in Denmark also receives one of the many free 'district weeklies'.

Ritzau's Bureau is the national news agency. It takes feeds from foreign agencies, notably Reuters, and in turn disseminates Danish news abroad. Eighty-six per cent of its material is news and about 11 per cent general information. The Bureau was established in 1866 and has been owned by the Danish press since 1947.

Danmarks Radio bears some similarities to the BBC. Program 1 (P1) offers a broad range of mainly informative and cultural programmes, Program 2 (P2musik) broadcasts mainly classical music, while Program 3 (P3) is a music and news channel catering principally for younger listeners. Program 4 (P4) mainly broadcasts entertainment and regional news. There is also a plethora of local radio stations.

National television began transmission in the early 1950s, and local television stations were set up in the early 1980s. The two state television channels have rules that guarantee a considerable amount of news coverage and educational programmes, giving them a serious and respectable image. Commercial stations are not governed by such restrictions, and concentrate instead on entertainment. According to government statistics, the average Dane watched television for two and a half hours per day during 2000, but whether they watched the latest news or the latest soap is not revealed.

Estonia

Estonia is the northernmost and smallest of the Baltic states, with a long history of fighting to maintain independence from its larger neighbours. With an old town that has kept its medieval turrets and winding cobbled streets, the Estonian capital Tallinn is opening up to tourists, and found itself the centre of attention when Estonia won the 2001 Eurovision song contest and hosted the event the next year.

Helped perhaps by its proximity to Finland, a country with which it has close cultural and linguistic links, Estonia has one of the most vibrant media scenes in the Baltics – it has no fewer than seven daily papers serving a population of 1.4 million (close to a world record) and four terrestrial television channels, plus numerous others available by cable and satellite. Human rights groups give the country a clean bill of health on freedom of the media, although some say Estonian journalists remain timid and deferential by comparison with their Western European counterparts. However, there remain a few concerns. In 2001 the publisher of a leading Russian language newspaper was shot dead. But one major issue was addressed in 2001 when parliament decriminalized defamation.

As elsewhere in the Baltic countries, the collapse of communism has led to much greater freedom of expression for journalists, which in Estonia has led to a new style of reporting – more investigative in substance and more tabloid in presentation. The ownership of newspapers passed rapidly from state to private hands, with a series of management/staff buyouts, but subsequently many titles have been bought by individuals or foreign companies. Newspaper editors maintain they are completely independent from the influence of political parties and the government, and in most cases this is true. Some parties have tried to set up their own papers but none has survived as a regular general-interest publication.

The top-selling daily is the tabloid *SL Õhtulet*, with a circulation of 65,000. It is half-owned by Norway's Schibsted and half by the Ekspress Group, whose owner is local publishing magnate Hans H Luik. The paper was created in 2000 as a result of the merger of two tabloids, *Sõnumileht* and *Õhtuleht*.

A close number two is the quality daily *Postimees*, with sales of 62,000. The Norwegian-owned broadsheet has seen its sales plummet from 200,000 under communism, when newspapers received state subsidies. The same applies to its bitter rival, *Eesti Päevaleht*, which now belongs to Hans H Luik. The two papers have been waging a circulation war for several years but *Eesti Päevaleht* has fallen behind with 35,000.

For Russian speakers the top-selling daily is *Estoniya*. For the business community, there is a daily title called *Äripäev* and a weekly *Eesti Ekspress*. The cultural elite of the country reads a weekly paper called *Sirp* and a weekly supplement of *Postimees* called *Arter*.

There is now only one news agency operating in Estonia. The Baltic News Service (BNS) covers all three Baltic republics. The Estonian News Agency (Eesti Teadete Agentuur, ETA) was the national agency but it went out of business in 2003.

On the television scene, Estonian-speaking viewers can watch the public channel Eesti Televisioon (ETV), which also includes a daily news bulletin in Russian, and two private national stations: Kanal 2 and TV3 Channels from Russia, which are no longer available on terrestrial TV, can be seen via cable and satellite, while Finnish television can be picked up by those living in the north of Estonia, which is near to Finland.

Estonia has a public service radio station, Eesti Raadio, which transmits on four channels, including one in Russian. The privately owned KUKU radio station is an important source of news and information for the country's key decision makers. There are more than 20 other private radio stations, most of which are local.

Finland

Finland – a huge country with a tiny population of only 5 million – is now best known as one of the world's leading producers of mobile phones. Almost everyone has one, along with access to the Internet. This strange and close-knit world is the result of centuries of invasion and occupation – first by Sweden, then by Russia – and of the country's hostile climate, with the north of the country experiencing four months of near continuous darkness in the winter months, and the white nights of the summer.

Not surprisingly in such a big country, communication is highly valued, and new forms of media are catching on fast. In early 1995, when the rest of the world was just waking up to the potential of home working, one of the authors visited a couple who both worked as journalists from their summer house about 60 miles from Helsinki. Their home consisted of a basic log cabin with outside toilets and water hauled from a nearby lake. But despite this seemingly primitive setting, both of them kept in close contact with their newsrooms and regularly filed stories on crime, politics and international affairs whilst contemplating a sauna or a trip to feed the sheep and two rabbits that lived in a pen in the back yard.

Finns, like other Nordic peoples, have always been avid readers of newspapers. Most of them are delivered well before the morning post so they can be perused over breakfast. So great is the Finns' appetite for print, in fact, that they come first in the EU league and third in the world, after the Japanese and the Norwegians. Official statistics show that half the population buy (not just read) an evening newspaper. There are over 55 daily newspapers, and 170 weeklies. Each provincial capital has its own paper, and there are also 14 (including 9 dailies) published in Swedish, the national minority language. Nine national dailies are published in the Helsinki area – the biggest sellers are the politically unaffiliated *Helsingin Sanomat* (441,000), the Swedish language *Hufvudstadsbladet* (51,000), the Social Democrat newspaper *Uutispaiva Demari* (17,000), the Centre Party newspaper *Suomenmaa* (8,000) and the independent left-wing paper *Kansan Uutiset* (8,000). If your appetite for news is still not satisfied, you can always turn to the evening papers: *Ilta-Sanomat* (205,000) and *Iltalehti* (126,000). Feeding all these publications with stories is the national news agency STT/FNB.

Yleisradio Oy – or YLE to those of us not yet versed in the mysteries of the Finnish language – is the state broadcaster. It started radio broadcasts in 1926 and now has four nationwide 24-hour Finnish language stations and two stations in Swedish. Advertising is banned on the main channels and a licence fee, as in the UK, funds its operations. YLE's Radio Finland, the country's international voice, broadcasts in English, German, French, Russian and – most curiously – Latin. It also has a joint operation with its Swedish and Norwegian neighbours to broadcast to the Sami people in Lapland. Radio City was the first private radio station to launch in 1985 and is still on air, but one of the most popular is Radio Nova, which proved a success despite tough competition from state stations. It now has around 14 per cent of listeners.

True to its high-tech reputation, Finland first tested cable television in 1950. The first real TV broadcast was in April 1955, thanks to the efforts of the Helsinki University of Technology and the Technical Research Centre of Finland. By the next year there were two hours of programming a week, but the experiment – named TES-TV – turned out to be too expensive and was taken over by the national broadcasting company YLE in 1964. The Finns also created Europe's first independent television station MTV Oy (now known as MTV3) in the 1950s.

YLE began regular broadcasting at the beginning of 1958 and now operates two main state channels, TV1 and TV2, and a commercial television network Channel Four, which started full-time broadcasting in June 1997.

For a very small place, Helsinki seems to have more than its fair share of international events, and is a likely port of call for you if you are hitting the European media trail. Thankfully, the Finns are very helpful and well organized – even down to publishing a free media guide in PDF format on the Web (http://virtual.finland.fi).

France

The French are an intellectual and analytical lot, and one of their great pastimes is to debate the hot topics of the day over coffee or a good meal. Moreover, their history and culture have given them an overwhelming respect for the rights and freedoms of the press (the NGO Reporters without Borders originated in France).

However, the French are not great buyers of national daily newspapers. Data from the World Association of Newspapers put the French amongst the lowest for the number of newspapers sold per 100 adults (just 18 compared with 35 in Germany and 72 in Norway). This trend in declining circulation prompted a former president of the French news agency AFP to declaim, 'People are reading fewer and fewer newspapers in France… the political press is dying.' His prediction is perhaps borne out by the fact that the bestselling daily is the sports paper *L'Equipe*. Still, it doesn't mean that the French shun news, merely that they begrudge paying high prices for newsprint. Café owners are now catching on by providing free newspapers for their clients to peruse, thereby prompting a rise in readership, even if the circulation itself stays low. Another area to buck the trend is the regional and local newspaper sector. Despite the fact that there are far fewer regional titles than in the UK or Germany, the French are fond of their local papers and hold them in great esteem. The largest seller is *Ouest France* with a circulation of nearly 800,000. Other regional newspapers of note include the *Dernières Nouvelles d'Alsace*, *Sud Ouest* and *La Voix du Nord*.

The biggest-selling mainstream newspaper in France according to the circulation figures is *Le Parisien*, with a daily total of 520,000 copies. Next in line is *Le Monde* with 425,000. France's newspaper of record, it was set up at the end of the Second World War in a bid to guarantee the freedom and diversity of a press that had been forced, or had chosen, to collude with the pro-Nazi Vichy regime.

Like *The Times*, *Le Monde* is an institution in itself, and is especially renowned in the world of diplomacy and politics. So much so that it produces the highly prestigious monthly edition *Le Monde Diplomatique*, which informs readers about the behind-the-scenes workings of international politics. It also has a stable of weekly theme-based newspapers – including *Le Monde de L'Education* and *Le Monde des Livres*. Written clearly and elegantly, the paper is an excellent tool for anyone trying to improve their French and gives a very full picture of French concerns.

France's other famous newspapers are *Libération* and *Le Figaro*. Born out of the popular movements of 1968, *Libération* still takes a consistently left-wing view of the world, and analyses current events and hot topics in great depth, while using much more colourful and inventive language than its rivals. On the right, there is the redoubtable *Le Figaro*. The other end of the spectrum – the French Communist Party – is served by the vintage newspaper *L'Humanité*. Set up in 1904 by the French statesman Jean Jaurès, it is still going strong. Even the Church has its own daily newspaper, *La Croix*, and a weekly, *Le Pélérin*.

Business newspapers are an important sector of the market and the leaders are *La Tribune*, *Les Echos* and the weekly supplement produced by *Le Figaro* newspaper, *Le Figaro Economie*.

The Sunday newspaper scene is quite different from Britain. There is only one newspaper published on a Sunday – *Le Journal du Dimanche* – with a circulation of just over 310,000. However, all the regional papers produce a Sunday edition – quite a contrast to their UK neighbours who would be amazed to discover their local paper coming out on the Sabbath.

Where the British have their Sunday nationals, the French enjoy their news and analysis in weekly magazine form. The publications divide on political lines. The *Nouvel Observateur* is on the left, while conservative French readers reach for the weekly magazine published by *Le Figaro*. Other news magazines include *Le Point*, *L'Express* and the cynical and sensational *Marianne*. *Paris Match* is the favourite read for lovers of gossip, but even that is much more inclined to run long, in-depth articles than tabloid chatter. The most iconoclastic of the French weekly magazines (although printed in newspaper format) is *Le Canard Enchainé*: a sort of French *Private Eye*, it mixes satire with investigative reporting to uncover some of the seedier stories. Its use of language borders on slang, and you need not only a very good grasp of the French language, but also a keen sense of the latest issues to be able to fully understand it.

For anyone interested in contrasting perspectives on global affairs, the *Courrier International* offers a weekly digest of press articles from the world's most prestigious newspapers.

Agence France Presse – the national news agency – is one of the giants of the media world, ranking alongside Reuters and AP on the international stage. Based in Paris, with bureaux throughout the world, it claims to be the world's oldest news agency, set up in 1835 by Charles Louis Havas, 'the father of global journalism' according to the AFP Web site. It provides services not only in French and English but in German, Russian, Arabic and Spanish.

Anyone used to the snappy presentation of Anglo-Saxon news will have some difficulties getting used to the slower pace and more analytical style of the French. Television news, especially, contrasts sharply. Whilst the British tune into half-hour news slots at around 6.00 pm or later in the evening, the main French television news lasts for 40 minutes, and covers not only the top news stories, but the latest cinema releases, local traditions and customs, and art exhibitions, sometimes including a long studio interview with a leading figure from the arts world. Whereas in the UK specialist programmes carry these sorts of subjects, the French seem to prefer their news in a more varied 'magazine' format. Similarly, whilst a British bulletin would be unlikely to devote more than a few minutes to any topic, French television can spend up to 10 minutes on a 'sujet'. As in the print world, regional news is very popular: people enjoy revelling in the quirks of their neighbours. The France 3 channel is divided into regional stations, all of which provide local news slots after the main national news. The difference between these and the UK variety is that hot news will tend to go into the national schedules – local programmes tend to concentrate on lighter stories such as culture and what is happening to the grape harvest. There is no French equivalent of the ITV regions, so viewers have only one source of local news – France 3.

French audiences are also very fond of documentaries and televised debate – and some well-known and excellent programmes specialize in this format (*Envoyé spécial* on France 2; *Des Racines et des Ailes* on France 3). These programmes are either made up of a number of mini documentaries on linked topics, or cover a specific theme, with an introductory film of around 20 minutes and a studio debate with experts to follow. They can easily last up to three hours – a length of time which would see other audiences either falling asleep through lack of attention or reaching for the zapper. Many French people watch these programmes, and they fuel the debates around coffee the next morning, so they are well worth thinking about as a vehicle for your story.

Perhaps the most interesting of all the French channels is the Franco/German collaboration ARTE. Based in the city of Strasbourg, its mission is to 'conceive, produce and broadcast television programmes of a cultural and international nature in the broadest sense of the term, designed to encourage understanding and cooperation'. This unconventional mandate leads to an unashamedly iconoclastic approach that often leaves them swimming against the tide. For example, their commemoration on the first anniversary of 11 September focused on the attitude of the Arabs rather than the Europeans. Their theme evenings – covering such diverse subjects as parents, beer, Marlene Dietrich, racism and the saxophone – are exceptionally well produced and thought provoking.

As everywhere else in Europe, radio is popular, with most listeners tuning in to music stations. Europe 1, France Info and France Inter are the most listened-to news stations. Radio France International (RFI) is the francophone equivalent of the BBC World Service.

Anyone wanting to find out more about the French media can visit the excellent site of the French Foreign Ministry (www.premier-ministre.gouv.fr) where they can consult the online version of the reference book *Média SIG*. Updated every year, it provides an exhaustive guide not only to the French media, but also to foreign journalists stationed in France and the press offices of major organizations based in the country.

Georgia

Under communism Georgia was the California of the Soviet Union, renowned for its high living standards, favourable climate, and thriving wine and film industries. Severing its political links with Moscow to become an independent state in 1991 has cost the country dear. Economic and business ties with Russia, Georgia's natural trading partner, were also disrupted, with the result that average income levels have plummeted to well below those of most other former Soviet republics, reversing the pre-independence situation. Independence was followed by a civil war between supporters of the country's first President, Zviad Gamsakhurdia, and opposition groups, who eventually drove him from office amid accusations of corruption and human rights violations.

The country has also suffered from a bloody conflict in the important coastal region of Abkhazia, which expelled 250,000 Georgians from its territory and is now independent from Tbilisi. Another region, South Ossetia, has also refused to accept the authority of the Georgian state, though like Abkhazia it remains officially a part of Georgia. To cap it all, Georgia shares a mountainous border with Chechnya, and has been accused by Russia of letting Chechen rebels take refuge there.

The country's political instability is mirrored in its media world. In 2001 the then president, Eduard Shevardnadze, dismissed his entire cabinet after security services raided an independent TV station, prompting mass demonstrations demanding the government's resignation. The US-based human rights monitor Freedom House reports widespread intimidation of journalists, especially outside the capital. The murder of a popular TV presenter and journalist in 2001 remains unsolved.

Although the press frequently criticizes the government, few newspapers are editorially independent and commercially viable. Two papers are financed by the state, while those which are privately owned often reflect the interests and opinions of their patrons in politics and business. Journalistic standards are generally poor, with lack of professional training, low pay and self-censorship among the main causes.

Georgia has 240 papers, with a total print run of about 400,000. Daily circulations range from 1,000 to 10,000, in a country with a population of more than 5 million. The most popular dailies, all based in Tiblisi, are *Alia* (around 10,000 copies), *Akhali Taoba* (7,000) and *Rezonansi* (3,000). Other leading dailies include *24 hours*, *Ertoba* and *Mtavari Gazeti*. Popular weekly digests include *Akhali Versia* (40,000), *Kviris Palitra* (35,000) and *Asaval-Dasavili* (23,000). The state-owned *Saqartvelos Respublica* sells 10,000 copies a day, twice the number of the Russian language daily *Svobodnaia Gruzia*. Circulation figures are unreliable, however, because some owners deliberately underestimate their sales figures in order to pay lower taxes. *Georgian Messenger* is an English language title aimed mainly at the foreign diplomats and businessmen living in the capital.

The state news agency in Georgia is Sakinformi, and in the independent sector, there are Kavkas-Press, Inter Press, Iprinda and Prime News.

On the TV scene, of the three channels that cover the whole country, two are owned by the public broadcaster Georgian State Television. The most popular station, however, is Rustavi 2, which is faced with a growing number of commercial rivals, such as Imedi, Mze, Channel 9, New Georgian Broadcasting, Cucasia and Iberia.

News and current affairs are an important element in the schedules of all the independents. As in most ex-communist states, viewers instinctively place a greater trust in non-official sources of information, and so news remains a major selling point for the commercial sector.

Georgian Radio, the state broadcaster, has two national channels, which have more factual programmes than their commercial counterparts. The head of the Georgian Orthodox Church, the Patriarch, has his own radio channel which is also heavily factual. Among the popular FM stations the ones with the highest proportion of information programmes are Fortuna+ (103.4), Europa+ (104.3) and Radio Imedi (105.9).

Germany

The land of beer, pretzels, sausages and large, fast cars is well known for its serious and analytical nature. Many a German philosopher and scientist has made a mark on the world – despite publishing tracts that challenge lesser brains with their sophistication and complexity (just try reading Karl Marx's *Das Kapital!*). The language of Goethe is rich and complex, and the people of Germany enjoy their information in industrial portions – with almost all daily newspapers and magazines resembling the Berlin telephone directory in size and verbosity.

And there is a lot to analyse. Consider Germany's recent history: the recovery from Nazism and Second World War destruction, the *Wirtschaftswunder* of economic prosperity, the fall of the Berlin wall and the reunification of a divided country – today's Germany is still coping with the ripples from its eventful past. Add to that the fact that the Germans have been at the forefront of many modern trends – the green movement and the Euro, for instance – and you quickly understand the popularity of in-depth news coverage.

Knowledge of the past is essential to understanding the story choices of German news desks. History shapes the agenda in a way that would be impossible in other European countries: even half a century after the end of the war the German nation struggles to make amends for the Nazi times, and any allusions to Hitler or perceived anti-Semitism can quickly blow up into a scandal. In fact, displays of swastikas and statements endorsing Nazism are outlawed. Other sensitive points include bioethics, human cloning and genetic engineering – a difficult subject to cover in a country that suffered the experiments of the Nazi scientist Dr Mengele. However, none of this is swept under the carpet – but analysed and debated almost constantly.

During the Nazi times (1933 to 1945), the media was strictly controlled. The shadow of this state censorship affected the country for a long time afterwards, creating an attitude that anyone and everyone should be able to express themselves in a democratic state, with the result that training for journalists was frowned upon. Although times have changed and journalism schools are now well established, many of the older generation of media professionals began their careers as amateurs.

Germany is a federal state, divided into 16 Länder, and this is reflected in the nature of its media. There are very few genuine national newspapers (*Die Welt* is one of the few examples) and some of the biggest sellers are in fact regional newspapers that are sold all over the country, such as the *Süddeutsche Zeitung*, the *Frankfurter Allgemeine Zeitung* (known colloquially as the Faz), and the *Frankfurter Rundschau*. The biggest seller of all is the tabloid *Bild Zeitung* (Picture Paper), which disproves the commonly held myth that Germans have no sense of humour. It is a cousin to the British *Sun*, challenging it for tackiness, clever punned headlines, and right-wing opinions. *Bild* has a circulation of around four and a half million, and a probable readership of twice or three times that amount, with people typically buying it on the way to work and bringing it home for the rest of the family in the evening. Fortunately, the *Bild* is not the only source of information, since many people also take one of the more sober and accurate regional newspapers as well, much the same as in Britain.

Bild is published by the Axel Springer company, one of a number of German publishing giants that dominate the media market throughout Europe. The company also publishes some of the highly successful regional newspapers – including the *Berliner Morgenpost*, which merged news desks with *Die Welt* in Spring 2002. The market for local and regional papers in Germany is exceptionally strong – there are around 355 daily newspapers in the whole of Germany, and many come from the stable of the WAZ (Westdeutsche Allgemeine Zeitung), including the *Westfälische Rundschau, die Thüringer Allgemeine*, the *Ostthüringer Zeitung* and many others. WAZ has made its mark on eastern Europe, buying up titles in the newly democratized countries and becoming an impressive player on the Eastern Europe media scene.

Germany's economic might can be seen through the strength of its business press. Newspapers and magazines catering for the financial and business sector such as *Handelsblatt* and *Wirtschaftswoche* sell well, and the *FT* prints a special edition for Germany.

One strong point of the news scene is the pre-eminence of news magazines. The week would not be complete for a German without their copy of the *Spiegel* (Mirror) or *Stern* (Star) or *Focus* magazine – all of them glossy confections. *Spiegel* is seen as the most influential political publication in Germany, with a reputation for good investigative journalism, and is considered internationally as one of the most independent weeklies worldwide. *Focus* is a relative newcomer, launched in 1993 and gaining ground, although many people find its coverage somewhat right wing.

Most countries with strong weekly news magazines tend not to have national Sunday newspapers. This is not the case in Germany, with three

Sunday choices to fill the weekend gap: the *Bild am Sonntag*, the *Welt am Sonntag* and the *Frankfurter Allgemeine Sonntagszeitung*. There is also a weekly newspaper, *Die Zeit*, which appears on Thursdays.

News agencies in Germany have a particularly interesting history. The biggest is the Deutsche Presse Agentur, which was set up in 1949 and now competes on the world stage with Reuters, Associated Press and Agence France Presse, sending out news in German, English, Spanish and Arabic. It also retransmits articles from the British *Guardian* newspaper and its sister Sunday newspaper, *The Observer*.

One aspect of the media scene unique in Western Europe is the grip of the Church – both Catholic and Protestant – on the media world. The Christian churches and Judaism have a special status with the German state (getting tax breaks, for instance) and that logically led to the churches establishing their own press outlets. The Catholic Church ran a number of newspapers in the past – including the liberal-minded *Public* newspaper – and at one time tried to lure readers with a *Bild Zeitung* look-alike called *Bild Post*. Today the Protestant Church edits a monthly called *Chrismon* which appears as a supplement of the *Süddeutsche Zeitung*, *Frankfurter Rundschau*, *Tagesspiegel*, *Sächsische Zeitung* and *Die Zeit*. The Catholic Church publishes the *Rheinischer Merkur*, founded in 1813 and one of the oldest newspapers in the world. More importantly, both the Catholic Church and the Protestant Church run their own press agencies, covering the news in a neutral fashion with reports that are taken by most media.

A British viewer watching German television would find it very familiar. The style is much the same as BBC or ITV, and news coverage differs only in the amount of airtime devoted to foreign stories. Both the two main channels ARD and ZDF produce high quality, accurate and succinct news broadcasts.

The German system also has some similarities to the British one in that viewers pay a television licence, the proceeds of which are shared out amongst the different public radio and television stations and, along with advertising, help fund them. The difference is that the regional channels come under the umbrella of ARD, but each is independent in its programming. The regional newsrooms nonetheless coordinate the national evening news, the *Tagesschau*, with reports sent from Munich, Frankfurt or Berlin airing on the same primetime news throughout the whole of Germany. Another good example of this coordination in action is the hugely popular cop show the *Tatort* (Scene of Crime) which is set in the different regional centres and filmed by the regional stations.

News programmes are as popular as in Britain, and some of the most influential have made star correspondents of their presenters. The best political commentators in Germany are women, and one of the most watched is Sabine Christiansen, who has a regular slot on a Sunday night, setting the political agenda by teasing out information from the hapless politicians in front of her.

Germany also has a wealth of private commercial stations, mainly broadcast by satellite, including Sat 1, RTL, RTL 2, ProSieben, Kabel 1, N-TV and N24. ARTE, the Franco-German station based in Strasbourg, is also a very popular choice for viewers who want intelligent entertainment and accurate commentary.

The public radio scene in Germany follows the same pattern as television, with national programmes working from coordinated regional centres. The ARD network acts as the umbrella company for radio and the nine regional radio broadcasting companies are based in the Länder (Bayerischer Rundfunk, Südwestrundfunk, Saarländischer Rundfunk, Hessischer Rundfunk, Westdeutscher Rundfunk, Mitteldeutscher Rundfunk, Rundfunk Berlin Brandenburg, Norddeutscher Rundfunk and Radio Bremen). One of the best and most quoted radio news sources is Deutschland Radio, the radio jointly run by ARD and ZDF, with two 24-hour news channels broadcasting nationally (DeutschlandRadio Berlin and Deutschlandfunk). They both provide news and high quality reports on political and cultural issues

On the commercial front, many stations feed listeners a diet of around 20 pop hits, played over and over again, interspliced with the latest news of where the traffic jams, bottlenecks and police speed traps are. This is especially important in a country which lives by the car, with the oldest motorways in Europe and a huge congestion problem. German drivers especially appreciate the special gadget that cuts out the CD player and switches to the radio as soon as the traffic news comes on. Nevertheless, there are many good stations catering for more refined tastes, and the regional centres generally broadcast a range of programmes – four, for instance, at the Stuttgart-based Südwestrundfunk.

Greece

One of the authors was introduced to the Greek media in all its glory at a press conference which took place in Athens during the Kosovo crisis. The theme of the conference – the effects of an ageing population on the European economy – was all but forgotten in a media feeding frenzy as journalist after journalist grabbed the microphone to demand why the assembled European Health Ministers were not doing something about pollution from the nearby conflict. The journalists were convinced we were attempting to block them in some way. In fact, our only concern was to help the poor interpreters, who were hanging on for grim life as questions in Greek succeeded questions in English, and Greek replies were interrupted with no microphone to relay the sound to the interpretation booths – and nobody understanding anything. Chaos reigned, and the conference lasted an hour and a half, ending only in English as the interpreters gave up in exasperation. But the greatest surprise came at the end – the Greek journalists came up to offer their thanks. They said they would never have had such access to their own public figures.

The home of democracy and debate has produced a rich media landscape – with electronic media playing a particularly important role, thanks to the nature of the country and the difficulties of distributing newspapers to the islands. Television style is especially colourful and loud – as witnessed in that anarchic press conference.

It was the expat Greeks who first adopted the idea of the newspaper from Enlightenment Europe: the first Greek newspaper was published in 1784 in Vienna, closing down shortly afterwards because of pressure from the Turks. But the idea refused to die, and another paper emerged from the same place – the *Ephimeris* – publishing news about the French Revolution and other current events. The first newspaper to appear in Athens was *Ephimeris ton Athenon* at the beginning of the 19th century. Newspapers became increasingly popular, and by the First World War 16 newspapers were being published in Athens, some of which still survive today.

There are more than 1,788 national, local and regional newspapers – 252 of them dailies. Of the nationals, most have a tabloid format, the main exception being *Kathimirini* and its Sunday edition. Journalists are well respected and trusted as key players in influencing social, economic and political debate. The main news agencies are the Athens News Agency and the Macedonian News Agency (based in the Greek province of Macedonia and not to be confused with MIA – the agency of the neighbouring republic of Macedonia).

Radio helped to shape Greek history – in a country consisting of dozens of islands, it played a key role in bolstering morale during the Second World War. Journalists of all types experienced their dark night of the soul during the days of the military junta between 1967 and 1974, but radio hams found a way around the censorship and pirate stations sprang up all over the country, although state radio was the only legal provider. It was not until the late 1980s that the state monopoly was challenged. The impetus for deregulation came from the political world itself, when the mayors of the three major towns – Athens, Piraeus and Thessaloniki – decided to promote media pluralism and set up municipal radio stations. Deregulation opened the doors to the private sector, and now more than 467 radio stations throng the airwaves, broadcasting a blend of music and debate, targeted either at the mainland or at local island communities.

Television broadcasting followed a similar route. Its history originates in the 1950s, when, curiously, regulation was the job of the military. The first regular television broadcasts began in Thessaloniki in the early 1960s, leading to the launch of Greek state television in 1966. State television was challenged in the 1980s, when the sector was deregulated. Almost overnight, dozens of private television stations were broadcasting, prompting in turn a huge development in Greek programme making, more foreign imports, lower advertising revenue and a general dumbing-down in the programme style. Today the main private stations are Antenna TV and the wonderfully named Mega Channel, along with the Alpha and Alter stations. There are a total of 157 television channels, with 10 of them broadcasting nationally.

One big embarrassment for Greece is its position at number 30 in the International Press Institute's press freedom index – the lowest for any EU country. Campaigning organizations such as Reporters without Borders are trying to turn the tide with international campaigns, but libel remains a criminal offence (as in many other countries in the region) and the Greek government has been known to threaten journalists with imprisonment. In fact, courts no longer hand down custodial sentences (although the law still allows five years' jail for 'insult' or 'dishonour') but newspapers are regularly having to pay fines of up to €290,000.

Corruption and nepotism used to be taboo subjects, but the Greek media are now tackling these issues with gusto – especially if there are any elections on the horizon. The issue of minorities, however, still remains a difficult subject for journalists. The Greek constitution recognizes only 'Muslims' as a minority – newcomers such as Albanians, Russians, Pakistanis, Polish, Romanians and Bulgarians are sometimes portrayed as transient nuisances by certain elements of the media.

Hungary

A country of 10 million, Hungary is at the heart of Europe, a melting pot of many cultures, and a pivotal location for the twists and turns of history. Part of the huge Habsburg empire until the end of the First World War, it helped to bring about the collapse of communism when, after tough negotiations with Germany and the USSR, it opened its borders with Austria in 1989, allowing thousands of East Germans to escape to the West. The first Eastern European country to join the Council of Europe in 1990, it is one of the newest members of the European Union in its enlargement to the east.

As with all the former Soviet bloc countries, the media style is coloured by the legacy of communism. Add in a need to appeal to a small market, the lure of foreign ownership and the appeal of Western-style tabloid journalism and you have a rapidly changing media scene, wide open to political influence.

The largest circulation broadsheet is *Nepszabadsag*, the former Communist party newspaper which has managed to adapt to its new role as the Hungarian newspaper of record. Its competitors in the quality market are the independent liberal broadsheet *Magyar Hirlap* (also left wing), the conservative-leaning – sometimes extreme right-wing – *Magyar Nemzet*, which supported the government coalition party Fidesz between 1998 and 2002, and *Nepszava*, which tends towards the left. No new political newspaper of quality was able to survive after the regime change in 1989, and circulation in all the big four went down. Meanwhile the Hungarians have discovered the pleasures of tabloids. *Blikk, Mai Nap* and *Mai Lap*, all foreign owned, vie for readers' attention.

The newspapers get their raw material from international agencies and the MTI – the Magyar Tavirati Iroda. State-owned, and run by a parliamentary board, MTI feeds news back from the key media centres of the world and runs correspondents out of Washington, London and Brussels. Given the mysterious nature of the Hungarian language, it might be a good bet to contact these foreign correspondents with your story, although most journalists in Budapest do speak either English or German.

Budapest is well served for English language newspapers, and English speakers planning a sortie in Hungary could do worse than to log on to the excellent Web site of the *Budapest Sun* (www.budapestsun.com). A main news page in English shows the stories running in the Hungarian press at the moment, and there are dozens of useful links to specialist subjects.

Another of the English language publications is the weekly *Budapest Business Journal* (BBJ). BBJ gives an insight into Hungarian business and economy, with special pages dedicated to the property market. There is also a German language weekly – *Budapester Zeitung* – and Russian and Chinese papers are also printed, but have not yet gained enough of a reputation for them to be described as quality products.

The biggest political weekly magazine in Hungary is *Heti Világgazdaság* (HVG), with a circulation of 80,000. A sort of Hungarian *Economist*, it covers world news, politics, economy and home affairs. Another political magazine, *Heti Válasz* (40,000), is backed (and financially supported) by Fidesz, and largely biased towards the right wing. *Magyar Narancs* is Hungary's trendy political weekly, attracting mostly youngsters and voters of the left-liberal party, the Alliance of Free Democrats.

The well-illustrated weekly business magazine *Figyelo* covers business, finance, economics, IT and science, and also produces a quarterly English language supplement.

The Internet boom and bust left its mark on the Hungarian media scene. After many experiments only two main Internet news portals survived: Origo and Index. Origo is the most popular, operated by Matav, the biggest Hungarian telecommunications company, which is owned by Deutsche Telekom. The other market leader, Index, was independent for a long time, but found it needed a more stable financial footing; at the moment it is owned by the Wallis Group, a huge Hungarian holding.

Hungary's public broadcaster, MTV, now a member of the European Broadcasting Union, was king of the air during the communist era. The advent of democracy not only brought a challenge to the monopoly, but has also led to funding problems, dwindling audiences and bitter debate about political influence. The situation has not been helped by each successive government viewing MTV as its propaganda machine. A 1996 media law attempted to remedy the situation and began the transformation of MTV from a state colossus to a slimmed-down broadcaster modelled on Western European traditions. Many Hungarians, however, remain cynical. MTV now operates two channels (M1 and M2). At the time of writing, state television is on the verge of bankruptcy and special government support is needed to save it.

A third state television station, Duna TV, broadcasts by satellite to expatriate Hungarians. In 1999 it won the UNESCO prize for the best cultural television worldwide.

Post-communist transition opened the TV market to foreign players. Apparently it was not uncommon to see lobbyists representing Western media megaliths such as Silvio Berlusconi and Rupert Murdoch prowling the corridors of the Hungarian parliament in the early 1990s. This has inevitably led to a mushrooming in foreign-owned commercial channels, both terrestrial and satellite, which now account for 70 per cent of the total audience.

RTL Klub is the most popular commercial TV, followed by TV2. A newcomer on the market is Hír TV, run and operated by business circles close to Fidesz and tending to follow their political line.

Radio is popular and music broadcasting dominates the airwaves in the land that bred Bartók and Liszt. Four national channels are complemented by a vast array of local radio stations, with many stations available on the web to target the large Hungarian expat community. News radio – especially on the more popular channels – is sometimes criticized for being politically biased.

Iceland

Only just over a quarter of a million people live in Iceland, a country the size of Greece – so it is not at all surprising that there is not a huge variety of media on the island. But Icelanders are nonetheless worth a mention for their unusual approach to news and public opinion.

As in some other Scandinavian countries, the news scene started with people of differing viewpoints and political allegiances pooling together enough money – or finding rich enough benefactors – to found their own newspapers. At one time there were a good number of newspapers on the market, but numbers fluctuated over time. The one that stayed the course was *Morgunblaðið* (*Morgunbladid*) – founded in 1913 – and still the most read paper in Iceland today, with almost every household taking it.

Morgunbladid's approach to the news used to be conservative, but the present editors have fought to get rid of the right-wing bias and give it more independence and objectivity. It has a huge influence on public opinion and one unique trait that makes it very different from national newspapers in the rest of Europe: the Icelandic tradition of earmarking part of the paper for public contributions. Anyone can send an article to the newspaper and fully expect it to be published – not the case in countries like the UK and France, where you need to be at least a well-known public figure to have any hope at all of getting your thoughts into print.

Nowadays *Morgunbladid* has been joined by two other national newspapers. *DV* is generally considered to be little challenge to the *Morgunbladid* monopoly: a tabloid, it survives mostly on advertising revenue. A couple of years ago, however, a newcomer arrived in the shape of the free publication *Fréttablaðið*, which means simply 'newspaper'. The paper has been well received in Iceland, offering as it does an alternative slant on the daily news.

Surprisingly perhaps for such a small population, Iceland also has a thriving magazine scene, dominated by several publishing groups. Frodi specializes in the women's market, while Heimur has three titles: *Frjals Verslun*, for business people, and *Iceland Review* and *Atlantica*, for tourists.

Summer holidays and days off proved something of a challenge to Icelandic state television in the 1970s and 80s, and one month in the summer would pass without anything at all on the small screen. Even throughout the year, the television broadcast nothing at all one day a week. Proud Icelanders claimed that it was to give the nation a chance to catch up on more intellectual pursuits, but the reality may have been more the lack of trained staff and the need to give employees a proper break. Now Icelandic television broadcasts full time and the Icelanders also have their own commercial channel Stoð 2 (Stod 2).

Radio stations are numerous, and many of them rely on the American model of music interspersed with news bulletins. State radio broadcasts the most comprehensive news and current affairs programmes, in a similar vein to BBC's Radio 4, even down to the shipping forecasts for Icelandic seafarers in the North Sea. The commercial station Stod 2 also gives good – but less complete – news coverage.

The advent of new media has been a great aid to the Icelandic nation and many of them are adept surfers of the Web. Interestingly, they have made a great effort to retain their own language, rather than swapping it for the ubiquitous English, with the result that the oldest Viking language is now being used for the most modern communications software.

Ireland

The Republic of Ireland justly holds a reputation as a country that delights in words, wordplay and wit. The homeland of Oscar Wilde is full of orators – and its media is full of the raw material for the many hot debates around dinner tables all over the country.

Story material has never been a problem in this land of rich history. Violence and crime, political debate and sporting events share the news schedules with quaint oddities of Irish life. The old traditional Roman Catholic values are giving way to new modes of life – many topics that would have been taboo even a couple of decades ago are now spoken about openly. Scandals involving the clergy and issues such as abortion and divorce are now tackled in the media, with every aspect, from the social to the salacious, coming up in talk shows and discussion programmes.

Ireland is also one of the countries to gain greatly from membership of the European Union – the adoption of the euro, along with a young, computer-literate and entrepreneurial workforce, has pushed it up the economic league. It has also given the country a highly educated population.

All this boils down to a thriving media scene – be it the old traditional workhorses such as the *Irish Times* and the *Irish Independent*, or new media. Newspaper sales have increased over the past few years, despite them being more expensive than their British counterparts. Four national dailies and one national evening newspaper serve the Republic, along with six national Sunday newspapers. Added to that, each town and region has its own newspaper and there are another 30 free newspapers in the urban areas.

Irish readers like their national newspapers to be factual in tone and format. The newspaper of record is the *Irish Times*, which has spread its name for excellence into new media and operates an informative Web site – but unfortunately with a subscription service. In circulation terms it comes second to its rival the *Irish Independent*. According to recent figures from the Audit Bureau of Circulation, the 100-year-old *Independent* is

Ireland's most popular paper, selling 50,000 more copies a day than the *Times*. The third-biggest seller is the *Irish Examiner*, which started its life as the *Cork Examiner* and still has its most loyal followers outside Dublin. It even claims bigger readership figures in general than the other two broadsheets.

Irish-produced tabloids do exist, for example the *Irish Daily Star*, a distant cousin to the UK paper of the same name, but with completely different content. Most gossip-fans prefer to get their fix from the British imports, which are widely available all over Ireland. Visitors to Ireland will often be surprised to find that the *Sun, Mirror* and *Star* ship out their Scottish editions rather than the ones sold on the streets of London. Sunday newspapers are as popular as in Britain, and at least a third are imported from across the Irish Sea. There is also a market in Irish-produced Sundays, the most reputable of which is the *Sunday Business Post*, with tabloids coming in the shape of *Ireland on Sunday* and the *Sunday World*. The *Sunday Tribune* is also respected as an 'agenda-setting' newspaper.

Radio is a thriving medium – and the talk show is especially strong in this land where no day would be complete without a heated argument on the hot topics of the day. Many a conversation is started with 'Did you hear the debate on the Gerry Ryan show?', one of the most popular programmes.

RTE, the state broadcasting giant, operates four radio stations (one of them in the Irish language) and at the time of writing there were over 40 licensed radio stations. Pirate radio stations are also very common. Where other countries rely on music to coax their listeners, the Irish know the power of speech, and debates ranging from the serious to the sensational are listened to by people from all walks of life – resulting in some very intelligent and interesting conversations with taxi drivers, who are tuned into the shows all day. This is partly a result of a law requiring broadcasters to ensure that 20 per cent of their content is news or current affairs based. In fact, the scene is so healthy that radio has its own news agency – the Independent News Network – that serves at least half the licensed stations.

Television is dominated by the state-owned station RTE, which operates three national television services – RTE 1, Network 2 and Telefis na Gaeilge (TG4). RTE 1 has a staple diet of news and current affairs, whilst Network 2 tries to jazz up its appeal with a mix of music, entertainment and film. Telefis na Gaeilge is a response to a language policy decision by the government to promote the Irish language and broadcasts an average of six hours per day. The commercial channel TV3 is a favourite for entertainment, and screens the popular UK soap *Coronation Street*. Many people can also pick up both terrestrial and satellite television from the UK.

Italy

On the positive side, Italy is renowned for beautiful cities such as Florence, Rome and Venice; for artists like Michelangelo, Leonardo da Vinci, Titian and Caravaggio and composers such as Verdi and Puccini; for its Roman history and last but not least, its delicious cuisine and majestic wines. Unfortunately the country also has a global reputation for bureaucracy, corruption, organized crime, frequent changes of government and a plodding legal system that can take decades to deal with a case. Many of these issues are being addressed; for example, the voting system has been reformed with the aim of producing clearer majorities and hopefully more stable governments. But other problems remain: employment prospects are brighter in the industrialized north, though the south is now developing fast. Italy also faces an acute demographic challenge – its birth rate is currently the lowest in Europe, with the population forecast to fall by a third over the next 50 years. If the trend continues, Italy will eventually overtake Japan and have the oldest population in the world.

The country's media scene is, like the rest of Italian society, inextricably linked with politics. Billionaire businessman and current Prime Minister Silvio Berlusconi owns the biggest slice of the Italian media, with most of the rest owned by other well-known entrepreneurs. Italy's most influential and independent paper is *Corriere della Sera*, which sells about 700,000 copies. The Milan daily criticizes the government and the opposition in equal measure. The second most popular paper is Rome-based *La Repubblica*, which sells 650,000 copies a day and is owned by Carlo De Benedetti, one of Mr Berlusconi's bitterest business rivals. Politically on the centre-left, it is more critical of the current government than *Corriere della Sera*. In third place comes *La Stampa*, owned by the Agnelli family. Its 400,000 circulation represents a substantial fall in sales in recent years. *Il Giornale* (230,000 copies) is a liberal-conservative paper read by supporters of the centre-right, and owned by Paolo Berlusconi, the Prime Minister's brother. There are a number of papers with much smaller print runs. Despite being owned by the Prime Minister's wife, Veronica Berlusconi, *Il*

Foglio (10,000 copies) can be highly critical of the government, thanks to its maverick editor Giuliano Ferrara, a former communist. *Il Foglio* is essential reading for journalists and politicians. *L'Unità*, which used to be owned by the Communist party, remains close to the left editorially. Mouthpieces for the extreme left are *Liberazione* and *Il Manifesto*, while at the other end of the political spectrum *Il Secolo d'Italia* is owned by the right-wing National Alliance Party. *Il Messaggero* is the leading paper for Rome and the surrounding region. For the Italian business community, the paper of choice is *Il Sole 24 Ore*.

Two important weekly news magazines are *Espresso*, owned by Carlo De Benedetti, which supports the centre-left, and *Panorama*, representing the centre-right.

The main news agency in Italy is Ansa, with Adnkronos another important source of information.

Silvio Berlusconi's Mediaset group is the major player in the world of Italian television. It owns three of the country's seven national channels: Canale 5, Italia 1 and Rete Quattro. The three public channels are Rai Uno, Rai Due and Rai Tre. The first public channel, Rai Uno, has a reputation for even-handed journalism. Rai Due is seen as sympathetic to the current government, while Rai Tre traditionally favours the centre-left opposition. Regional programmes (mostly news and documentaries) are shown only on Rai Tre. The seventh national TV channel in Italy is La7. Owned indirectly by Telecom Italia, La7 is perceived as being objective in its news coverage. On satellite and cable only there are two rolling news channels: Rai News 24 and its private sector rival Sky TG24, owned by Rupert Murdoch's News Corporation.

As far as radio is concerned, two of the best stations for news are Radio 24, owned by the same group as the business daily *Il Sole 24 Ore* (not surprisingly, their radio station is particularly strong on business and financial news) and Radio Radicale, owned by the Radical party of former EU commissioner Emma Bonino. The public broadcaster RAI runs four national networks, the first of which is best for news.

Latvia

The middle country of the Baltic states, sandwiched between Estonia and Lithuania, Latvia's recent politics has been coloured by the issue of minorities. Latvia has the largest Russian minority (29 per cent) of all the Baltic states. There are also smaller Belarusian, Polish and Ukrainian minorities. Latvians themselves make up 58 per cent of the total. This may explain why relations with Russia and the Russian minority living in Latvia are sensitive. Citizenship is only granted to those who can pass Latvian language and history tests, and without citizenship there is no right to vote or enter certain professions.

There are around 220 newspapers in Latvia. Some are published only in Latvian, some only in Russian, and some are available in separate Latvian and Russian editions. Of the national dailies, the market leaders are *Lauku Avīze* (particularly strong on economic, agricultural and rural issues) and *Diena*, both with more than 60,000 copies. The nearest rivals are *Neatkarīga Rīta Avīze* (known popularly as NRA), with over 40,000 copies a day. The bestselling Russian dailies are *Vesti Segodnja* (30,000) and *Telegraf* (more than 13,000).

There is also a healthy market for national evening newspapers. The top seller is *Rīgas Balss*, with 35,000 copies, followed by *Vakara Zinas* (13,000 copies).

For business people, there are several options – the market leader is *Dienas Bizness*. In the Russian language there is *Komersant Baltii* and *Bizness & Baltiya*, which is also read by Latvians.

There are two news agencies – LETA, which is privately owned, and the Baltic News Service, which covers all three Baltic republics.

On the television scene, the most popular channel is the commercial Latvian Independent Television LNT (Latvijas Neatkarīga Televīzija), which broadcasts a mixture of news, sports and entertainment. The state broadcaster Latvian Television (LTV) has two channels, with the second carrying 20 per cent of its output in minority languages. The latest arrivals are the Swedish-owned TV3 and TV5, both oriented to younger people. As well as the national networks, there are also more than 20 local and regional TV stations, as well as a satellite company, Baltcom TV, an American-Latvian joint venture.

As far as radio is concerned, the most popular national channels are those of the public broadcaster Radio Latvia, which provides news, current affairs and documentaries, as well as most kinds of music. The national commercial networks are Radio SWH, Star FM and Latvian Christian Radio. There are also 21 local radio stations in Latvia, all of them commercial.

Lithuania

Lithuania, the southernmost of the Baltic states, has the biggest population (more than double the size of Estonia) and the fastest-growing economy. The Lithuanians have gained a reputation as being friendly, open and quirky – in the place of the usual municipal worthies, they have erected a statue of the eccentric American singer Frank Zappa. One of the reasons for this more laid-back attitude could be the significantly smaller Russian minority, making for a more peaceful coexistence. Another important difference is that the country's main religion is Catholicism, in contrast with the Lutheran and Orthodox traditions of Estonia and Latvia. One clue to this divergence lies in Lithuania's close historic ties with Poland, the country on its southern border.

Like its northern neighbours, Lithuania has a free press, which in little over a decade since the collapse of communism has passed from state to private hands.

The market leader is *Lietuvos Rytas*, with a circulation of about 65,000 on weekdays and more than 200,000 for its weekend edition. While its circulation has slumped from communist times, it has increased the number of pages in an average issue from 4 to 56, with numerous specialized supplements. The paper produces a free online version which is popular with Lithuanians living abroad, and with the rapidly growing number of Internet users in the country itself.

The national daily *Respublika*, with about a third of the circulation of its bigger rival *Lietuvos Rytas*, is well known for its focus on crime stories and social issues. It is often labelled as a tabloid, though in recent years it has become much less sensational. *Lietuvos Žinios* is another national rapidly gaining in popularity. *Lietuvos Aidas*, on the other hand, is in decline, with a tiny circulation and big financial problems.

Vakaro Žinios is a new daily with a clear orientation towards tabloid sensationalism.

In addition to their main sections, all national papers have local supplements, serving the country's major cities. The paper aimed at the business community, *Verslo Žinios*, has expanded in recent years from a weekly to a daily newspaper.

Important regional newspapers include *Kauno Diena*, which covers Kaunas and the surrounding region, and *Vakaru Ekspresas* and *Klaipeda*, serving the Klaipÿÿda region in the western part of Lithuania.

Other influential publications are *Veidas*, a quality weekly magazine specializing in social and political issues, and *Atgimimas*, a weekly analytical paper with a loyal following among politicians and academics. The same people also tend to buy the country's weekly news magazine, *Ekstra*.

If you are targeting decision makers, the most influential publications are *Lietuvos Rytas*, *Verslo Žinios* and the magazine *Veidas*.

There are two news agencies in Lithuania – the newly privatized ELTA, which was formerly run by the government, and the Baltic News Service (BNS), which covers all three Baltic republics.

Three out of four of the country's national TV networks are privately owned. The exception is the state broadcaster LRT (Lietuvos radijas ir televizija), which has only a 16 per cent share of the total audience. The most popular channel is LNK, followed by TV3, which is well known for high quality news and documentary programmes. In third place is TV4 (formerly known as Baltijos TV). All three channels broadcast for 16 hours a day, with American films and drama series making up a high proportion of their output.

In addition to the national networks, there are about 20 local channels and 13 cable companies. Of these, Vilnius TV is the most popular, reaching about 5 per cent of the national TV audience through its broadcasts in the capital Vilnius and the surrounding area.

In the radio sector, the public broadcaster LRT runs two radio stations, the first of which is the country's most listened-to radio network. There are six national commercial broadcasters, with the most popular channels being M-1, M-1 Plus, Radiocentras (pop music and news) and Znad Vilii (which specializes in Polish and Russian programming).

While most of Lithuania's media caters for native speakers, there are a healthy number of minority language publications and broadcasts. For example, there are 12 periodicals in Russian, 7 in Polish, and 15 in other languages, including Belarusian, German, Latvian and Ukrainian. For English speakers, the weekly *Baltic Times* covers the whole region, while *Lithuanian Weekly* concentrates on events in Lithuania.

Luxembourg

Luxembourg's media landscape is influenced by its position as the country in Europe with the biggest proportion of immigrants, and the success it has made of their integration. Foreigners make up 40 per cent of the population, and schools teach not only the Letzembergish language, but also French, German, and the language of the immigrant's country of origin. Another quirk of the country is that its daytime population is larger than the evening one because workers from France and Germany drive home across the border.

The daily press is published in all the main languages. The papers reflect political interests, trade unions or other institutions: for example, the biggest-selling German language newspaper, the *Luxemburger Wort*, belongs to the Catholic Archbishop of Luxembourg and has close links with the Christian Social Party. The second bestseller *Tageblatt*, in German, is connected to the Socialist Party. The French language newspaper *Le Jeudi* is owned by the same group that publishes the Portuguese language weekly *Correio*, serving the large expat community. The two papers published in the Luxembourg language – a language in its own right, but close to German – are owned by the Liberal party (*Letzeburger Journal*) and the Communist Party (*Zeitung vum Letzeburger*). There is also a weekly newspaper in the native language – *Letzeburger Land* – which can claim the title of the only truly independent publication.

Despite its tiny size, Luxembourg has an influential media. Many non-Luxembourgers remember tuning into Radio Luxembourg on a tinny transistor radio, and the pop music station is not the only Luxembourg-based media to stretch beyond the borders of the Grand Duchy.

In the broadcasting world RTL is a giant on the European scene. Its radio and television operation extends to France, Germany and the Netherlands. In fact, so wide is its influence that it can make life very confusing if you are trying to track down a certain programme – was it on French RTL, or German? The company is now expanding into Eastern Europe, so it is more important than ever to establish precisely which branch you are dealing with.

Macedonia

Macedonia is a fertile land; its symbol is the tomato, and it was the greenhouse for the whole of former Yugoslavia. Now struggling to get back on its economic feet after the collapse of the Yugoslav state, it managed to avoid the outright wars that blighted its neighbours, but has been troubled by ethnic tensions in the north.

The modern-day state of Macedonia is officially known as 'the former Yugoslav Republic of Macedonia' in international circles because Greeks dislike the use of the word Macedonia, the term for the region straddling the borders of Macedonia, Bulgaria and Greece. This makes it difficult for authors and diplomats alike, since the Macedonians themselves react badly to being called by their full official name, or even the shortened FYROM. The Greeks also complain about the Macedonian flag. It is a huge yellow sun on a red background, called the star of Vergina, the place where Alexander the Great was born – now in Greece.

Following the pattern of other countries in South East Europe, the Macedonian media is going through great changes, as journalists flex their professional muscles and enjoy new freedoms. The media scene in Macedonia exploded within a couple of years of independence in 1991, with the arrival of hundreds of private newspapers and magazines and more than 250 private broadcasters. However, many media outlets suffer from a lack of money and resources, and watchdog groups such as the International Journalists' Network have noticed a slip in balanced reporting as opinions polarized over the dispute with the Albanian minority.

The benchmark of success for a Macedonian newspaper is a circulation of around 50,000 a day. Poverty and illiteracy are the biggest problems for the newspaper world, but there is nevertheless a thriving national daily market. *Dnevnik* is the most popular newspaper, covering stories in a balanced and political way. Its main rival is *Vest*, a relative newcomer to the Macedonian newspaper scene that draws inspiration from the traditional standards of British journalism, basing its layout on the old-style *Daily Mirror* and approaching stories in a way that appeals to an everyday audience. The most serious paper is *Utrinski Vesnik*. All three titles are now owned by the German WAZ group, which has taken over many publications in Eastern Europe.

The two newspapers that have fallen from grace are the tabloid *Vecer* and the old state news-sheet *Nova Makedonija*, both now owned by a Slovenian company. *Nova Makedonija* fell prey to industrial action by journalists when lay-offs were threatened as a means of saving money. When it came back on the streets after the strike, circulation had fallen drastically.

Recent action to ease tensions between Macedonians and the ethnic Albanian minority has resulted in new rights for the Albanian population, including the official use of Albanian as a language. The Albanian minority have their own titles, such as *Flakka* and *Fakti*. Although some of the journalists are very open-minded, the general pitch of the news tends to be mistrustful about the Macedonian majority.

The best source of information is the national Macedonian Information Agency. Launched in 1998, it provides news in a professional manner, and has a well-designed Web site, in Macedonian, Albanian and English. Another reliable agency is Makfaks, which was formerly the Macedonian outpost of the Belgrade-based agency Tanjug.

The only media outlet under direct government control in Macedonia is the state-run MRTV. The station has gone through a difficult patch, with controversy about the appointment of a series of different directors by the government and complaints about poor programming. The director is now a former journalist who is struggling to bring MRTV up to date with a minimal budget. The second channel broadcasts in Albanian.

The most popular television channel in Macedonia is the privately owned A1, which celebrated its 10th anniversary in 2003. It broadcasts a range of popular programmes and makes efforts to cover news both accurately and in a way that can be easily digested by the person in the street. A1's news editor recently defected to Kanal 5 television with a number of journalists, giving Kanal 5 a boost in popularity. Other stations with high ratings are Sitel and Telma.

Commercial radio has mushroomed in the past 10 years, and particular favourites are Antenna 5, broadcasting nationwide, and City Radio, which is limited to Skopje and Ohrid. Radio Uno and Radio Ravel are also popular. The Albanian language Radio Vat started broadcasting in 1994 and gained huge audiences during the Kosovo war by helping people track down missing relatives. There are also four stations broadcast by the state service, MRT.

Malta

The tiny Mediterranean islands of Malta, Gozo and Comino boast a population of only 381,000, most of whom are hooked on radio. Many a Maltese will sigh with nostalgia at the memory of the old Rediffusion sets that had pride of place in homes from 1935 onwards, when the British – who then colonized the island – brought in the company to set up the first broadcasts. The Rediffusion monopoly carried on until the mid-1970s, when the new Maltese government took broadcasting under its wing. Malta now has one of the largest concentrations of radio stations per population in the world, broadcasting bilingually everything from music to deep political debate.

Maltese papers divide neatly along linguistic lines, with two English language dailies and two Maltese language dailies, three English language Sundays and three Maltese language Sundays, and two English language weeklies and two Maltese language weeklies. However, the Maltese are not great fans of newspapers and only 51 per cent said they read a paper in the most recent research. The biggest seller is the *Times of Malta* and its sister paper the *Sunday Times*, which arrived on the scene in the 1920s and 30s respectively. A recent addition to the English language newspaper market is the *Malta Independent*, but despite promising launch figures its future remains uncertain.

The biggest sellers amongst the Maltese language papers are the daily *L-Orizzont* (Horizon) and the weekly *It-Torca* (Torch), both published by the General Workers Union. The Malta Labour Party owns, publishes and heavily influences the Sunday tabloid *KullHadd* (Every Sunday) and the Partit Nazzjonalista has its own mouthpieces in the daily *In-Nazzjon* (The Nation) and the Sunday *Il-Mument* (The Moment).

The existence of these papers is a testament to the dominance of institutions in the country. In fact the state, political parties and the Catholic Church have done more than anything to shape the media landscape. Their influence is particularly strong in the broadcasting sector – all the institutions own a radio and/or a television station. An audience survey in

2002 showed that over three-quarters of the Maltese population regularly tuned into a radio station owned by one of the institutions.

Television arrived in Malta in early 1957 when the Italian public broad-caster RAI set up a booster on the island of Sicily to strengthen the signal. Malta Television (TVM) was inaugurated in September 1962, and at the end of 2002 there were also nine private television stations.

Moldova

Moldova is Europe's poorest country, with its citizens earning an average €30 a month – if indeed they are lucky enough to receive anything at all, given the parlous state of the nation's economy. This is a great shame since it is a picturesque country, verdant and charming outside the Stalinist cities, with vineyards producing the sort of wine Western connoisseurs would give their right arms for.

Squeezed between Romania and Ukraine, the country suffers from an ongoing identity crisis: Moldova is one of the countries finding it most difficult to shake off the Soviet influence. Part of the country broke away in the early 1990s to form the unrecognized republic of Transdniestr. In 1999 – a decade after the fall of the old regime – a communist government was returned to power, and began behaving in a way that has raised concerns for media freedom.

There is also much ambivalence towards the nearest neighbour to the west, Romania. The official language is identical to Romanian, but the Moldovan Constitution calls it 'Moldovan'. Some of the population want to bond with Romania to make a unified state; others are sceptical about the idea. Yet even though two-thirds of Moldovans are of Romanian descent, about 35 per cent of the population speaks Russian, including the Ukrainian minority who account for about 14 per cent. These contradictions found their expression in 2002 when the whole country ground to a halt as crowds took to the streets to protest against government plans to reinstate Russian as a mandatory subject in Romanian-language schools, as was the case in Soviet times.

Add to this an ever-growing tendency to censorship and a huge lack of resources, and you end up concluding that life as a reporter in Moldova is an uphill struggle. Salaries are low – some journalists receive only about €25 a month – encouraging a temptation to accept gifts or money from patrons who want favourable reporting. Independent journalists are obliged to fight almost constantly against state censorship, and often this leads to self-censorship. One of the most dramatic moments was the strike of around 500 employees of the Moldovan state broadcasting corporation in February and June 2002. Their protest against government censorship resulted in sackings and lockouts, and the deployment of troops around the television station. A newly adopted legal framework has set up an independent board to supervise the company's activities, but questions remain over the effective editorial independence of TeleRadio-Moldova, given the presence of representatives of the authorities on the supervisory board and the fact that the company is funded directly from the state budget.

Print journalists can also feel the heavy hand of the state if they try any sort of investigative journalism. Moldova has a constitutional guarantee of freedom of the press, but defamation and insulting public officials remain criminal offences and journalists often find themselves harassed and under threat of lawsuits. For instance, the independent weekly *Accente* fell foul of Moldova's government after exposing how certain top officials were involved in people and organ trafficking. Its offices were raided and the editor arrested.

Nevertheless, Moldova manages better than some other countries in international censorship indexes. Freedom House considers it to be 'Partly Free' and the European Institute for Media said that the last election had been reported in a balanced way in the state-run media, although private media were accused of carrying out smear campaigns and lacking objectivity. In general, newspapers and magazines are able to report on diverse subjects, as long as they do not overstep the mark and upset the government.

Moldova has many newspapers and magazines, but many only exist to express the views of their owners. Even so, only one in two Moldovans read a newspaper, and of these, most choose the Russian language *Nezavismaya Moldova* and *Kishinevskie Vesti*. The most popular Moldovan language daily is *Moldova Suverana* – a free newspaper financed by the state. The weekly *Saptamana* sells well, probably because it is a good read at a cheap price. Whatever the language they are published in, the papers are very proud of being Moldovan, and stories tend to extol the national spirit and concentrate on national politics, economics and scandal. They are fed by three national agencies, Basa-Press, Interlic and Moldova News.

It is almost impossible for an independent newspaper to survive in the breakaway Transdniestr region, owing to severe state restrictions. The self-proclaimed authorities own two major newspapers in Tiraspol. Moldovan newspapers do not circulate in the area and Transnistrian publications are not available in the rest of the country.

Language policy also has its impact in the radio world. Some time ago a law was passed stipulating that 65 per cent of all broadcasting should be in Moldovan. When it failed to have much effect, the law was amended to apply only to domestic stations, leaving the field open for retransmissions of Russian programmes from Moscow. These are more popular than the Moldovan equivalents – there is more advertising revenue, more resources and therefore better programming. The upshot of this is that Moldovan radio stations are not encouraged to put scarce funds into better broadcasts.

The broadcast media has recently had a rocky ride. Government control and the sensitive issue of Romanian influence affect this sector as well. Transmissions from TVR1, the Romanian public service channel, were blocked by the Moldovan government in 2002. Even before the strikes, the state broadcaster TeleRadio-Moldova faced difficulties, with parliament dismissing its directors in 2001 for unbalanced programming. Surveys show that the population does not trust state television, believing it to be involved in manipulation and propaganda, and the Moldovan Independent Journalism Centre has accused it of poor standards. Channel One Russia (formerly known as ORT) remains the most watched in the country – possibly because of its daily staples of Hollywood movies and South American soaps.

The Netherlands

Anyone who has wandered the streets of Amsterdam will realize how highly prized freedom of expression is to the average Dutch citizen. Not only are the Dutch great champions of individual style, they are a serious-minded lot, with great respect for accuracy and analytical information. Newspapers and journalists are accorded respect – and in turn they respect their readers. In fact, the Dutch media scene is remarkable for a number of things – the complete lack of tabloid newspapers in the style of the *Sun* (the UK's leading tabloid), no sports papers at all and a highly unusual state broadcasting service.

Newspapers, magazines and books are avidly devoured in this nation of print addicts. The Dutch, indeed, are near the top of the world league for newspaper reading, although the market is succumbing to the general European trend of declining readership. Twenty years ago 90 per cent of households bought a newspaper – now it has dropped to 70 per cent. Seven national dailies are on sale, and although a couple can be described as 'popular' for their use of larger type and more colour, there are no scandal rags. Tabloids never saw the light of day in the Netherlands, and nor are there any Sunday newspapers, as in most of the other European countries.

Of the national newspapers, three are based in Amsterdam (*De Telegraaf, De Volkskrant* and *Trouw*) and two in Rotterdam (*Algemeen Dagblad* and *NRC Handelsblad*). *De Telegraaf* and *Algemeen Dagblad* (sometimes referred to as *AD*) pursue a more populist style and tend towards the right, *Volkskrant* and *Trouw* are left leaning and *NRC Handelsblad* – the only evening paper in the stable – is considered independent and liberal-minded. There are also two right-wing Christian newspapers – *Nederlands Dagblad* and *Reformatorisch Dagblad*.

For business news, the leading papers are *NRC Handelsblad* and *Financieele Dagblad*.

Besides the national newspapers, each city has its own paper – making 29 regional titles in all. There is also a thriving market in free weekly newspapers.

The leading news agency is Algemeen Nederlands Persbureau (ANP) which is based near The Hague, home of the Dutch government. It has a near monopoly of the agency market.

The broadcast world is unique and public broadcasting is structured quite differently from any other European country. This is partly a result of history – for many years, the Dutch had a very compartmentalized society, with newspapers divided into religious and political camps. The newspaper world has changed with the times and today's publications are no longer strictly tied to a church or political party. This system, however, still applies to state broadcasting, which began in the 1920s. Radio started with programmes presented by diverse organizations (socialist, liberal, Catholic, Protestant etc) that paid for their airtime. Having proved successful for radio, the same structure was adopted for public service television, when it started in 1955. A licence fee similar to the British model was introduced, with quotas for the types of programme that should be shown (news, documentaries, entertainment, drama etc).

There are three public television channels, supplied with programmes by about 10 broadcasting associations, with overt religious or political loyalties. All work together in the Netherlands Broadcasting System (NOS). Since the early 1990s the public broadcasters have had competition from commercial rivals such as Luxembourg-based RTL and home-grown channels like SBS6 and Yorin. The whole system is overseen by a neutral broadcasting authority. Thanks to cable TV, which is in 90 per cent of Dutch households, viewers can also watch a wide range of foreign channels. In addition, people living near the coast can pick up BBC and ITV programmes from the UK.

The main news providers of television news are NOS, RTL 4 and SBS6. The latter has a popular evening news bulletin which rather oddly covers only national news, leaving out all foreign stories.

There are five national public radio stations in the Netherlands, with healthy competition from the private sector. Dutch commercial radio stations had an unusual origin – many of them started life as 'pirates', broadcasting from boats in the North Sea to get around legal restrictions. There are now around 400 local radio stations. The country's international radio voice is Radio Nederland, aimed at Dutch people living abroad and foreigners interested in Dutch culture. It broadcasts in Dutch, English, Spanish, Bahasa Indonesian and Papiamento.

Norway

Norway has one of the world's most indented coastlines, with fjords that make communications difficult – doubly frustrating for a people with a strong oral tradition of folk tale and myth. This penchant for telling stories may partly explain the Norwegians' love affair with the newspaper – an obsession that continues even in our modern, Internet-dominated world.

The Norwegians hold the title of being the world's greatest newspaper readers. Not only does each Norwegian faithfully buy each day's version of their favourite rag, they are also inclined to read quite a few others bought by their family and friends. A nation of less than 5 million boasts a grand total of 220 different titles, and the bestseller – the *Verdens Gang* or *VG* as it is commonly known – is estimated to be read daily by over a quarter of the population.

Norwegian newspaper style is colourful and inventive. The *VG* – and the other tabloid bestseller *Dagbladet* – practises the kind of cheeky approach to politics that you find in the English tabloid market. One of the author's first encounters with the Norwegian press came in the run-up to the European Union referendum when the Norwegians famously voted 'No'. Newspapers rejoiced in stories about how EU membership would lead to price hikes, curbs on freedom and even poisoned food. All this gloom and doom was presented in the best journalistic traditions of finding the human angle, adding a dash of national pride and a touch of humour, and serving it up to a population already half convinced of the need to stay outside Euroland.

Another similarity to the British system is the absence of VAT on newspapers, making them not only cheerful, but relatively cheap. Many Norwegians are in fact quite happy to spend their hard-earned cash on both a tabloid and a broadsheet. *Aftenposten* heads the league table as the favourite serious read, with *Bergens Tidende* in second place.

Christianity's grip on Norway, in the form of the particularly austere faith of the Lutheran church – had its own influence on the way the media developed. Sunday newspapers were at one time banned altogether, and even now only 12 papers appear on the day of rest.

Most of the national newspapers are printed in Oslo. There is also a thriving market in city and community-based publications – the one area that is constantly growing, despite the challenge of the Internet.

Such a wealth of publications needs raw material, and this is provided by the news agencies, led by the Norsk Telegrambyra (NTB).

Not surprisingly, the dominance of the printed word makes television and radio less attractive to the average Norwegian. Statistics show that they watch three hours' television a day and listen to the radio for two hours – far less than in most other European countries. NRK, the state broadcaster, held a monopoly for 50 years from its inception in the 1930s, and it was only when satellite television began to catch on (with Rupert Murdoch's Sky television making inroads into Norway) that the broadcast scene began to expand. Norway had to wait until 1992 for its first private commercial television, and until 1996 for the launch of the second NRK channel. Norway now has two terrestrial channels (NRK 1 and TV2) and two channels with terrestrial and satellite distribution (NRK TO and TV Norge).

Radio was a state monopoly at national level until 1993, when the private station P4 started broadcasting. Locally the monopoly was broken in the 1980s, when independent local radio stations were allowed to broadcast. Norway has five national channels: P1, with a fairly formal style and an elderly audience; P2, the culture channel; Petre, for a younger audience; P4, appealing to the 25 to 45 age group; and Kanal 4, a private channel offering a mix of music and serious-minded speech with an eye to attracting female listeners. Channels P1, P2 and Petre are run by NRK, while P4 and Kanal 4 are privately owned.

Poland

A nation with a proud cultural heritage, Poland has lived through turbulent and violent times, to emerge in the late 20th century as the country that gave the world its first Eastern European pope and challenged Soviet domination. Now one of the first former communist countries to successfully knock at the door of the European Union, its media market is blossoming and proving a magnet for investment.

Poland's news media played a pivotal role in the country's fight against Soviet domination. Poland's ambassador to the USA, Przemyslaw Grudzinski, was quoted in 2001 as saying that the underground press during the 1980s created 'a powerful state that was more real than the real state'. Freedom of speech and information were highly prized, and a keystone of the Solidarity (Solidarnosc) movement which led the rebellion. For 46 years, communist governments gagged and censored the press: newspapers read like propaganda bulletins and TV and radio put out the party line.

Since independence the media has begun to enjoy new freedom, assuming the sort of watchdog role associated with journalism in the established democracies of Europe. Polish journalists were amongst the first to adopt Western practices, despite the difficulties of dumping the habits of political diatribes in favour of the 'who, what, where, when' approach. The media is now free – and in fact, journalists are just as quick to grumble about the likelihood of editorial interference from their commercial masters as they were to buck against the political diktats of former years.

Despite a strong tradition of the written press, the Poles are not great newspaper readers, and statistics show that only an estimated 30 per cent of the population read a newspaper daily. Nonetheless, there is a rich print market. There are about 5,500 periodicals on sale throughout the country and the 16 national dailies sell around 4 million copies daily. These split into two different types – the old-time communist newspapers that have reinvented themselves for the new era through privatization, and new arrivals. The most widely read is the tabloid *Gazeta Wyborcza*, launched by Solidarnosc in 1989 and privately owned from the very start. *Super Express* (with a name like that, it can't be anything but a tabloid) is second in popularity, and broadsheet *Rzeczpospolita* takes a fair share of the market. Other popular papers are *Przeglad Sportowy*, *Nasz Dziennik* (the Catholic newspaper) and *Trybuna*, which leans to the left. For the English-speaking community there is the *Warsaw Voice* and the *Warsaw Business Journal*.

The regional and local press have grown since the fall of communism, and are particularly strong in the regions of Pomorze, Wielkopolska and Slask. Polish readers are also very fond of weekly news magazines – the most prestigious and well respected are *Polityka*, *Newsweek Polska* and *Wprost*.

Poland is blessed with a good complement of news agencies – a useful resource for the many newspapers published abroad for expats. The state news agency PAP (Polska Agencja Prasowa) took longer than the rest of the press to shake off the shackles of the old regime, but is now privatized and fully committed to objective and impartial reporting, both in Polish and in English. The agency's recently launched Web site has been a huge success and is one of the most frequently visited in Poland. Their competitors are PAI (Polska Agencja Informacyjna – Polish Information Agency) and KAI (Katolicka Agencja Informacyjna – the Catholic Information Agency).

The broadcasting market is one of the largest and fastest growing in the whole of Central and Eastern Europe, attracting much foreign investment, particularly from the French and Germans. The latest estimates for radio and TV channels put the number of national and regional radio stations at 250, with about 70 television channels. The state broadcasters still lead the field. Polish Public Radio is modelled along the lines of the old-style BBC, with PR1 and PR3 covering general news, PR2 providing a cultural slant with classical music and literature and Radio Bis giving an educational service. It also operates 17 different regional radio channels. Commercial radio is very successful, with the usual diet of music and populist news. And in this devoutly Catholic country, the Catholic networks – especially the controversial Radio Maryja – have a large share of the market.

The state-owned television, Telewizja Polska, still commands the largest audience share, providing 2 national channels and 11 regionally based channels, along with the satellite channel TV Polonia. During the past few years, a myriad of commercial channels have sprung up, and cable TV is growing in popularity. About a quarter of the population also tune in to foreign channels via satellite. The most popular private channels are TVN and Polsat.

Portugal

Portugal's proud history as a nation of explorers and sailors has given it a much larger international influence than might be expected from a country of only 10 million. A dictatorship which lasted half a century under the rule of Salazar (died 1969) and then Caetano came to an end in 1974 with the 'Carnation Revolution', ushering in a new era of democracy and freedom, and helping to create what is today a thriving media scene.

One important educational factor shapes the media landscape in Portugal – more than 10 per cent of the population are illiterate and more than 20 per cent never went to school or never completed more than four years of schooling. The knock-on effect of this for the newspaper industry is obvious – they struggle, and the only papers that really sell well are the sports papers.

This does not imply that the newspaper world is deficient, just that it has a hard time making money. The four main titles are *Jornal de Noticias* (circulation just over 100,000), *Correio da Manha* (89,000), *Diario de Noticias* (65,500) and *Publico* (53,000). There are several weeklies, but the most influential is undoubtedly *Expresso* (155,000), the only Portuguese paper to keep the broadsheet format. Several financial titles (eg *Diario Economico*) and online publications (eg *Diario Digital*) have also recently appeared on the press scene.

Another odd fact about Portugal is that it has the lowest number of telephones and televisions per household in the European Union. Commercial channels vie for viewers with the state broadcaster RTP, and about 2 million homes receive television via cable and satellite. RTP had a monopoly on television until the 1990s and now operates two domestic channels and external services targeting Africa and the international market. The commercial channel SIC, broadcasting terrestrially, has the largest audience, closely followed by TV1, the television station established by the Catholic Church, but now owned by an independent group. It may seem strange to outsiders, but the Catholic Church is one of the main media players: the country's most popular national radio is the Catholic-owned Radio Renascença, and the Church has another 60 or so regional radio stations in its stable, not to mention 600 small newspapers and magazines, most of them aimed at parishioners.

Romania

Romania has deep historical roots, beautiful countryside, a fine literary and musical tradition and a claim to fame as the home of the vampire Count Dracula. After decades under the particularly mean-spirited communist leader Ceausescu, the people are now emerging and reclaiming their pride in their country.

Like many countries in Central and Eastern Europe, Romania has undergone tremendous change during the past decade, and the momentum is likely to continue with greater investment and the election of Western-leaning governments.

Romania's varied and numerous news sources are one of the few indisputable achievements of the country since the fall of the communist regime, but standards vary. Journalists are all fairly serious in their coverage of 'foreign' stories, and as a country whose dearest wish is to join the European Union one day, they are very keen to cover any story with a 'European' angle. They nevertheless have a tendency to pass off their personal opinions as facts: but the Romanians are a people who love debate, much like the Irish, so they enjoy information of any kind, and luckily for them there is a wide range of sources in the new wave of newspapers, magazines, TV and radio programmes that are making an appearance.

Romanian journalists tend to divide into two categories – the older generation whose work in communist times consisted of official communiqués, and newcomers, either those who have trained in the UK, the USA and Germany and have an idea of the profession, or fairly ill-trained beginners looking for a career opening. Ceausescu's time was defined by strict censorship, and some of the journalists from that period have found it difficult to adapt to a freer society. There are many, however, who make an effort. This older generation tends to speak French as a second foreign language (Romanian is a Latin language and the country has always had close links with France). They can mostly be found in what was previously the main government newspaper, *Romania Libera*, in the national news agency Rompres, or in the state television and radio (although television is changing rapidly, and radio was less affected by the strictures of communist censorship).

More than 10 years on from the revolution, there are over 14 Bucharest-based daily newspapers. They range from the serious-minded to the out-and-out tabloid, but the best of Romanian journalism can be seen in publications such as *Adevarul*, a broadsheet with a young enthusiastic staff, *Jurnalul National*, which models itself on the British *Guardian* newspaper (even launching with the exact same layout, although it later changed its style) and the tabloid *Evenimentul Zilei*, which tries to present serious issues in a popular way. An alternative broadsheet, *Cotidianul*, sells well and the tabloid *Ziua* presents serious news with a sensational slant. Romanian entrepreneurs turn to the business paper *Curentul*, which attempts to be the *Financial Times* of Romania. *Nine o'clock* is Bucharest's English language newspaper, run by the same people and in the same office as the French language newspaper *Le Matin*.

In the main cities, you can choose between three or four local daily newspapers. About a hundred magazines and monthly publications are distributed nationwide.

Romania has two press agencies – illustrating the contrasting style between the old guard and the modern media. Rompres was the communist-era agency, and is still housed in the Press House in central Bucharest, a huge Stalinist building with Kafkaesque corridors. Rompres suffers from a lack of resources but is bravely attempting to provide a more up-to-date service, and many young reporters pass through the agency before moving on to higher things. By contrast, the private agency Mediafax employs the newer brand of journalist and is housed in a modern building with complete online facilities. It now takes a larger slice of the market than Rompres, catering also for foreign media.

New private broadcast media outlets have been launched, mostly after 1993. In Bucharest, the national station Antena 1 started operating in 1993; the Tele-7 abc channel came on air in 1994; Pro TV in December 1995; and Prima TV was launched in 1997. Numerous smaller TV stations operate in other cities.

Public television has three channels. The first is national and its programming contains mainly news, current affairs, and entertainment. The second public TV channel airs more educational and cultural programmes and the third station, TVR International, is for keeping Romanians abroad in touch with events back home. They also have a section that produces programmes in the minority Hungarian language. The state television struggles financially against the might of the dollar and the euro, with Fox and the German-funded Pro TV cornering a large share of the market with a popular mix of news programming and Romanian-subtitled American imports such as *Buffy the Vampire Slayer*.

Public radio programmes are balanced and radio plays a big role in daily life, especially in the countryside, where lower wages make buying a newspaper a luxury. Radio Romania is a respectable outfit that has modelled itself on the BBC, with the same structure of Radios 1, 2, 3, with Radio Four (Actualitati) acting as the news channel.

Russia

When St Petersburg celebrated its 300th anniversary in Summer 2003, it also coincidentally celebrated 300 years of Russian journalism. Peter the Great – founder of the city and one of the most flamboyant Tsars – created not only the first newspaper, *Vedomosti o voennykh i inykh delakh*, he also instituted the modern Cyrillic alphabet. The idea of press freedom, however, took a little longer to come about, and many still doubt its existence.

Russia is a huge country – one-sixth of the world's land surface – and home to 143.2 million people. A strong information network is essential to bind the country together, and no one knew that better than Vladimir Ilich Lenin, whose theories of revolution were based on the idea of a controlled and centralized press. From the 1917 revolution onwards, not only was the press controlled and centralized, but also heavily censored. Russians nonetheless developed the habit of reading one of the Communist Party dailies – not only were they state subsidized and incredibly cheap, but front pages were posted up in the street for the edification of passers-by. During the period between 1970 and 1990, almost every Russian household subscribed to at least two leading newspapers such as *Pravda*, *Izvestiya*, *Trud*, or *Sovetskaya Rossiya*. There was also a very rich market in local and regional papers and magazines.

The trend for reading continues to this very day – although the papers themselves are very different from those of the communist era. Gorbachev's policy of *perestroika* brought a breath of fresh air to the media world, as journalists shook off the shackles of censorship. It was a heyday for the journalists, who could enjoy new-found freedoms – but waiting round the corner were other problems: the economic imperatives of the market and new forms of restrictions on what could be published. Newspapers have also faced new difficulties as they were forced to put up prices, despite the falling standard of living of most of their readers. Most Russians can now only afford to buy one newspaper a week, and that has led to an expansion of weekly round-ups by the main newspapers, which have proved extremely popular with cash-strapped customers.

Today the Russian print market is still growing, with 37,425 outlets officially recorded with the Ministry of Press in 2002, including 22,181 newspapers and 12,725 magazines. The main papers from communist times have adapted to the new scene and still lead the market. Top seller is the *Moskovsky Komsomolets*, selling around two and a quarter million. *Komsomolskaya Pravda*, which sells about a quarter of a million on a normal day; sees its sales boosted to 2,800,000 on a Friday. *Trud* sells around one and a quarter million. A number of papers appeared after the break-up of communism, including *Nezavisimaya Gazeta* (circulation 50,000), *Kommersant* (117,000) and *Novaya Gazeta* (670,000). Proving the success of weekly newspapers, *Argumenty I Fakty* has nearly 3 million circulation, while the monthly newspaper *Sovershenno Sekretno* (Top Secret) sells 3.5 million copies. *The Moscow Times* is the most popular English-language daily in Russia.

The popularity of local newspapers has grown even more as economic hardship has prompted Russians to choose their local news over the Moscow-based equivalent. Up until the break-up of the Soviet Union, the media was traditionally Moscow-controlled, but according to the Ministry of Press there are now more than 3,500 regional and city newspapers in Russia, with a total circulation of around 32 million.

News agencies play an especially important role in such a large and diverse country. There are around 30 information and news agencies – some of them specializing exclusively in financial and economic news. Most of them cover all aspects of the news, and many provide online services in Russian and often English. The old state agency TASS began its transformation at the end of communism by changing its name to ITAR-TASS (the TASS part was the Russian acronym for the Soviet Union Press Agency, but it was decided to keep it for the sake of continuity). ITAR-TASS is now a joint stock company, but the government is still the majority shareholder, leaving some doubt about its independence. The agency has benefited from its position as the former state agency and has by far the biggest and the best network, with correspondents operating abroad. The state agency is RIA Novosti, which is 100 per cent government controlled. The newcomer on the scene is Interfax. Established at the beginning of the Gorbachev era, it is generally considered to be more open, but its coverage is limited to the former Soviet territory.

The electronic media are of increasing importance, and television takes the crown as the most popular way of receiving information. Today's broadcasters benefit from the network put in place in Soviet times – and just about every Russian household owns at least one television set that can pick up at least two national, one regional and one local TV channel. Satellite TV is also making inroads into Russia.

Over 2,300 radio stations are officially registered with the Ministry of Press. Many of them – in fact the most popular – are music stations that carry only scant news. The market leaders in news programmes are Radio Mayak, Radio Rossii and Radio Echo Moscow (see Chapter 6 for more details).

Over 3,000 television channels are registered with the Ministry of Press, but there are six main channels at federal level: Channel One Russia (formerly ORT), RTR, NTV, Cultura, TVC and RTR-Sport. Euronews, the Lyon-based Europe-wide channel, broadcasts in Russian on the RTR channel outside of peak viewing hours. However, the field is dominated by Channel One Russia – a joint stock company with 51 per cent of shares owned by the Russian state. It broadcasts to 98 per cent of the landmass of Russia and reaches an estimated 140 million viewers. TV Channel Russia (RTR) – fully state-owned – is only available to 50 million viewers. One of the most respected channels is third in the Russian league, NTV. A professional, American-style outfit, it previously represented the only real opposition to the government, and still remains the only voice of criticism, even though that voice has been somewhat muted by government action.

A cynic might observe that the popularity and influence of television in Russia can be assessed by looking at the government's attempts to bring broadcasting under control. For a few years now, the Kremlin has tightened the reins on all journalists, and in 2002 the Committee to Protect Journalists put President Vladimir Putin in its top 10 worst enemies of the press. So Byzantine has the story become that, at the time of writing, two of the leading media barons of the Yeltsin era – Vladimir Gusinsky and Boris Berezovsky – had fled abroad.

Part of the problem was President Putin's election commitment to reduce the power of the so-called oligarchs – fabulously wealthy businessmen who prospered in the new Russia. This was a popular pledge, because the tycoons have a bad reputation amongst ordinary Russians, who believe them to be corrupt. One of the leading oligarchs is Vladimir Gusinsky, who owned Russia's biggest independent channel NTV, which won international acclaim for its coverage of the war in Chechnya. His problems began when Gazprom, a state-owned gas monopoly, called in debts and was given the right to change the managing board, effectively wresting control of the TV station from him.

Another victim is TV-6, an independent channel. At the time of writing, it had been taken off air and replaced by a state-run sports channel, leading to criticisms of government manipulation in advance of elections. And it is not only television journalists who are under threat – laws are being drawn up that would allow the authorities to close any media outlet that indulges in 'biased reporting' in the election run-up. Even critics of President Putin's administration who often disagree with each other have complained about Kremlin attempts to control the media.

According to the *Financial Times*, the Putin years have seen more arrests of journalists and legal cases opened than throughout the whole of the Yeltsin era. International groups such as Amnesty, the CPJ and organizations such as the Council of Europe and the European Union maintain pressure on Russia to change its ways. But despite the obvious difficulties faced by journalists, and the inevitable concomitant self-censorship, there are still many examples of campaigning journalists who are courageous enough to face up to the state machine.

Serbia and Montenegro

The newly born nation of Serbia and Montenegro, voted into life at the beginning of 2003, is what remains of the former Yugoslavia. It has a population of about 10.5 million, with a political scene that is at once volatile and fascinating for outsiders. Now rebuilding after the reign of Slobodan Milosevic, the government's main challenge is to stabilize the economy, combat organized crime (one of Milosevic's political gambits was to encourage the rise of a mafia class) and raise social standards to the level approved by the European institutions it dearly wants to work alongside.

A changing society has meant a changing media, and Serbian journalists have had more than their fair share of drama. Heavy censorship characterized the Milosevic era: so much so that the NATO bombing of Belgrade in 1999 targeted the state-owned radio and television, claiming the lives of 16 journalists and technicians.

Even then, however, a core of courageous independent journalists battled against censorship. Radio B92 was the most famous symbol of the resistance – it changed its name to B292 when its offices were raided and closed, but continued guerrilla broadcasts until the fall of the regime, when it resumed its original name. Many independent journalists risked their careers – and their lives – to beat the censor, and some were indeed murdered. When Milosevic fell from power in October 2000, these journalists were the ones who spearheaded sweeping changes.

Journalists based in Belgrade and the Montenegrin capital Podgorica are for the most part highly competent professionals. Many of them trained and began their journalistic careers under Tito, when the country was the freest of the then communist bloc. Citizens travelled without restrictions and were encouraged to learn other languages – the result is a generation of articulate and inquisitive journalists.

There is a rich newspaper market in the country. The former state-run paper, *Politika*, which kept its retro style until very recently, using Serbian Cyrillic rather than the Latin alphabet, has been bought by a German company and is modernizing rapidly. There are a host of tabloids, led by the best-selling *Blic*, which follows an independent line and covers stories much more fully than Western European tabloids, spiced up with a naked girl or two. Another bestseller is *Vecernje Novosti*. Both of these are excellent targets for your story – they sell throughout the whole area and even have editions in the Serbian part of Kosovo and the Republika Srpska in Bosnia and Herzegovina. The intellectuals' paper is *Danas*, printed in the Latin alphabet and very conscious of its duty to bring factual news and thoughtful opinion to the public.

These papers are fed by three main agencies. The oldest is Tanjug, the communist news agency that spread throughout the whole of ex-Yugoslavia and still keeps correspondents in each area. Many of the independent journalists started their careers at Tanjug. The agency has a good reputation but is struggling to restore its credibility since the fall of Milosevic.

There are two independent agencies. The larger, Beta, is a competitor to Tanjug, and the smaller, Fonet, specializes in multi-media, covering television, radio, written press and photographs. Both provide impartial and well-researched news in Serbian, and have Web sites in English. Another agency, SENSE, is not a news agency as such, but specializes in feature and analytical pieces, and covers the whole of the Balkan region from its Belgrade base.

There are two main venues for press conferences in Belgrade. The first is the Independent Media Centre, a leading meeting point for the anti-Milosevic campaigners in the past. They can efficiently provide refreshments, press conference and interpretation facilities at a reasonable price. The competitor is the Tanjug International Media Centre. Tanjug is based in more prestigious surroundings, but is somewhat tainted by its previous links with the state regime

Around 500 radio stations and 200 TV channels operate in Serbia, but only 10 per cent of these provide news. The main state-run media is RTS. Now installed back in central Belgrade after their premises were destroyed by the NATO bombing, RTS is receiving financial help from international organizations who want to foster independent media in the region. Radio B92 also now operates a television station, and Television Pink – the news channel set up by Milosevic's wife Mira Markovic – has made a U-turn and now attempts to provide news and comment in the style of Western European TV.

Montenegro is fiercely proud of its own identity, and this is reflected in its media. Montenegrins tune into their own television programmes and read their own locally produced newspapers and magazines. Their media was less affected by the Milosevic censorship, so changes have been less dramatic. The main newspaper of record is *Vijesti*, which is professionally run and produced. It is complemented by a news magazine called *Monitor*.

Kosovo is still internationally recognized as part of the territory of Serbia and Montenegro, although it is at present administered by the

United Nations. The northern part of the region is Serbian, and the Kosovo Serbs take the papers from Belgrade. Further south the people are Albanians, and tensions are such that Serbian newspapers are very rarely seen.

There are a number of newspapers in Kosovo, but only one that can aspire to the standards of international journalism. That is *Koha Ditore*, based in the centre of the Kosovo capital Pristina and staffed by a young team who have benefited from outside help and grants for international travel.

The radio and television station RTK is funded and run by the United Nations and the Organization for Security and Cooperation in Europe (OSCE). Many international organizations and non-governmental organizations are involved in the development of an independent media in Kosovo, with radio playing an especially important role in bringing together the different communities who are attempting to recover from a devastating war and decades of persecution.

Slovakia

Part of Czechoslovakia until the 'Velvet Revolution' of 1993, Slovakia was one of the Eastern European countries to enjoy a period of democracy before the Second World War. For the first half of the 1990s, it laboured under the authoritarian prime ministership of Vladimir Meciar, but a new government is now leading the country in a more enlightened direction, with EU and NATO membership gained, and a freer media able to report the changes.

The immediate post-communist period was a difficult one for the media, with Mr Meciar trying to restore some degree of state control through taxes and reduced access to newsprint. His attempts only partially succeeded, and most journalists continued to report freely, if carefully. The media is now free to report without harassment, and you can find a wide variety of opinions in the press, although some professionals complain that many of their colleagues are unaware of the existence of a written code of ethics for Slovakian journalists.

The Slovak newspaper scene is thriving. Latest government studies show readership going up – with 61 per cent of the population aged over 14 reading a newspaper every day. The top three newspapers are *Novy Cas*, *Pravda* and *Sme*. *Novy Cas* (New Times) is owned by the German Bertelsmann Group and has a Czech-born editor who has given it a gloss of scandal and gossip. But the re-launch has provoked a lot of mistrust amongst the population, who now consider it a less reliable source than previously. *Pravda* (Truth) barely takes 16 per cent of the market, but is seen as a newspaper of record, which can influence the political mood in the country. A left-leaning daily, it too has a Czech editor in chief. Despite the official figures, both papers claim to be the country's most popular read. The third title, *Sme*, is well known for being read in political circles.

One title now lagging behind is *Narodna Obroda*. Established in the 1990s, it soon gained a reputation for accuracy and in-depth commentaries. However, it is now widely considered to be a propaganda sheet for the ANO (Alliance of New Citizens) political party. Another paper with close political ties is *Novy Den* (New Day), which backs the populist HZDS (Movement for a Democratic Slovakia). Hungarian language newspapers are also on sale, including the Slovak-produced *Uj Szo* and imports from Budapest, especially the popular tabloid *Blikk*.

These morning papers are complemented by three evening publications – *Vecernik, Presovsky Vecernik* and *Kosicky Vecer*, and there is also a network of regional newspapers (*Kosicky Dennik, Presovsky Dennik, Gemersky Dennik, Spissky Dennik, Tatransky Dennik, Zemplinsky Dennik, Hlas Ludu* and *Smer*).

Slovakia has two news agencies – both of them set up after the transition to democracy. TASR is state-supported, and the prime minister personally appoints its director. Discussions are under way on whether it should move towards greater political and financial independence. SITA (Slovak Information and Press Agency) was set up in January 1997 and is privately owned, although it does receive some state subsidies.

Television and radio are very popular. Government figures show that up to 88 per cent of the population tune into radio, with Radio Slovensko taking the lion's share with 46.8 per cent of listeners. An information channel, it covers current affairs both at home and abroad and is one of the channels broadcast by Slovak Radio as a public service. Arts and culture are covered by Radio Devin, youth culture and music by Radio Rock FM, broadcasting for minorities is to be found on Radio Patria, and there is also an international service in five languages – Radio Slovakia.

For a small country Slovakia has a vast number of private radio stations, broadcasting mostly at regional and local level. They include Radio Okey, Fun Radio, Radio Lumen and Radio Twist. Most of them are supported by wealthy entrepreneurs or by political parties. Like most Europeans, the Slovaks listen whilst driving, so perhaps it is no surprise that it is the traffic information station Radio Express which people often tune into first, along with Slovak Radio's music channel.

The Slovak state television service cannot claim the same success as its radio counterpart. Slovak citizens are less likely to tune into its two channels than they are to switch to the private TV Markiza. Slovak television has also had a rocky ride politically over the past few years, and many people have expressed doubts that the radio and television councils are now truly unbiased, since many board members belong to political parties, even if they stand as independents.

TV Markiza has broadcast since August 1996, and attracts half the Slovak audience. It is owned by the ANO political party, who are also proprietors of *Narodna Obroda* and Radio Okey.

The third television company is TV Joj, and there is also an international rolling news channel TA3 which models itself on Euronews and CNN. Many Slovaks also tune into Czech or Hungarian national television.

Slovenia

The beautiful Alpine country of Slovenia was the closest to Western Europe of all the former communist countries, both geographically, since it borders with Italy and Austria, and also philosophically. It was the most prosperous region of Tito's Yugoslavia, and benefited from the 'open communism' of the Yugoslav states, making its transition to democracy easier than for most of its neighbours. It was also exceptional for being the only Yugoslav state not to descend into violence: its breakaway was relatively bloodless.

This has left a legacy of a free and diverse media landscape, but in common with many of the former communist countries, the Slovenians choose to get their news via the electronic media rather than newspapers. The six daily newspapers share a total daily circulation of only 345,000 copies. New titles that tried to enter the Slovenian markets in the 1990s failed for the most part, and it is the old newspapers from the communist times – *Delo*, *Dnevnik* and *Vecer* – that now lead the way. *Vecer* is the paper with the longest tradition – and is published not in the capital Ljubljana, but in Maribor. *Delo* – the main broadsheet – is the market leader with an average circulation of 93,000 copies, and tabloid *Slovenske Novice* is the only daily newspaper to be set up in the 1990s and to have survived. Two specialist productions also made the grade after launching in the 1990s – *Finance*, produced for the business market, and *Ekipa*, the sports daily.

Slovenia is unique in being a country with no real regional daily newspapers, although at the time of writing plans were afoot to try to launch some. Quite a number of regions have bi- or tri-weekly newspapers. They include *Primorske Novice*, publishing three times a week, *Gorenjski Glas* which appears twice a week, and three weeklies – *Dolenski List*, *Novi Tednik* and *Vestnik*. Strangely enough, one of the strongest papers on the media market is the national weekly *Nedeljski Dnevnik*, which is read by about a third of the population (32 per cent), and deals in general news. Weekly news magazines also do very well and include *Jana* (readership 13 per cent), *Nedelo* (10 per cent), *Razvedrilo* (10 per cent), *Stop* (7 per cent), and

Kmecki Glas (7 per cent). There are also two highly influential political weeklies, *Mladina* and *Mag*. The main news agency is the STA.

The electronic media is the most popular way for Slovenians to receive their daily dose of news. The pre-eminent broadcaster is Radio Television Slovenia (RTS), which began life 40 years ago under the communist system. Today, with 2,300 employees it is the largest communications outfit in the country. It operates three national radio channels and broadcasts to the regions, including programmes in Italian. There are also many small commercial radio stations broadcasting mostly music and chat shows.

RTV – the television arm of RTS – runs two national channels in Slovenian and a third in Italian, and there are also plans to set up a channel broadcasting in Hungarian. Amongst the commercial operators, Kanal A was the first private broadcaster to be granted a licence under the communist regime, and still broadcasts today. The free market era has meant a boom in commercial broadcasting and today five private channels compete with the state station, with Pop TV the market leader.

Spain

A country with four official languages (Spanish – which is usually called 'castillian', Catalan, Basque and Galician) is sure to be a country with a mixed personality, and such is the case of Spain. With 40 million people and a complex political scene, Spain is marked by a diversity that is reflected in its media landscape.

National or regional media, public or private, operate in the various languages, and even journalistic style can differ from place to place, with Madrid being known for a more aggressive kind of political debate than in the provinces.

Today's media scene has developed out of Spain's history, and this generation would find it hard to recognize the style that dominated the life of their parents. Modern Spain is a very different place to the Spain of Franco (1939 to 1975). With his death, Spain changed beyond recognition – and the media scene changed with it. Only the Spanish national television (TVE), some radio stations and a couple of the main newspapers have survived.

The most international Spanish newspaper, *El País* (The Country), was founded in 1976. It was the first newspaper to give information about the newly born democracy without the censorship of the past. It is still the bestseller amongst the national press.

El País (circulation 435,000) is a quality newspaper in a tabloid format, with front page colour added to the mix in 2001 (Spanish readers don't see the point of buying a paper that you cannot open on public transport).

The newspaper *El Mundo* (The World) was also born out of the transitional period. Today it is the second most read paper (300,000) and the one that makes the most use of investigative journalism. The third paper in the sales league, and the most conservative, is ABC (262,000).

All these papers have central offices in Madrid and publish special editions for the different autonomous communities (regions) of Spain. But each region has its own bestselling newspapers, sometimes in the regional language. For example, *La Vanguardia* (The Vanguard) or *El Periodico* (The

Journal) in Catalonia; *La Voz de Galicia* (The Voice of Galicia) in Galicia and *El Correo Español* (The Spanish Mail) in the Basque country.

The trashy tabloid style much loved by the British or German tourists simply doesn't exist. Spain has rejected attempts to place a Spanish version of the *Sun* or *Bild* onto the news-stands. For example, *El Periodico* recently tried to change its style by using big formats, large photos and different colours. The experiment proved a flop with readers and the paper was forced to reinstate its classic look.

On the other hand, the Spanish revel in romantic gossip, with the 'prensa del corazón' (heart press) taking a large slice of the market, mostly in the form of weekly magazines. The most famous one is *Hola!*, the main (and possibly only) example of a Spanish press product that has found a niche in other countries (its UK version is *Hello!*).

One new growth area has been the trend towards free newspapers, which are available in most of Spain's big cities. *Metro* and *20 Minutos* (20 minutes) are two popular examples of the genre. The free press covers the same news as bought papers, but in less depth. Relying heavily on agency copy, they employ fewer journalists than the mainstream press, and are frequently criticized for a lack of originality. However, their success, particularly with younger readers, has dented the sales of some of the country's leading bought papers.

Sports news is big business in Spain, with the most popular sports paper, *Marca* (Brand), coming second only to *El País* in terms of circulation (380,000). Mainly bought by men, the sales figures of sports papers can vary with the fortunes of the football teams they support. *Marca* and *As* (Ace) are on the side of Real Madrid, while *El Mundo Deportivo* (The Sporting World) supports FC Barcelona.

Nearly half the news stories published by Spanish newspapers come from the main news agency: EFE. Created at the end of the Civil War (1936–39), it now has a presence in a hundred countries, and is especially strong in South America. The second-largest agency is Europa Press, which offers news in the four official Spanish languages.

Whilst all newspapers are private, TV and radio stations can be both public and private. Controlled by the central government, TVE operates the two public national television channels, TVE-1 and La 2, also broadcasting in the regional languages.

Since 1989 Spanish viewers have been able to watch two private terrestrial channels: Tele 5, whose main owner is the Italian group Fininvest, and Antena 3, mainly owned by the Spanish telephone company, Telefónica. A third one, Canal+, imported from France, is a subscription channel, but news and popular programmes can be picked up by viewers without a subscription – including the Spanish version of the satirical show *Spitting Image – Las noticias del Guiñol*. There are also two digital satellite channels: Canal Satélite Digital and Vía Digital, which began operations in 1997.

The regional TVs are TV3, 33 (Catalonia), ETB 1 and 2 (Basque Country), TVG (Galicia), Canal Sur (Andalucía), Canal 9 (Valencia) and Telemadrid (Madrid).

Most of the public television channels also operate radio stations, and the most important private radio networks are Ser (owned by Prisa), Onda Cero (Telefónica) and Cope, whose main owner is the Catholic Church. There are also 500 local public radio stations, usually broadcasting in the regional language.

When trying to sell your story to Spanish journalists, take into account that timetables there are slightly different than in Northern Europe: the main TV and radio news shows are broadcast around 2.00 pm (TVE and Antena 3 at 3.00 pm) and 8.30 pm. Similarly, it is not easy to find somebody at their desk before midday as most of the work is done after 4.30 pm. This makes lunchtime and early afternoon a good moment to organize a press conference, and most big cities have venues – such as the Centre Internacional de Premsa in Barcelona.

Sweden

Sweden has the distinction of having one of the world's first Freedom of the Press laws, dating from 1766, and of leading the world in the technological revolution. The home of Ericsson, Saab, Volvo and Ikea, Sweden is adapting fast to new technology but retains its affection for newsprint.

Swedes are great newspaper consumers and, in common with their Scandinavian neighbours, tend to subscribe to their favourite read, rather than buying a copy on the way to the office. That the papers arrive on the doormat each morning with regularity and efficiency is remarkable in a country with some very remote areas. It is estimated that more than 80 per cent of the adult population read a newspaper on an average day. There are around 160 papers, although about a third of them appear only once or twice a week and have very low circulation. Regional and local publications are strong and some of the national papers are based in regional cities.

In terms of the national press, both broadsheets and tabloids are popular. They are produced in Sweden's three main cities: Stockholm, Gothenburg and Malmö. The broadsheets – *Dagens Nyheter*, *Göteborgs-Posten* and *Sydsvenska Dagbladet* – make up a quarter of all newspaper circulation and appear in the morning. The main tabloids are *Aftonbladet* and *Expressen*. Two other papers are tabloid in appearance but broadsheet in content: *Svenska Dagbladet* (which used to be a broadsheet until quite recently) and *Dagens Industri*, which specializes in financial and business news.

Sweden has a sizeable Finnish-speaking minority, and they have their own press, of which *Ruotsin Sanomat* (daily) and *Ruotsinsuomalainen* (weekly) are two market leaders.

Tidningarnas Telegrambyrå (TT) is the much-respected state news agency.

Radio arrived in Sweden in 1925 and television in 1956, under the wing of the Swedish Broadcasting Company – Sveriges Radio – which still rules the airwaves. Its three channels are P1 for news and current affairs, P2 for classical music, and P3 aimed at young people. Regional programmes are the remit of P4, the most popular channel, capturing 37 per cent of the audience. There is also a channel for Finnish-speakers – SR Sisuradio, which broadcasts for 16 hours every day. The international voice of Sweden is SR International, which broadcasts in 18 languages.

Commercial stations such as Energy, Mix Megapol, Rix FM and Fria Media do not have national coverage and cater instead for the local market. So local in fact, that some stations broadcast only within a radius of 10 kilometres. These stations survive thanks to a system of state support.

The state broadcasters are the biggest players in television. The main channel is SVT1, with the second channel SVT2 serving the 10 television regions. Swedish television broadcasts special programmes for the Finnish-speaking minority living in Sweden, and in March 1999 launched a 24-hour rolling news channel SVT24.

Commercial stations arrived fairly late in Sweden, but from the late 1980s onwards the cable and satellite market took off. The main commercial broadcaster is TV4, and there are five satellite channels – TV3, Kanal 5, Z-TV, TV6 and TV8.

Switzerland

Switzerland has zealously guarded its neutrality for over 300 years and consistently votes against membership of the European Union, although it has been a member of the Council of Europe for the past 40 years. In the film *The Third Man* the Orson Welles character Harry Lime makes a famous speech that unfavourably compares the peaceful Alpine country with the Italy of the Borgias. He concludes that the greatest achievement of 500 years of Swiss democracy and peace has been the cuckoo clock (for some reason he forgot to mention the Swiss army knife, an equally successful export).

The reality is of course more flattering than Harry Lime would have us believe. Switzerland is one of the world's richest nations, with a thriving banking sector, several world-class pharmaceutical giants, a huge tourist industry and a big exporter of cheese, chocolate, and yes, cuckoo clocks! With its four-way regional split on linguistic lines (French, German, Italian and Rhaeto-Romanic) and a highly decentralized democracy, the country is truly unique in Europe.

From a media point of view, Switzerland is important for several reasons: it is one of the world's leading financial centres, and hosts many international organizations, including the World Health Organization, the United Nations, the International Red Cross and the World Trade Organization. The European Broadcasting Union (EBU), based in Geneva, is the hub through which most international television news passes on its way to newsrooms throughout Europe, and further afield.

To work with the Swiss press, you have to bear in mind the country's federal structure, and its different language groups. German, French and Italian speakers are in the majority and are well provided for in terms of print media. Around 40,000 speak the Rhaeto-Romanic language – their main means of communication is local radio and there are no newspapers in this language.

This cumbersome structure means you have to target each linguistic group separately. There is little or no contact between the different groups and no shared news desks. A good way of tracking the media is through the *PR Verzeichnis* guide, which is published every year and gives details of all the media active in the country. The Swiss press agency SDA ATS also serves all language groups.

Switzerland has 90 daily newspapers, 77 weekly and a total newspaper circulation of 4 million copies. The market for newspapers in Switzerland is going through a tough time. Advertising – the main way of funding production – is down sharply, and it is causing the market to shrink. Reading habits are also changing with the increasing popularity of online information. In 2003 eight newspapers closed down. At the time of writing, various mergers between the different papers were being discussed, with at least one in danger of disappearing. The most likely survivor is the much-respected *Neue Zürcher Zeitung*.

Broadcasting is dominated by public television and radio, which operates in all languages, and the regions are well covered by private operators. The main evening news is shown at 7.30 pm and covers the big political stories of the day. The late bulletin is usually just before midnight. Many Swiss also receive television from cable and satellite – over 90 per cent of households have access.

Turkey

Once the centre of the mighty Ottoman empire, Turkey straddles the border between Europe and Asia, with the bulk of its landmass in the Orient. It already plays a key strategic role in the NATO military alliance, but its dream is to join the European Union. With this end in mind, in recent years Turkey has made great advances in human rights and democracy, and is expecting soon to enter into accession negotiations. The EU application is a source of endless speculation for the Turkish media, along with two other running political stories: the future of Cyprus and the situation of Turkey's population of Kurdish origin (20 per cent), many of whom want greater recognition for their cultural identity.

Although Ankara, located in central Turkey, is the country's seat of government and parliament, the media capital is Istanbul, a sprawling, vibrant city on the Bosphorus – the narrow strait that separates the Mediterranean from the Black Sea, and the symbolic link between Europe and Asia. The US-based media monitor Freedom House classified the Turkish media as 'Partly Free' in 2003, claiming that some journalists who discussed sensitive issues such as the Kurds, the military (which still plays an important role in Turkish society) and political Islam were imprisoned. Although official censorship is a thing of the past, many older journalists who experienced it still have a tendency to self-censorship when writing about controversial issues.

Newspapers have existed in Turkey since the 19th century. There are now 30 national dailies, many of them also available on the Internet. The biggest-selling title is *Hürriyet*, with a circulation of more than 500,000. Other big sellers are *Posta* (450,000), *Sabah* (380,000), *Vatan* (310,000), *Milliyet* (290,000), *Zaman* (280,000), *Takvim* (220,000), *Star* (216,000) and *Akşam* (216,000). Two smaller but influential papers are *Cumhuriyet* and *Radikal*, both with circulations of fewer than 50,000. Although these two titles lean to the left, on the whole it is difficult to classify Turkish newspapers politically. Most succeed in reflecting a wide spectrum of views, by employing columnists of different political colours. Less laudable is the lack of restraint shown by many picture editors, who frequently use graphic photos of accidents, often showing the dead and injured.

The leading English language paper is the *Turkish Daily News*, read widely in expat and diplomatic circles.

For the Turkish business community, the most important paper is *Hürriyet*, followed by *Dünya* (World). *Dünya* has substantial subscription sales. By contrast, *Finansal Forum*, which models itself on the *Financial Times*, is sold mainly over the counter.

The leading news agency in Turkey is Anadolu Ajansı, which is partly state-owned. Ankara-based Anka concentrates on political news. İHA (İhlas Haber Ajansı) is a television news agency which supplies pictures to many Turkish and foreign TV stations. It has a particularly strong network of correspondents in the Middle East and Central Asia.

Television viewers in Turkey are spoilt for choice, with 38 national channels, available by terrestrial transmission, cable and satellite. The state broadcaster is TRT, which has one international and four domestic channels. The first, TRT 1, carries a range of programming including entertainment, news and documentaries. TRT 2 specializes in news, TRT 3 in sport, and TRT 4 focuses on culture, education and learning. TRT International targets Turkish communities abroad, and countries with a cultural affinity to Turkey, such as Azerbaijan.

Channels that offer mixed programming include ATV, Kanal D, Kanal 6, Kanal 7, Show TV, Star, TGRT and HBB. There are also several rolling news channels, including CNN Türk, NTV, Sky Türk, Habertürk and TRT 2.

In addition, foreign outfits such as Eurosport, MGM, Fox Kids, Discovery Channel and National Geographic are also targeting the Turkish market.

The result of all this choice is that the TV market is extremely fragmented, with few channels capturing more than 15 per cent of the audience. Advertising income is therefore spread thinly, with the result that resources for home-grown programme making are limited. Most channels belong to one of several large industrial groups, the biggest of which is Doğan Medya, the creation of media magnate Aydın Doğan. He owns Kanal D and CNN Türk, along with daily papers such as *Hürriyet*, *Milliyet*, *Posta*, *Radikal* and *Finansal Forum*. However, unlike their counterparts in the UK, Turkish media barons do not insist that all their media outlets follow the same political line.

Prior to the 1990s radio in Turkey was the preserve of the public broadcaster TRT, which offers a range of channels specializing in news, culture and different kinds of music. In the past decade there has been a huge increase in the number of private FM stations, nearly all of which broadcast music in one form or another, with a short news bulletin on the hour. If you want to reach the decision makers and opinion formers of Turkey, the best radio channels to target are NTV Radyo and Radyo D, which broadcasts CNN Türk news.

Internet news is expanding fast in Turkey, with more than 30 sites, most of them operating on a shoestring. One of the most reliable and independent is www.ntvmsnbc.com, an offshoot of the TV news channel NTV, in partnership with MSNBC. News sites have a reputation for being more independent than traditional media, and providing news which does not appear anywhere else.

Ukraine

Europe's second-biggest country in terms of territory, Ukraine gained independence in 1991 following the downfall of the Soviet Union. Known as the 'bread basket' of the USSR because of its fertile land, its agricultural sector suffered a big setback when the nuclear reactor at Chernobyl caught fire in 1986, contaminating large parts of Ukraine and many other countries, which lay in the path of the ensuing dust clouds. Post-communism, the country hit the headlines when sensational allegations were made that President Kuchma was implicated in the murder of a journalist whose headless corpse was discovered after he vanished in mysterious circumstances in 2000. Tapes purporting to prove the claims were never authenticated, and the case remains unsolved. However, all human rights groups agree that criticizing the government of Ukraine can be a dangerous and even deadly pursuit for a journalist. Reporters Sans Frontières (Reporters Without Borders) noted in March 2002 that 10 journalists had died in suspicious circumstances in the previous four years, and another 41 suffered serious injuries from attacks. The US-based media monitor Freedom House recently downgraded its classification of the media in Ukraine from 'Partly Free' to 'Not Free', citing among its complaints the failure of the authorities to adequately investigate attacks against journalists.

Ukrainian and Russian are quite different languages, though very similar in structure. However, most newspapers in Ukraine are printed in Russian, reflecting both the country's large Russian minority (20 per cent) and a continuing preference among many citizens for what was until fairly recently the official – and most commonly used – language. The daily circulation of the Russian language press is around 25 million copies, compared with 16 million for Ukrainian. Generally speaking, Russian language titles and editions sell best in the east and south (nearest to Russia) while their Ukrainian counterparts are most popular in the west.

Political parties or politicians own most of the country's newspapers. The biggest-selling title is *Fakty i Komentarii* (1,000,000). The daily political paper *Golos Ukrainy* sells around 170,000 copies. Other popular dailies are *Kievskiye Vedomosti* (130,000) and *Segodnya* (122,000).

Favourite papers of key decision makers in Ukraine are *Kommersant* (a Russian title) and *Kievskiye Vedomosti*. For politicians, academics and journalists, the most influential papers are *Den* (the Day) and *Zerkalo Nedeli* (Mirror of the Week). *Uryadoviy Kourrier*, an official paper, is also widely read in elite circles.

For business people, the papers of choice are *Delovoy Zhurnal* (Business Journal), *Companion, Invest Gazeta* and *Galitsky Kontrakty* (published in Lvov but available nationwide) and *Delovaya nedelya-FT* (Business Week), which has a licence to reprint articles from the British *Financial Times*. Most of these titles are weekly, but there is a business section every day in *Kievskie Vedomosti*.

News magazines are beginning to emerge in Ukraine. Two of the best-known titles are *PIK* and *Korrespondent*.

As in Russia, sales of newspapers and news magazines have plummeted in post-communist Ukraine, owing to falling real incomes on the one hand and the rising prices of papers on the other. Only 60 copies are sold per 1,000 people compared with 440 in the years prior to the break-up of the USSR. Most people in Ukraine now turn to TV as their main news source.

There are three leading news agencies in Ukraine: the state-owned Ukrinform distributes information at home and abroad, in Ukrainian, Russian and English. The other two agencies are Interfax-Ukraine, a branch of the Russian news agency Interfax, and UNIAN, which is one of the main sources of information for the Ukrainian media, and particularly renowned for its photo service.

On the TV scene the most watched national channels are Inter, Studio '1+1', Noviy Canal, STB, UT-1 and ICTV. As well as home-grown channels, Ukrainians living in cities can watch the main Russian stations such as Channel One Russia (formerly ORT) and NTV on cable and satellite. In rural areas without access to cable TV, terrestrial channels like UT-1 and Inter are more popular, as is regional television.

Radio is less politicized than either the press or television. The leading FM stations (mostly available in the Kiev area) are Dovira, Continent, Hromadske Radio and Era, all of which carry news bulletins. Local re-broadcasts of the Ukrainian service of the BBC are also popular, because they are considered to be more objective than many of their home-grown rivals.

Internet news is of increasing importance in Ukraine. Unlike traditional media, which require a lot of capital, setting up an Internet site is comparatively cheap. They are also quick to get out the news, and tend to be more independent than the mainstream media, which often represent a political party or business group. Some of the best known sites are Ukrainska Pravda, Forum, Glavred, Versii, Mignews, Korrespondent, Podrobnosti and Ukraine.

The Ukrainian media can also be categorized according to where their political loyalties lie, which unsurprisingly nearly always coincides with who owns them.

In the state sector the president controls UT-1, the main public channel. The newspaper *Golos Ukrainy* answers to the Ukrainian parliament, while *Uryadoviy Kourrier* is a mouthpiece for the Cabinet of Ministers of Ukraine.

Other media are allied to a range of political parties and groups, most of whom support President Kuchma and his government. The United Social Democratic Party (USD) controls three TV channels – Studio '1+1', Channel Inter and TET. STB is partly owned by Viktor Pinchuk, a wealthy businessman and son-in-law of President Kuchma (the Russian Lukoil group also has a stake in STB). Mr Pinchuk and another Russian conglomerate, the Alfa group, jointly own Noviy Canal, and he is also a major shareholder in ICTV. Ukraine's best-selling paper *Fakty I Komentarii* is also part of the Pinchuk media empire.

Elsewhere in the print world, the news agency UNIAN and the daily paper *2000* belong to the USD party. Finally, the Donetsk financial group owns *Segodnya*, the popular daily, and partly owns *Delovoy Zhurnal* (Business Journal) and *Invest Gazeta* (Investment Paper).

There are a small number of independent newspapers, but none of them are big players in terms of circulation and influence: *Zerkalo Nedeli* (Mirror of the Week) and *Vechirni Visti* (Evening News).

United Kingdom

ENGLAND

The green English countryside, a cup of tea, the sound of leather on willow... and a newspaper to scan – the very essence of Britishness could not exist without newsprint somewhere on the scene. The British may not be the world's champion newspaper readers – that honour goes to the Scandinavians and the Japanese – but they are not far behind. The Newspaper Society has calculated that 84 per cent of British adults read a regional newspaper and 67 per cent a national.

Furthermore, it would be no exaggeration to say that many British media institutions can claim a place as world leaders. London-based publications such as *The Economist* and the *Financial Times* are so respected worldwide that they merit a mention in the chapter on the European media scene. The BBC is the giant of broadcasters, and the news agency Reuters – although founded by a German – has always had its main offices in London.

But there are darker aspects to the media picture – Britain is the home of the gossip-fuelled tabloid, the country where media barons put their personal stamp on the editorial independence of journalists and the European capital of 'spin' – the manipulation of news to politicians' ends.

The British passion for newsprint dates back to the mid-18th century, although most of the national press developed between 1850 and 1900 as literacy levels improved and workers earned enough to be able to afford a daily paper. Britain's biggest-selling tabloid *The Sun*, generally known for its right-wing, conservative slant, began its life in 1911 (when it was called the *Daily Herald*) as a journal for striking workers.

As newspapers developed, so too did a journalistic mythus. The image of a reporter in a dirty overcoat, with a shorthand pad and a nose for the news, became something of an archetype for the profession. The intellectuals of the newspaper world emphasized the importance of accuracy in reporting – C P Scott, editor of the *Manchester Guardian* (which later became the national newspaper *The Guardian*) famously stated that comment is free but facts are sacred. By contrast, media baron Lord Beaverbrook admitted to a parliamentary committee that he ran the *Daily Express* purely for propaganda purposes.

One of the reasons papers are so popular in Britain is that they are not taxed. This makes them cheaper to buy and has triggered numerous price wars in recent decades. *The Sun* now retails at 30 pence and even the quality newspapers sell at a very reasonable price by European standards.

Today newspapers are described according to their format – broadsheets are the larger newspapers that need constant folding on public transport, the tabloids are small and easy to read. Tabloids are generally the gossip papers, and the worst of them are called the 'redtops'. In other European countries, quality newspapers have also taken to the tabloid format (for example, *El País* in Spain).

The redtops are read and enjoyed by many British people. It would be wrong to say they do not cover politics and current affairs – they do, but briefly, colourfully and interspliced with pictures of celebrities and practically naked young men and women (some attempt has been made to avoid accusations of sexism by balancing the genders!). Sports enthusiasts are especially fond of the tabloids, many of which give excellent coverage of football and horseracing. The leader in the field is *The Sun*, with the *Daily Star* and the *Daily Sport* attempting a similar sort of style. The *Daily Mirror* is considered the most serious of the redtops. A left-wing newspaper, it had a strong tradition of investigative journalism in the 1960s and 70s that it has recently tried to revive.

At the more conservative end of the tabloid market are the *Daily Mail* and the *Daily Express*. They take themselves a lot more seriously, with commentators and columnists discussing the latest hot topics, and more emphasis on political news. They are pitched mainly at women, and carry a lot of 'lifestyle' features.

There is a similar range amongst the broadsheet market. All broadsheet newspapers give much more significant coverage to political and social issues, but their approaches are very different. The fattest of the daily newspapers in terms of sheer volume is the left-inclined *Guardian*, which covers news issues in the main section and features in the tabloid pullout, which has a different theme for each day of the week. Those who buy the European edition of the paper have to make do with a slimmed-down version of the British product.

The Independent (and its sister paper *The Independent on Sunday*) was one of the few papers launched in the 1980s that managed to survive and now has a faithful following. True to its name, the 'Indy' often refuses to follow the rest of the press crowd, notably boycotting the Westminster lobby system of unattributable Downing Street briefings in the 1980s (the paper decided to resume attending the twice-daily briefings after the government agreed that they could be attributed to Downing Street). Another distinctive characteristic is a tendency to downplay stories about the royal family that receive blanket coverage in other newspapers. In 2003 the paper made history by becoming the first in the world to offer its readers a choice between a broadsheet and tabloid format. Everything offered in the bigger size is available in the smaller version, which sells for the same price.

The Times is one of the world's oldest and best-known papers. It was founded in 1785 by John Walter, and by 1861 its reputation had grown to such an extent that the US president, Abraham Lincoln, said: '*The Times* is one of the greatest powers in the world – in fact, I don't know anything which has more power, except perhaps the Mississippi.' He was probably thinking of the reports sent from the Crimean War by the legendary journalist William Howard Russell. His dispatches were highly critical of the handling of the war, and led to the downfall of Lord Aberdeen's government. In today's crowded media marketplace the paper has much less influence. Politically it leans towards the right, and tends to attract conservative, establishment types. Its archrival in the battle for right-wing readers is *The Daily Telegraph*. The 'Torygraph' is the chosen read of the well-to-do segment of British society that enjoys stories about the royal family, the Anglican Church, and scandalous court cases (it carries more court reports than any other broadsheet).

Although fairly stereotypical, these readership profiles were recently confirmed by a study carried out by the market research company Claritas, which came up with one surprise result – that readers of the *Financial Times* are the youngest, and (less surprisingly) the richest, newspaper readers of all.

One unique aspect of the British way of life is the Britons' love of Sunday newspapers. For many people, these replace the weekly analytical magazines popular in the rest of the continent. Some of them, indeed, are excellent ways to catch up on the events of the week over a lazy Sunday breakfast. The weightiest of these is *The Sunday Times*, which takes some hefty lifting thanks to its many different sections. *The Sunday Times* still basks in a reputation as an incisive investigative newspaper, gained in the 1970s when the legendary Harold Evans edited the paper. Its Insight team uncovered many a scandal, famously exposing the dangers of the drug Thalidomide, for example. The other heavyweights include *The Guardian*'s sister paper, *The Observer* (established in 1791, making it the world's oldest Sunday newspaper) and *The Independent on Sunday*.

The tabloid sector includes the Sunday versions of the main daily newspapers. The bestseller is the *News of the World*, *The Sun*'s sister paper and part of the Murdoch stable.

The influence of Rupert Murdoch is pervasive in the British media scene. In the print world his empire spans the tabloid and broadsheet market – he owns the *Sun*, the *News of the World*, *The Times* and *The Sunday Times*. Sky TV has changed the face of British television forever, by using new technology to launch successful pay TV channels for sport and films. Traditional broadcasters such as the BBC and ITV have lost ground in terms of both access to live sporting events and audience share.

Besides the world-renowned Reuters, Britain also has its home-grown news agency, the Press Association. PA feeds both the nationals and the regional media.

The regional newspaper scene in Britain is one of the healthiest in the world, and every local community has its own weekly or daily newspaper. Many a top journalist has begun their career with their local newspaper group, and local communities hold their press in a lot of affection – not least because they tend to publish photographs of all their friends and relations.

In London, the regional media takes on a different character – the London *Evening Standard*, by rights the regional evening paper for the capital, aspires to be a national newspaper, although it has less impact in the provinces. Londoners can also get metropolitan news and gossip from the free morning paper *Metro*, which is distributed mainly at railway and Underground stations.

Radio also has a strong presence at local and regional level. The BBC has the largest network, but many areas also have successful commercial stations. The phone-in talk show is particularly popular in Britain, and much information as well as some eccentric late-night opinions can be gleaned by tuning in.

The BBC dominates national radio. It operates 10 national channels, which provide news and sports coverage, entertainment, music, documentaries and drama. The best and most cherished of the BBC channels for news and current affairs aficionados is Radio 4, whose early morning *Today* programme sets the daily agenda for much of the serious media. Five Live, a rolling news and sports channel, has won praise for its innovative programming.

In the commercial sector, Independent Radio News (IRN) supplies national and international news to many local radio stations. In the London area, London Broadcasting Company (LBC) is a popular rolling news station, well known for its phone-ins, but the highest ratings go to Capital Radio, a music station with an award-winning news team.

The British Broadcasting Corporation (BBC) was born in 1922 (though it was initially called the British Broadcasting Company). The government decided that the fledgling broadcaster should be funded directly by the public through a licence system, which meant that it depended neither on the government nor on advertising for its income. This formula assured the organization's legendary independence from government or commercial influence. Under the motto 'Nation shall speak peace unto nation', the

189

BBC began its life under John Reith, the first Director General. His aim was to create a 'trustee for national interest' which should 'inform, educate and entertain'. This philosophy has served the corporation well for many years. The BBC's budget now exceeds 2.6 billion pounds a year, which funds all its domestic TV, radio and multimedia services (the world services of BBC radio and TV are funded separately).

The BBC operates two free-to-air TV channels BBC 1 and BBC 2, and six digital channels, including BBC News 24, a rolling news channel, and BBC Parliament, which covers proceedings at Westminster. Its main terrestrial rivals are ITV and Channel 4. Established in the late 1950s as a network of regional franchises, ITV quickly gained viewers with its informal, homely style and aggressive approach to ratings. Channel Four was set up in 1982 and immediately became popular with more radical, liberal elements of society. Since 1997 the UK has had a fifth terrestrial channel, simply known as Five. With a much smaller budget than the other free-to-air channels, Five has a reputation for canny scheduling in its battle for survival in the ever-diminishing advertising market. News is provided by ITN (Independent Television News) who also supply news to ITV and Channel Four.

The biggest revolution in British TV came with the advent of satellite technology. Sky television hit the scene in the 1990s, and soon made satellite the popular choice for many Britons, offering specialist sports and film channels as well as 24-hour news.

News programmes on British television tend to be short and succinct, with regional editions following the main national news bulletins. As at national level, there is keen competition between the BBC and commercial rivals. For example, in Birmingham, England's second-largest city, BBC Midlands Today competes with Carlton News for the attention of the region's viewers.

For more in-depth coverage of daily events, the UK has a number of daily current affairs shows that run from Monday to Friday. The most influential are *Channel Four News*, at 7.00 pm, and BBC 2's *Newsnight* at 10.30 pm. Both have a small but upmarket following, which includes many politicians, journalists and business people.

Weekend current affairs are concentrated on Sunday morning and early afternoon. First up is *GMTV*, the ITV breakfast show whose Sunday edition is a popular forum for leading politicians trying to set the day's news agenda. At 9.00 am *Breakfast with Frost* on BBC 1 relies on the tried and tested interview skills of the British TV icon, Sir David Frost. At midday BBC 1's *Politics Show* is the main focus. Finally, on Sunday evenings, *Panorama*, the BBC's flagship news documentary programme, is a showcase for the Corporation's investigative journalism.

For Internet news and features, the BBC is pre-eminent, with one of Europe's biggest and most visited Web sites. Nearly every other news organization also has an online version of its output.

SCOTLAND

Visitors to the UK often make the mistake of thinking that the London scene covers everything. This approach is not only erroneous, it might also risk offending the many people who live outside the capital.

The Scottish media landscape is quite different from England. Scotland has its own newspapers, television and radio, and its newsbeat is quite different from the London-based media. The top seller is the tabloid *Daily Record*, and the London-based tabloids also produce special editions with stories for the Scottish market. The two top quality newspapers are *The Herald* and *The Scotsman*, both highly respected, and running foreign correspondents out of the main European press centres in the same way as the London-based dailies.

There are four Scottish Sunday newspapers – the *Sunday Mail*, *Scotland on Sunday*, the *Sunday Herald*, and the *Sunday Post*, with its famous and much-loved cartoons the Broons and Oor Wullie. Regional and local news-papers also sell strongly throughout Scotland, from the far north *Shetland Times* to *Border Telegraph* in the south.

Radio and TV are provided by the BBC and television by the independent channel Scottish TV (STV) and Grampian TV.

WALES

The Welsh language has equal official status with English, and the country is a fine example of how to protect and sustain a minority culture through bilingualism. In the media though, English has the edge, with more news-papers, radio stations and television channels using the language of William Shakespeare than that of Owain Glyndwr (a 15th-century Welsh freedom fighter who became a national legend).

The *Western Mail* is the national newspaper of Wales, but it can also be found on news-stands as far away as London. A quality two-section broadsheet, it is Wales' only national morning daily paper. The Welsh equivalent of *The Scotsman*, it is particularly strong on political events at the Welsh Assembly in Cardiff. In North Wales, however, some people prefer to read the Welsh edition of an English morning newspaper, the *Daily Post*, which is based in Liverpool. The *South Wales Echo*, the evening newspaper for Cardiff and neighbouring areas, is Wales' biggest-selling home-grown paper. Since 1989 the Principality has had its own Sunday paper, *Wales on Sunday*.

The leading Welsh language publications are *Golwg*, a weekly magazine, and *Y-cymro*, a weekly paper. *Cymru'r Byd* is an Internet news site operated by the BBC. There are also more than 50 local papers in Welsh.

Radio in Wales is dominated by the BBC, which runs two networks, Radio Wales and Radio Cymru, broadcasting in English and Welsh respectively. They each offer a mix of news, current affairs, sport, drama, arts and religious programming. Local radio is left to the commercial stations, including Swansea Sound, Bridge FM, Valleys Radio, Real Radio and Red Dragon (South Wales), Radio Ceredigion and Magic 756 (mid-Wales) and Marcher Gold, MFM, Coast FM and Champion FM (North Wales).

Since 1982 Welsh language viewers have had their own channel – S4C, the Welsh version of Channel Four. It carries a wide range of programmes, including drama, sport and news, all in the Welsh language. Its bestselling export has been the cartoon character Super Ted. BBC 1 Wales and HTV (the ITV franchise for Wales) cover Welsh affairs, but in the English language. BBC 2 Wales also has regional programmes in English.

NORTHERN IRELAND

Though its population (1.3 million) is substantially below that of either Wales or Scotland (3 and 5 million respectively), for more than a quarter of a century Northern Ireland has punched above its weight in terms of making the news. The sectarian conflict euphemistically known as 'The Troubles' has consistently thrust the area into the international limelight. Nowadays the shaky but still intact peace process has led to a scaling down of media coverage by the British national media and their foreign counterparts, while local journalists are now happily concentrating on a more balanced news agenda.

The main morning paper in Northern Ireland is the *News Letter*, with a circulation of around 31,000. This title has the distinction of being the oldest daily paper in the United Kingdom. Editorially, it supports the unionist position – that Northern Ireland should remain a part of the United Kingdom. Another morning publication, the *Irish News*, gives more weight to the nationalist viewpoint – that the Irish Republic should be given more of a say in the running of affairs north of the border. However, in recent years it has signed up some columnists from the unionist side. This more balanced approach, together with a decision to print the paper in an unusual new size – between a broadsheet and a tabloid – has paid off in terms of increased sales.

Northern Ireland's main evening paper, the *Belfast Evening Telegraph*, enjoys a healthy circulation of 111,000, and is broadly unionist in its politics.

Appendices

Appendices

Appendix 1

Europewide Media

Newspapers and news magazines

Courrier International
64–68, rue du Dessous-des-Berges
75647 Paris Cedex 13
France
Tel: +33 1 46 46 16 00
Fax: +33 1 46 46 16 01
Web site:
www.courrierinternational.com

Economist Newspaper
25 St James's Street
London SW1A 1HG
United Kingdom
Tel: +44 20 7830 7000
Fax: +44 20 7839 2968
Web site: www.economist.com

Financial Times
1 Southwark Bridge
London SE1 9HL
United Kingdom
Tel: +44 20 7873 3000
Fax: +44 20 7407 5700
Web site: www.ft.com

International Herald Tribune
6 bis, rue des Graviers
92521 Neuilly-sur-Seine Cedex
France
Tel: +33 1 41 43 93 00
Fax: +33 1 41 43 93 38
Web site: www.iht.com

Le Monde
21 bis, rue Claude-Bernard
75242 Paris Cedex 05
France
Tel: +33 1 42 17 20 00
Fax: +33 1 42 17 21 21
Web site: www.lemonde.fr

News Agencies

Agence France Presse
11–13–15, place de la Bourse
75061 Paris Cedex 02
France
Tel: +33 1 40 41 46 46
(no general fax number)
Web site: www.afp.com

Associated Press News Agency
12 Norwich Street
London EC4A 1BP
United Kingdom
Tel: +44 20 7353 1515
Fax: +44 20 7353 8118
Web site: www.ap.org

Deutsche Presse-Agentur
Mittelweg 38
D-20148 Hamburg
Germany
Tel: +49 40 4113 0
Fax: +49 40 4113 2219
Web site: www.dpa.de

Information Telegraph Agency of Russia (ITAR-TASS)
10–12 Tverskoy blvd
Moscow 125993
Russia
Tel: +7 095 229 7925
Fax: +7 095 203 3049
Web site: www.itar-tass.com

Reuters Ltd
85 Fleet Street
London EC4P 4AJ
United Kingdom
Tel: +44 20 7250 1122
Fax: +44 20 7542 7921
Web site: www.reuters.com

Tanjug
11000 Belgrade
Obilicev venac 2
Serbia-Montenegro
Tel: +381 11 32 81 608
Fax: +381 11 633 550
Web site: www.tanjug.co.yu

Distributors of television news

Associated Press Television News (APTN)
The Interchange
Oval Road
London NW1 7DZ
United Kingdom
Tel: +44 20 7410 5200
Fax: +44 20 7410 5210
Web site: www.ap.org

Europe by Satellite
Avenue d'Auderghem 45
1040 Brussels
Belgium
Tel: +32 2 295 1173
Fax: +32 2 296 5956
Web site:
www.europa.eu.int/comm/ebs

European Broadcasting Union
Ancienne Route 17a
CH-1218 Geneva
Switzerland
Tel: +41 22 717 21 11
Fax: +41 22 747 40 00
Web site: www.ebu.ch

European News Exchange
45, boulevard Pierre Frieden
Kirchberg
L-1543 Luxembourg
Tel: +352 42 142 3101
Fax: +352 42 142 3768
Web site: www.enex.lu

Reuters Video News
85 Fleet Street
London EC4P 4AJ
United Kingdom
Tel: +44 20 7250 1122
Fax: +44 20 7542 3237
Web site: www.reuters.com

Television channels

ARTE
4, Quai du Chanoine Winterer
F-67080 Strasbourg Cedex
France
Tel: +33 3 88 14 22 22
Fax: +33 3 88 14.22.00
Web site: www.arte-tv.com

BBC World
Room 2524
Television Centre
Wood Lane
London W12 7RJ
United Kingdom
Tel: +44 20 8576 2062 / 20 8624 9443
Fax: +44 20 8749 7435
Web site: www.bbcworld.com

CNBC Europe
10 Fleet Place
London EC4M 7QS
United Kingdom
Tel: +44 20 7653 9427
Fax: +44 20 7653 9393
Web site: www.cnbceurope.com

CNN International
Turner House
Great Malborough Street
London W1F 7HS
United Kingdom
Tel: +44 20 7693 1000
Fax: +44 20 7693 1001
Web site: www.turner.com

DW-TV
Voltastrasse 6
D-13355 Berlin
Germany
Tel: +49 30 4646 0
Fax: +49 30 4631 998
Web site: www.dwworld.de

EuroNews
BP 161–60
Chemin des Mouilles
69131 Lyon Ecully Cedex
France
Tel: +33 4 72 18 80 00
Fax: +33 4 72 18 93 71
Web site: www.euronews.net

Radio stations

BBC World Service
News Intake
Room 440 SE
PO Box 76
Bush House
London WC2B 4PH
United Kingdom
Tel: +44 20 7240 3456
Fax: +44 20 7836 1810
Web site:
www.bbc.co.uk/worldservice

DW-RADIO
Kurt-Schumacher Strasse 3
D-53113 Bonn
Germany
Tel: +49 228 429 0
Fax: +49 228 429 3000
Web site: www.dwworld.de

Radio France Internationale (RFI)
116, avenue du Président-Kennedy
75016 Paris
France
Tel: +33 1 56 40 12 12
Fax: +33 1 56 40 44 71
Web site: www.rfi.fr

Radio Free Europe/Radio Liberty
Vinohradska 1
110 00 Prague 1
Czech Republic
Tel: +420 221 12 1111
Fax: +420 221 12 3630
Web site: www.rferl.org

Other journalists' organizations

European Institute for the Media
Düsseldorf headquarters
Zollhof 2A
DE-40221 Düsseldorf
Tel: +49 211–90 10 40
Fax: +49 211–90 10 456
Berlin Office
Ludwigkirchplatz 3–4
10719 Berlin
Tel: +49 30 880 07–218
Fax: +49 30 880 07–100

European Journalism Centre
Postal address:
Sonneville-lunet 10
6221 KT Maastricht, the Netherlands
Visiting address:
Avenue Ceramique 50
Maastricht, the Netherlands
Tel: +31 43 325 40 30
Fax: +31 43 321 26 26
Web site: www.ejc.nl

International Federation of Journalists
IPC-Residence Palace, Bloc C
Rue de la Loi 155
B-1040 Brussels
BELGIUM
Tel: +32 2 235 22 00
Fax: +32 2 235 22 19
Web site: www.ifj.org

Journalists@your service (help for journalists arriving in Brussels)
Résidence Palace
(Metro Schuman)
155 rue de la Loi, Bloc C
1040 Brussels
Tel: +32 2 235 22 07
Fax: +32 2 235 22 20
Web site:
www.brusselsreporter.org

Reporters without borders (Reporters sans frontières)
5, rue Geoffroy-Marie
75009 Paris – France
Tel: +33 1 44 83 84 84
Tel: +33 1 45 23 11 51
Web site: www.rsf.org

Appendix 2

European Broadcasting Union – active members

Albania

RTVSH – Radiotelevisioni Shqiptar
Rruga Ismail Quemali 11
AL – Tirana
Tel: +355 42 56 059 / 42 283 10
Fax: +355 422 77 45 / 423 08 42

Andorra

RTVA – Radio i Television d'Andorra SA
Baixada del Moli 24
AND – Andorra La Vella
Tel: +376 873 777
Fax: +376 863 242
Web site: Web site: www.rna.ad

Austria

ORF – Österreichischer Rundfunk
TV:
Würzburggasse 30
A-1136 Vienna
Tel: +43 1 878 78 0
Radio:
Argentinierstrasse 30A
A-1040 Vienna
Tel: +43 1 501 01 18 70 1
Fax: +43 1 501 01 18 699
Web site: www.orf.at

Belarus

Belarussian Radio Broadcasting
Ul. Krasnaya 4
BY-220807 Minsk

BTRC – Belaruskaja Tele-Radio Campanija
Ul. Makayonka 9
BY-220807 Minsk
Tel: +375 17 263 43 01
Fax: +375 17 264 81 82
Web site: www.tvr.by

Belgium

BE/RTBF-Radio-Télévision Belge de la Communauté Française
Cité Reyers – Local 11M31
Boulevard August Reyers 52
B-1044 Brussels
Tel: +32 2 737 21 11
Fax: +32 2 737 42 10
Web site: www.rtbf.be

VRT-Vlaamse Radio en Televisieomroep
Omroepcentrum
52 August Reyerslaan
B-1043 Brussels
Tel: +32 2 741 31 11
Fax: +32 2 734 93 51
Web site: www.vrt.be

Bosnia-Herzegovina

JSBIH/PBSBIH – Javni Radio Televizijski Servis
Public Broadcasting Service
Bosnia-Herzegovina
Blvd. Mese Selimovica 12
BIH – 71000 Sarajevo
Tel: +387 33 455 124 / 33 450 963
Fax: +387 33 461 523 / 33 455 104
Web site: www.rtvbih.ba

Bulgaria

BNR – Balgarsko Nationalno Radio
4, Dragan Tzankov Blvd.
BG-1040 Sofia
Tel: +359 2 933 64 63
Fax: +359 2 963 44 64

BNT – Balgarska Nationalna Televizija
29 San Stefano Str
BG-1504 Sofia
Tel: +359 2 661 149
Fax: +359 2 963 40 45

Croatia

HRT – Hrvatska Radiotelevizija – TV
Prisavlje 3
HR-10000 Zagreb
Tel: +01 6342–634
Fax: +01 6343–712
Web site: www.hrt.hr

Cyprus

CY/CBC –Cyprus Broadcasting Corporation
Broadcasting House
PO Box 4824
CY-Nicosia
Tel: +357 22 422 231
Fax: +357 22 314 050
Web site: www.cybc.com.cy

Czech Republic

CR-Cesky Rozhlas
Vinohradska 12
CZ – 120 99 Prague 2
Tel: +420 2 215 511 11
Fax: +420 2 232 10 20
Web site: www.rozhlas.cz

CT – Ceska Televise
Kavci Hory
CZ-14070 Prague 4
Tel: +420 2 6113 1111
Fax: +420 2 6121 2891
Web site: www.czech-tv.cz

Denmark

DK/TV2 – TV2 Danmark
Rugaardsvej 25
DK-5100 Odense
Tel: +45 65 91 12 44
Fax: +45 65 91 33 22
Web site: www.tv2.dk

DR – DR
TV – Byen
DK-2860 Soeborg
Tel: +45 35 20 30 40
Fax: +45 35 20 35 99
Web site: www.dr.dk

Estonia

ER – Eesti Raadio
Gonsiori 21
EE-15020 Tallinn
Tel: +372 611 4115
Fax: +372 611 4457
Web site: www.er.ee

ETV – Eesti Televisioon
12 Faehlmanni Street
EE-15029 Tallinn
Tel: +372 628 41 33
Fax: +372 628 41 55
Web site: www.etv.ee

Finland

FI/MTV – MTV Oy
00033 MTV 3
Ilmalantori 2
FIN-00240 Helsinki
Tel: +358 9 1500 1
Fax: +358 91 500 707
Web site: www.mtv3.fi

YLE – Yleisradio Oy
Radiokatu 5
FIN-00024 Yleisradio
Tel: +358 9 148 01
Fax: +358 9 1480 32 16
Web site: www.yle.fi

France

E1 – Europe 1
26 bis rue François 1er
F-75008 Paris
Tel: +33 1 44 31 90 00
Fax: +33 1 47 23 19 13

FT – France Télévision
Maison de France Télévision
7 Esplanade Henri de France
F-75907 Paris Cedex 15
Tel: +33 1 56 22 60 00
Fax: +33 1 56 22 61 08
Web site: www.francetv.fr

**GRF – Groupement des
Radiodiffuseurs Français de l'UER**
Maison de Radio France
116 avenue du Président Kennedy
F-75220 Paris Cedex 16
Tel: +33 1 56 40 50 32
Fax: +33 1 56 40 50 30

GRF/C+ – Canal +
85/89 Quai André Citroën
F-75711 Paris Cedex 15
Tel: +33 1 44 25 10 00
Fax: +33 1 44 25 12 34
Web site: www.cplus.fr

GRF/FT2 – France 2
Maison de France Télévision
7 Esplanade Henri de France
F-75907 Paris Cedex 15
Tel: +33 1 56 22 42 42
Fax: +33 1 56 22 60 89
Web site: www.france2.fr

GRF/FT3 – France 3
Maison de France Télévision
7 Esplanade Henri de France
F-75907 Paris Cedex 15
Tel: +33 1 56 22 30 30
Fax: +33 1 56 22 60 89
Web site: www.france3.fr

GRF/RFI – Radio France Internationale
116 avenue du Président Kennedy
BP 9616
F-75762 Paris Cedex 16
Tel: +33 1 56 40 12 12
Fax: +33 1 56 40 30 71
Web site: www.rfi.fr

GRF/SRF – Radio France
Maison de Radio France
116 avenue du Président Kennedy
F-75786 Paris Cedex 16
Tel: +33 1 56 40 22 22
Fax: +33 1 56 40 35 87
Web site: www.radiofrance.fr

GRF/TF1 – Télévision Française 1
1 quai du Point-du-Jour
F-92656 Boulogne Cedex
Tel: +33 1 41 41 12 34
Fax: +33 1 41 41 34 00
Web site: www.tfl.fr

Germany

ARD
Bertramstrasse 8
D-60320 Frankfurt
Tel: +49 69 59 06 07
Fax: +49 69 155 20 75
Web site: www.ard.de

ARD includes the following organizations:

ARD/BR – Bayerischer Rundfunk
Rundfunkplatz 1
D-80335 Münich
Tel: +49 89 5900 2324
Fax: +49 89 5900 3290
Web site: www.br-online.de

ARD/DFS – Deutsches Fernsehen
Arnulfstrasse 42
D-80335 Münich
Tel: +49 89 590 001
Fax: +49 89 590 032 49
Web site: www.DasErste.de

ARD/DLR – Deutschlandradio
Funkhaus Köln
Raderberggürtel 40
D-50968 Cologne
Tel: +49 221 345 0
Fax: +49 221 380 766

ARD/DLRB – Deautschlandradio – Berlin
Funkhaus Berlin
Hans-Rosenthal-Platz
D-10825 Berlin
Tel: +49 30 8503 0
Fax: +49 30 8503 9009

ARD/DW – Deutsche Welle
Kurt Schumacher Str.3
D-53113 Bonn
Tel: +49 228 429 0
Fax: +49 228 429 3000
Web site: www.dwworld.de

ARD/HR – Hessischer Rundfunk
Bertramstrasse 8
Postfach 101001
D-60320 Frankfurt
Tel: +49 69 155 1
Fax: +49 69 155 29 00
Web site: www.hr-online.de

ARD/MDR – Mitteldeutscher Rundfunk
Kantstr. 71–73
PO Box 67
D-04275 Leipzig
Tel: +49 341 300 7702
Fax: +49 341 300 7760
Web site: www.mdr.de

ARD/NDR – *Norddeutscher*
Rundfunk
Rothenbaumchaussee 132–134
D-20149 Hamburg
Tel: +49 40 415 60
Fax: +49 40 447 602
Web site: www.ndr.de

ARD/RBB – *Rundfunk Berlin-*
Brandenburg
Standort Berlin
Masurenalleÿ"ÿ5 8–14
D-14057 Berlin
Tel: +49 30 30 31 0
Fax: +49 30 30 15 0 62
Standort Potsdam
Marlene-Dietrich Allee 20
D-14482 Potsdam
Tel: +49 331 731 0
Fax: +49 331 731 35 71
Web site: www.rbb-online.de

ARD/RB-*Radio Bremen*
Bürgermeister-Spitta-Allee 45
D-28329 Bremen
Tel: +49 421 246 0
Fax: +49 421 246 10 10
Web site: www.radiobremen.de

ARD/SR – *Saarländischer Rundfunk*
Funkhaus Halberg
D-66100 Saarbrücken
Tel: +49 681 602 0
Fax: +49 681 602 38 74
Web site: www.sr-online.de

ARD/SWR – *Südwestrundfunk*
Neckarstrasse 230
D-70190 Stuttgart
Tel: +49 711 929 10 00
Fax: +49 711 929 10 10
Web site: www.swr.de

ARD/WDR – *Westdeutscher*
Rundfunk
Appellhofplatz 1
D-50667 Cologne
Tel: +49 221 220 21 00
Fax: +49 221 220 85 72
Web site: www.wdr.de

DW-TV
Voltastrasse 6
D-13355 Berlin
Tel: +49 30 4646 0
Fax: +49 30 4631 998

ZDF – Zweites Deutsches
Fernsehen
ZDF Strasse
D-55127 Mainz
Tel: +49 6131 70 1
Fax: +49 6131 70 21 57
Web site: www.zdf.de

Greece

ERT – Elliniki Radiophonia
Tileorassi SA
432 Messoghion Avenue
153 42 Aghia Paraskevi
GR-Athens
Tel: +30 210 606 60 00
Fax: +30 210 639 0652

Hungary

HU/MTV – Magyar Televizio
Szabadsag ter 17
H-1810 Budapest 5
Tel: +361 373 43 03
Fax: +361 373 41 33
Web site: www.mtv.hu

MR – Magyar Radio
Brody Sandor u. 5–7
H-1800 Budapest
Tel: +361 328 84 17
Fax: +361 328 70 04

Iceland

RUV – Rikisutvarpid (Icelandic National Broadcasting Service)
Efstaleiti 1
IS-150 Reykjavik
Tel: +354 515 30 00
Fax: +354 515 30 10
Web site: www.ruv.is

Ireland

RTE – Radio Telefis Eireann
Donnybrook
IE-Dublin 4
Tel: +353 1 208 3111
Fax: +353 1 208 3082
Web site: www.rte.ie

Italy

RAI –Radiotelevisione Italiana
Viale Mazzini 14
I-00195 Rome
Tel: +39 06 3686 4046
Fax: +39 06 3622 6422
Web site: www.rai.it

Latvia

LR – Latvijas Radio
Doma Laukums 8
LV-1505 Riga
Tel: +371 7 206 722
Fax: +371 7 206 709
Web site: www.latvijasradio.lv

LT – Latvijas Televizija
Zakusalas Krastmala 3
LV-1509 Riga
Tel: +371 720 03 16
Fax: +371 720 00 25
Web site: www.ltv.lv

Lithuania

LRT – Lietuvos Radijas Ir Televizija – TV
S.Konarskio 49
LT-2600 Vilnius
Tel: +370 52 363 209
Fax: +370 52 363 208
Web site: www.1rt.lt

Luxembourg

CLT – CLT Multi Media
45 Boulevard Pierre Frieden
L-2850 Luxembourg
Tel: +352 421 421
Fax: +352 421 427 790

ERSL – Establissement de Radiodiffusion Socioculturelle du Grand-Duché du Luxembourg
B.P. 1833
L-1018 Luxembourg
Tel: +352 44 00 441
Fax: +352 4400 44 980
Web site: www.100komma7.lu

Former Yugoslav Republic of Macedonia

MKRTV – MKRTV
Bulevar Goce Delcev bb
MK-1000 Skopje
Tel: +389 2 311 33 70
Fax: +389 23 225 212
Web site: www.mtv.com.mk

Malta

MT/PBS – Public Broadcasting Services Ltd
PO Box 82
MT-Valletta CMR 01
Tel: +356 21 249 060
Fax: +356 21 244 601
Web site: www.pbs.com.mt

Moldova

TRM – Teleradio-Moldova
64 Hincesti Str.
MD-2028 Chisinau
Tel: +373 22 739 194
Fax: +373 22 73 94 84

Monaco

GRMC – Groupement de Radiodiffuseurs Monégasques
6 bis Quai Antoine 1er
MC-98011 Monaco Cedex
Tel: +377 93 15 14 15
Fax: +377 93 50 66 97
Web site: www.rmc.mc

GRMC/MCR – Monte-Carlo Radiodiffusion
10–12 quai Antonie 1er
MC-98000 Monaco
Tel: +377 97 97 47 00
Fax: +377 97 97 47 07
Web site: www.mcr.mc

GRMC/TMC – Télé Monte-Carlo
6 bis Quai Antonie 1er
MC-98011 Monaco Cedex
Tel: +377 93 15 14 15
Fax: +377 93 50 66 97

Netherlands

NL/NPB – Nederlands Public Broadcasting
Postbus 26444
NL-1202 JJ Hilversum
Tel: +31 35 677 92 22
Fax: +31 35 677 26 49
Web site: www.omroep.nk or www.publickeomroep.nl

NPB/AVRO – Algemene Omroepvereniging AVRO
Postbus 2
NL-1200 JA Hilversum
Tel: +31 35 671 79 11
Fax: +31 35 671 70 59
Web site: www.avro.nl

NPB/EO – Vereniging de Evangelische Omroep
Postbus 21000
NL-1202 BB Hilversum
Tel: +31 35 647 47 47
Fax: +31 35 647 47 27

NPB/KRO – Katholieke Radio Omroep
Postbus 23000
NL-1202 EA Hilversum
Tel: +31 35 671 39 11
Fax: +31 35 671 31 28

NPB/NCRV – Nederlandse Christelijke Radio Vereniging
Postbus 25000
NL-1202 HB Hilversum
Tel: +31 35 671 99 11
Fax: +31 35 671 92 85

NPB/NOB – Netherlands Broadcasting Services Corporation
Postbus 10
NL-1200 JB Hilversum
Tel: +31 35 677 91 11
Fax: +31 35 677 4727
Web site: www.nob.nl

NPB/NOS – Nederlandse Omroep Stichting
Postbus 26600
NL-1202 JT Hilversum
Tel: +31 35 677 92 22
Fax: +31 35 624 20 23
Web site: www.omroep.nl/nos

NPB/NPS – Nederlandse Programma Stichting
PO Box 29000
NL-1202 MA Hilversum
Tel: +31 35 677 93 33
Fax: +31 35 677 45 17
Web site: www.omroep.nl

NPB/RNW – Radio Netherlands International
Postbus 222
NL-1200 JG Hilversum
Tel: +31 35 672 42 11
Fax: +31 35 672 42 07
Web site: www.rnw.nl

NPB/TROS – Televisie Radio Omroep Stichting
Postbus 28450
NL-1202 LL Hilversum
Tel: +31 35 671 57 15
Fax: +31 35 671 54 60

NPB/VARA – Omroepvereniging Vara
Postbus 175
NL-1200 AD Hilversum

Tel: +31 35 671 19 11
Fax: +31 35 671 13 13

NPB/VPRO – Omroepvereniging VPRO
Postbus 11
NL-1200 JC Hilversum
Tel: +31 35 671 29 11
Fax: +31 35 671 21 00

Norway

NO/TV2 – TV2 Gruppen AS
Postbooks 2 Sentrum
N-0101 Oslo
Tel: +47 22 314 700
Fax: +47 22 314 701
Web site: www.tv2.no

NRK – Norsk Rikskringkasting As
N-0340 Oslo
Tel: +47 23 04 70 00
Fax: +47 23 04 77 99
Web site: www.nrk.no

Poland

PRT/PR – Polskie Radio SA
AL. Niepodleglosci 77/85
PL-00977 Warsaw
Tel: +48 22 645 90 00
Fax: +48 22 645 59 24
Web site: www.radio.com.pl

PRT/TVP – Telewizja Polska SA
UI.J.P. Woronicza 17
Box 211
PL-00999 Warsaw
Tel: +48 22 547 76 14
Fax: +48 22 547 42 28
Web site: www.tvp.com.pl

Portugal

RDP – Radiodifusao Portuguesa Ep
Avenida Eng. Duarte Pacheco 26
P-1070–110 Lisbon
Tel: +351 21 382 0000
Fax: +351 21 385 4137
Web site: www.rdp.pt

RTP – Radiotelevisao Portuguesa – Servico Publico de Televisao S.A.
Avenida 5 de Outubro 197
P-1050 Lisbon
Tel: +351 21 7 947 000
Fax: +351 217 947 669
Web site: www.rtp.pt

Romania

RO/TVR – Televiziunea Romana
Calea Dorobantilor nr.191
PO Box 63
RO-79757 Bucharest 1
Tel: +40 21 230 5710
Fax: +40 21 230 71 01
Web site: www.tvr.ro

ROR – Societatea Romana de Radiodifuziune
Strada General
Berthelot no 60–64
RO-70747 Bucharest
Tel: +40 21 303 1432
Fax: +40 21 312 1057

Russia

C1R – Channel One Russia
Akademika Koroleva Street 12
RU-127000 Moscow
Tel: +7 095 217 88 27
Fax: + 7 095 215 12 84
Web site: www.1tv.ru

RDO – Radio Dom Ostankino
Pyatniskaya Street 25
RU-113326 Moscow
Tel: +7 095 950 65 07
Fax: +7 095 959 42 04

RDO/MK – Radio Mayak
Pyatniskaya Street 25
RU-115326 Moscow
Tel: +7 095 950 67 67
Fax: +7 095 959 42 04
Web site: www.radiomayak.ru

RDO/OP – Radio Orpheus
Pyatnitskaya Street 25
RU-115326 Moscow
Tel: +7 095 222 01 93
Fax: +7 095 222 01 93

RDO/VOR – Voice of Russia
Pyatnitskaya Street 25
RU-115326 Moscow
Tel: +7 095 950 63 31
Fax: +7 095 950 63 21
Web site: www.vor.ru

RTR – Rossijskoe Teleradio All-Russian State TV and Radio Broadcasting Company
5th Yamskogo Polya Street 19/21
RU-125124 Moscow
Tel: +7 095 745 4978
Fax: +7 095 975 2611
Web site: www.ptp.ru

San Marino

SM/RTV – San Marino RTV
Viale J. F. Kennedy 13
San Marino A-3
SM-43031 San Marino
Tel: +378 882 000
Fax: +378 882 850

Serbia and Montenegro

UJRT/RTCG – Radiotelevizija Crne Gore
Cetinjski put b.b.
CS-81000 Podgorica
Tel: +381 81 244 911
Fax: +381 81 225 930

UJRT/RTS – Radiotelevizija Srbije
Abardareva 1
PO Box 880
CS-11000 Belgrade
Tel: +381 11 321 2200
Fax: +381 11 321 2211

UJRTSCG – Association of Public Broadcasting Services of Serbia and Montenegro
Beogradska 70   PO Box 284
CS-11000 Belgrade
Tel: +381 11 323 0194
Fax: +381 11 323 4355

Slovakia

SK/SR – Slovensky Rozhlas
Mytna 1
PO Box 55
SK-817 55 Bratislava 15
Tel: +421 2 57 27 35 60
Fax: +421 2 52 49 89 23
Web site: www.slovakradio.sk

SK/STV – Slovenska Televizia
Mlybska Dolina
SK-845 45 Bratislava
Tel: +421 2 6061 1111
Fax: +421 2 6061 4403
Web site: www.stv.sk

Slovenia

RTVSLO – Radiotelevizija Slovenija
Kolodvorska 2
SI-1550 Ljubljana
Tel: +386 1 475 21 51
Fax: +386 1 475 21 50

Spain

COPE – Cadena Cope Radio
Alfonso XI, 4
E-28014 Madrid
Tel: +34 91 309 00 00
Fax: +34 91 401 23 54

RNE – Radio Nacional de Espana
Casa de la Radio
Prado del Rey
E-28223 Pozuelo de Alarcon
(Madrid)
Tel: +34 91 346 16 12
Fax: +34 91 346 12 49

RTVE – Radio Television Espanola
Centro RTVE
Prado del Rey
E-28223 Pozuelo de Alarcon
(Madrid)
Tel: +34 91 581 70 00
Fax: +34 91 581 54 12
Web site: www.rtve.es

SER – Sociedad Espanola de Radiodifusion
32 Gran Via
Apt. de Cor. 745
E-28013 Madrid
Tel: +34 91 347 07 00
Fax: +34 91 347 07 09

TVE – Television Espanola
Centro RTVE
Prado del Rey
E-28223 Pozuelo de Alarcon
(Madrid)
Tel: +34 91 346 80 00
Fax: +34 91 346 30 55
Web site: www.kftv.com

Sweden

STR/SR – Swedish Radio Ltd
Oxenstiernsgatan 20
S-105 10 Stockholm
Tel: +46 8 784 50 00
Fax: +46 8 660 15 84

STR/SVT – Swedish Television Company
Oxenstiernsgatan 26–34
S-105 10 Stockholm
Tel: +46 8 784 00 00
Fax: +46 8 784 15 00
Web site: www.svt.se

STR/UR – Swedish Educational Broadcasting Company
Tulegatan 7
S-113 95 Stockholm
Tel: +46 8 784 40 00
Fax: +46 8 784 43 91

Switzerland

SRG SSR idée suisse / SF DRS – Schweizer Fernsehen DRS
Fernsehstrasse 1–4
CH-8052 Zürich
Tel: +41 1 305 66 11
Fax: +41 1 305 56 60
Web site: www.sfdrs.ch

SRG SSR idée suisse / SSR – Sociéte Suisse de Radiodiffusion et Télévision
Giacomettistrasse 1
Case postale 26
CH-3000 Berne15
Tel: +41 31 350 91 11
Fax: +41 31 350 92 56
Web site: www.srgssrideesuisse.ch

SRG SSR idée suisse/ SR DRS – Schweizer Radio DRS
Novarastrasse 2
CH-4059 Basle
Tel: +41 61 365 34 84
Fax: +41 61 365 34 83
Web site: www.srdrs.ch

SRG SSR idée suisse/RR – Radio Rumantsch
Via dal Teater 1
CH-7002 Cuira
Tel: +41 81 255 75 75
Fax: +41 81 255 75 00
Web site: www.rtr.ch

SRG SSR idée suisse/RSR – Radio Suisse Romande
Maison de la Radio
Avenue du Temple 40
CH-1010 Lausanne
Tel: + 41 21 318 11 11
Fax: +41 21 652 37 19
Web site: www.rsr.ch

SRG SSR idée suisse/RTSI – Radiotelevisione Svizzera di Lingua Italiana
Via Canevascini
Casella postale
CH-6093 Lugano
Tel: +41 91 803 51 11
Fax: +41 91 803 53 55
Web site: www.rtsi.ch

**SRG SSR idée suisse/swissinfo –
Swissinfo/Radio Suisse
Internationale**
Giacomettistrasse 1
Case postale
CH-3000 Berne 15
Tel: +41 31 350 92 22
Fax: +41 31 350 97 44
Web site: www.swissinfo.ch

**SRG SSR idée suisse/TSR –
Télévision Suisse Romande**
20 Quai Ernest Ansermet
CH-1205 Geneva
Tel: +41 22 708 20 20
Fax: +41 22 708 98 00
Web site: www.tsr.ch

Turkey

**TRT- Turkiye Radyo-Televizyon
Kurumu**
TRT Sitesi, 4, Kat
A Blok No 427
TR-06109 Ankara
Tel: +90 312 490 10 58
Fax: +90 312 490 11 09
Web site: www.trt.net.tr

Ukraine

**NRU – Natsionalna
Radiokompanya Ukrainy**
Hreshchatyk Street 26
UA-01001 Kiev
Tel: +380 44 221 61 24
Fax: +380 44 229 34 77

**NTU – Natsionalna
Telekompanya Ukrainy**
42, vul. Melnykova
UA-04119 Kiev
Tel: +380 44 241 38 95
Fax: +380 44 211 08 56
Web site: www.ntu.com.ua

United Kingdom

**BBC – British Broadcasting
Corporation**
Broadcasting House
Portland Place
GB-London W1A 1AA
Tel: +44 207 580 44 68
Fax: +44 207 637 16 30
Web site: www.bbc.co.uk

BBC Network Radio
Broadcasting House
Portland Place
GB-London W1A 1AA
Tel: +44 207 580 44 68
Fax: +44 207 765 29 03

BBC Television
Television Centre
Wood Lane
GB-London W12 7RJ
Tel: +44 208 743 80 00
Fax: +44 207 749 75 20

ITV Wales
The TV Centre
Culverhouse Cross
GB-Cardiff CF5 6XJ
Tel: +44 2920 59 05 90
Fax: +44 2920 59 71 83

UKIB/C4 – Channel 4 Television
124 Horseferry Road
GB-London SW1P 2TX
Tel: +44 207 396 44 44
Fax: +44 207 306 83 66
Web site: www.channel4.com

UKIB/ITV – ITV Network Ltd.
200 Gray's Inn Road
GB-London WC1X 8HF
Tel: +44 207 843 80 00
Fax: +44 207 843 81 58
Web site: www.itv.co.uk

**UKIB/ITV/ANG – Anglia
Television**
Anglia House
GB-Norwich NR1 3JG
Tel: +44 1603 61 51 51
Fax: +44 1603 63 10 32

**UKIB/ITV/BTV – Border
Television**
Television Centre
GB-Carlisle CA1 3NT
Tel: +44 1228 5251 01
Fax: +44 1228 5413 84

**UKIB/ITV/CAR – Carlton
Television**
101 St. Martin's Lane
GB-London WC2N 4AX
Tel: +44 207 240 40 00
Fax: +44 207 240 41 71

**UKIB/ITV/CEN – Central
Independent Television**
Carlton Broadcasting
Gas Street
GB-Birmingham B1 2JT
Tel: +44 121 643 9898
Fax: +44 121 634 4606

**UKIB/ITV/CHA – Channel
Television**
Television Centre
La Pouquelaye
GB-St Helier, Jersey, Channel
Islands
Tel: +44 1534 816 816
Fax: +44 1534 816 817

**UKIB/ITV/GPN – Grampian
Television Ltd**
Queen's Cross
GB-Aberdeen AB15 3XJ
Tel: +44 1224 848 848
Fax: +44 1224 848 800

**UKIB/ITV/GRA – Granada
Television**
Quay Street
GB-Manchester M60 9EA
Tel: +44 161 832 72 11
Fax: +44 161 827 20 29

UKIB/ITV/HTV – HTV
UKIB/ITV/LWT – London
Weekend Television
South Bank Television Centre
Kent House Upper Ground
GB-London SE1 9LT
Tel: +44 20 7620 1620
Fax: +44 20 7737 8431

**UKIB/ITV/MER – Meridian
Broadcasting**
Television Centre
GB-Southampton SO14 OPZ
Tel: +44 23 8022 2555
Fax: +44 23 8033 5050

**UKIB/ITV/STV – Scottish
Television**
200 Renfield Street
GB-Glasgow G2 3PR
Tel: +44 141 300 3000
Fax: +44 141 300 3030

**UKIB/ITV/TTT – Tyne Tees
Television**
Television Centre
City Road
GB-Newcastle-upon-Tyne NE1 2AL
Tel: +44 191 261 01 81
Fax: +44 191 261 23 02

**UKIB/ITV/UTV – Ulster
Television**
Havelock House
Ormeau Road
GB-Belfast BT7 1EB
Tel: +44 2890 32 81 22
Fax: +44 2890 24 66 95

UKIB/ITV/WES – Westcountry Television
Langage Science Park
Western Wood Way
GB-Plymouth PL7 5BQ
Tel: +44 1752 33 33 33
Fax: +44 1752 33 30 33

UKIB/ITV/YTV – Yorkshire Television
Television Centre
Kirkstall Road
GB-Leeds LS3 1JS
Tel: +44 113 243 82 83
Fax: +44 113 242 38 67

UKIB/S4C – Sianel 4 Cymru
Parc Ty Glas
Llanishen
GB-Cardiff CF14 5DU
Tel: +44 29 2074 7444
Fax: +44 29 2075 4444

Vatican City State

RV – Radio Vaticana
Direzione Generale
VA-00120 Citta del Vaticano
Tel: +39 06 69 88 39 45
Fax: +39 06 69 88 32 37
Web site: www.vaticanradio.org

Appendix 3

European and International Organizations based in Europe

European Union

Allée du Printemps
BP 1024/F
F – 67070 Strasbourg
France
Tel: + 33 3 88 17 40 01
Web site: www.europarl.eu.int

Bâtiment Eastman

135, Rue Belliard
B – 1040 Brussels
Belgium
Tel: + 32 2 230 50 90/230 64 83
Web site: www.eca.eu.int

Committee of the Regions

Rue Montoyer, 92 – 102
B – 1000 Brussels

Belgium
Tel: + 32 2 282 22 11
Fax: + 32 2 282 23 25
Web site: www.cor.eu.int

Council of the European Union

Rue de la Loi 175
B – 1048 Brussels
Belgium
Tel: + 32 2 285 61 11
Fax: + 32 2 285 73 97/81
Press and current information:
Tel: +32 2 285 81 11/68 08/
74 59/63 19
Fax: + 32 2 285 80 26/ 85 41
http://ue.eu.int/

Court of Auditors
12, Rue Alcide de Gasperi
L – 1615 Luxembourg
Tel: + 35 2 43 98 43 981
Fax: + 35 2 43 93 42

Court of First Instance
Rue du Fort Niedergrunewald
L – 2925 Luxembourg
Tel: + 35 2 43 031
Fax: + 35 2 43 03 210 0

Court of Justice of the European Communities
Palais de la Cour de Justice
Bd Konrad Adenauer
Kirchberg
L – 2925 Luxembourg
Tel: + 35 2 43 031
Fax: + 35 2 43 03 260 0
Web site: www.curia.eu.int

European Central Bank
Eurotower
Kaiserstrasse 29
D-60311 Frankfurt am Main
Germany
Tel: + 49 69 1344 0
Fax: +49 69 1344 6000
Web site: www.ecb.int

European Commission
Rue de la Loi 200
B – 1049 Brussels
Belgium
Tel: + 32 2 299 11 11
Fax: + 32 2 295 01 38
http://europa.eu.int/comm

European Economic and Social Committee
Rue Ravenstein 2
B – 1000 Brussels
Belgium
Tel: + 32 2 546 90 11

Fax: + 32 2 513 48 93
Web site: www.esc.eu.int

European Investment Bank (EIB)
Bld Konrad Adenauer 100
L – 2950 Luxembourg
Tel: + 35 2 43 791
Fax: + 35 2 43 77 04
Web site: www.eib.eu.int

European Ombudsman
1, Av. du Président Robert
Schuman
B.P. 403
F – 67001 Strasbourg Cedex
France
Tel: +33 3 88 17 23 13
Fax: + 33 3 88 17 90 62
Web site: www.euro-ombuds-man.eu.int

European Parliament
Plateau du Kirchberg
B.P. 1601
L – 2929 Luxembourg
Tel: + 35 2 43 001
Fax: + 35 2 43 00 294 94
Rue Wiertz, 60
B-1047 Brussels
Belgium
Tel: + 32 2 284 21 11

EUROPOL (European Law Enforcement Cooperation)
Europol Headquarters
Raamweg 47
The Hague
The Netherlands
Postal address:
PO Box 90850
NL-2509 LW
The Hague
Tel: + 31 70 302 5000
Fax: + 31 70 345 5896
Web site: www.europol.eu.int

Humanitarian Aid Office (ECHO)
Rue de Genève 1
B – 1140 Brussels
Belgium
Tel: + 32 2 295 42 49/299 29 69
Fax: + 32 2 295 45 78

Other International Organizations based in Europe

Assembly of Western European Union
43 Avenue du Président Wilson
F-75775 Paris Cedex
France
Tel: + 33 1 53 67 22 00
Fax: + 33 1 53 67 22 01
Web site: www.assembly.weu.int

Council of Europe
Avenue de l'Europe
F – 67075 Strasbourg Cedex
France
Tel: +33 3 88 41 20 00
Fax: +33 3 88 41 27 81
Web site: www.coe.int

European Bank for Reconstruction and Development (EBRD)
One Exchange Square
London EC2A 2JN
United Kingdom
Tel: + 44 20 7338 6000
Fax: + 44 20 7338 6100
Web site: www.ebrd.com

European Conference of Ministers of Transports (ECMT)
2–4 rue Louis David
F-75016 Paris
France
Tel: + 33 1 45 24 97 10/ 16
Fax: + 33 1 45 24 97 42 / 13 22
Web site: www.oecd.org/cem

European Court of Human Rights
Avenue de l'Europe
F – 67075 Strasbourg Cedex
France
Tel: +33 3 88 41 20 18
Fax: +33 3 88 41 27 30
Web site: www.echr.coe.int

European Cultural Foundation (ECF)
Jan van Goyenkade 5
NL – Amsterdam 1075 HN
The Netherlands
Tel: + 31 20 676 02 22
Fax: + 31 20 675 22 31 / 20 573 38 68
Web site: www.eurocult.org

European Free Trade Association (EFTA)
9–11 rue de Varembé
CH – 1211 Geneva 20
Switzerland
Tel: + 41 22 749 1111 / 22 332 2626
Fax: + 41 22 733 9291 / 22 332 2699
http://secretariat.efta.int

European Organization for Nuclear Research (CERN)
CH – 1211 Genena 23
Switzerland
Tel: + 41 22 767 6111
Fax: + 41 22 767 6555
Web site: www.cern.ch

European Organization for the Safety of Air Navigation (EURO-CONTROL)
Rue de la Fusée, 96
B – 1130 Brussels
Belgium
Tel: + 32 2 729 90 11
Fax: + 32 2 729 90 44
Web site: www.eurocontrol.be

European Patent Organization (EPO)
Erhardstrasse 27
D – 80331 Munich 2
Germany
Tel: + 49 89 2399 0
Fax: + 49 89 2399 4465
Web site:
www.european-patent-office.org

European Space Agency (ESA)
8–10 rue Mario-Nikis
F – 75738 – Paris Cedex 15, France
Tel: +33 1 53 69 71 55/ 53 69 76 54/
53 69 75 60
Fax: + 331 53 69 76 90
Web site: www.esa.int

European Trade Union Confederation (ETUC)
Boulevard Roi Albert II, 5
B – 1210 Brussels
Belgium
Tel: + 32 2 224 04 11/39
Fax: + 32 2 224 04 54/55
Web site: www.etuc.org

Food and Agricultural Organization of the United Nations (FAO)
Via delle Terme di Caracalla
I – 00100 Rome
Italy
Tel: + 39 06 57051
Fax: + 39 06 5705 3152
Web site: www.fao.org

International Atomic Energy Agency (IAEA)
Wagramerstrasse 5
PO Box 100
A – 1400 Vienna
Austria
Tel: + 43 1 260 00

Fax: + 43 1 260 06/7
Web site: www.iaea.or.at

International Committee of the Red Cross (ICRC)
19 Avenue de la Paix
CH – 1202 Geneva
Switzerland
Tel: + 41 22 734 6001
Fax: + 41 22 733 2057
Web site: www.icrc.org

International Court of Justice (ICJ)
Peace Palace
Carnegieplein 2
NL – 2517 KJ The Hague
The Netherlands
Tel: + 31 70 302 2323
Fax: + 31 70 364 9928
Web site: www.icj-cij.org

International Criminal Police Organization (OIPC)
General Secretariat
200, Quai Charles de Gaulle
F – 69009 Lyon
France
Tel: +33 4 72 44 70 00
Fax: +33 4 72 44 71 63
Web site: www.interpol.int

International Criminal Tribunal for the former Yugoslavia (ICTY)
Churchillplein 1
PO Box 13888
NL – 2501 EW La Haye
The Netherlands
Tel: + 31 70 416 5000/5343
Fax: + 31 70 512 534
Web site: www.un.org\icty

International Federation of Red Cross and Red Crescent Societies
17 Chemin des Crêts
Petit-Saconnex
PO Box 372
CH – 1211 Geneva 19
Switzerland
Tel: + 41 22 730 4222
Fax: : + 41 22 733 0395
Web site: www.ifrc.org

International Fund for Agricultural Development (IFAD)
107 Via del Serafico
I – 00142 Rome
Italy
Tel: + 39 06 54591
Fax: + 39 06 504 34 63 / 504 25 13
Web site: www.ifad.org

International Labour Organization (ILO)
4, route des Morillons
CH – 1211 Geneva 22
Switzerland
Tel: + 41 22 798 6111
Fax: + 41 22 798 8686/85
Web site: www.ilo.org

International Maritime Organization (IMO)
4 Albert Embankment
UK – London SE1 7SR
United Kingdom
Tel: + 44 20 7735 7611
Fax: + 44 20 7587 3210
Web site: www.imo.org

International Organization for Migration (IOM)
17 Route des Morillons
PO Box 71
CH – 1211 Geneva 19
Switzerland

Tel: + 41 22 717 9111
Fax: + 41 22 798 6150
Web site: www.iom.int

International Telecommunication Union (ITU)
Place des Nations
CH – 1211 Geneva 20
Switzerland
Tel: + 41 22 730 5115 (SG)
Tel: + 41 22 730 5595 (Vice SG)
Fax: + 41 22 733 5137
Web site: www.itu.ch

Interparliamentary Union (IPU)
Chemin du Pommier 5
PO Box 330
CH – 1218 Le Grand-Saconnex
Geneva
Switzerland
Tel: + 41 22 919 4150
Fax: + 41 22 919 4160
Web site: www.ipu.org

Nordic Council of Ministers
Store Strandstraede 18
DK – 1255 Copenhagen K
Denmark
Tel: + 45 33 96 02 00
Fax: + 45 33 96 02 02
Web site: www.norden.org

North Atlantic Treaty Organization (NATO)
Blvd Leopold III
B – 1110 Brussels
Belgium
Tel: + 32 2 707 41 11
Fax: + 32 2 707 46 66/ 12 52
Web site: www.nato.int

Nuclear Energy Agency of the OECD (NEA)
La Seine St Germain
12 blvd des îles
F-92130 Issy-Les-Moulineaux
France
Tel: + 33 1 45 24 82 00/10 10
Fax: + 33 1 45 24 11 10
Web site: www.nea.fr

Office of the High Representative in Bosnia & Herzegovina (OHR)
Emerika Bluma 1
71000 Sarajevo
Bosnia and Herzegovina
Tel: +387 33 283 500
Fax: +387 33 283 501
Web site: www.ohr.int

Office of the United Nations High Commissioner for Human Rights (OHCHR-UNOG)
Palais des Nations
8–14 avenue de la Paix
CH – 1211 Geneva 10
Switzerland
Tel: + 41 22 917 9000
Fax: + 41 22 917 0111/917 90 16
Web site: www.unhchr.ch

Organization for Economic Co-operation and Development (OECD)
2 rue André Pascal
F-75775 Paris Cedex 16
France
Tel: + 33 1 45 24 82 00
Fax: + 33 1 45 24 85 00
Web site: www.oecd.org

Organization of the Petroleum Exporting Countries (OPEC)
Obere Donaustrasse 93
A – 1020 Vienna
Austria
Tel: + 43 1 211 12 279
Fax: + 43 1 214 98 27
Web site: www.opec.org

OSCE Parliamentary Assembly
Rådhuustraede 1
DK – 1466 Copenhagen K
Denmark
Tel: + 45 33 37 80 40
Fax: + 45 33 37 80 30
Web site: www.oscepa.org

OSCE Secretariat
Kärntner Ring 5–7, 4th Floor
A – 1010 Vienna, Austria
Tel: + 43 1 514 36 0
Fax: + 43 1 514 36 96
Web site: www.osce.org

Southeast European Cooperative Initiative (SECI)
OSCE Congress Center
Office of the SECI Co-ordinator
Heldenplatz 1
A – 1600 Vienna
Austria
Tel: + 43 1 531 37 422/423
Fax: + 43 1 531 37 420
Web site: www.secinet.org or www.unece.org/seci

Stability Pact for South-Eastern Europe
rue Wiertz 50
B-1050 Brussels
Belgium
Tel: +32 2 401 87 00
Fax: +32 2 401 87 12
Web site: www.stabilitypact.org

The Commonwealth
Marlborough House
Pall Mall
London SW1Y 5HX
United Kingdom
Tel: + 44 20 7747 6500
Fax: + 44 20 7930 0827
Web site: www.thecommon-
wealth.org

**Union of Industrial and
Employer's Confederation of
Europe (UNICE)**
Avenue de Cortenbergh, 168
B – 1000 Brussels
Belgium
Tel: + 32 2 237 65 11
Fax: + 32 2 231 14 45
Web site: www.unice.org

**United Nations Children's Fund
(UNICEF)**
5 – 7 Avenue de la Paix
CH-1211 Geneva 10
Switzerland
Tel: + 41 22 909 5111
Fax: + 41 22 909 5900
Web site: www.unicef.org

**United Nations Conference on
Trade and Development
(UNCTAD)**
Palais des nations
8–14 Avenue de la Paix
CH – 1211 Genena 10
Switzerland
Tel: + 41 22 907 1234
Fax: + 41 22 907 0043
Web site: www.unctad.org

**United Nations Educational,
Scientific and Cultural
Organization (UNESCO)**
7 Place de Fontenoy
75732 Paris 07 SP

France
Tel: + 33 1 45 68 10 00
Fax: + 33 1 45 67 16 90 / 68 57 02
Web site: www.unesco.org

**United Nations High
Commissioner for Refugees
(UNHCR)**
Case Postale 2500
CH – 1211 Geneva 2 Dépôt
Switzerland
Tel: + 41 22 739 8502/ 8111
Fax: + 41 22 739 7315/ 7377
Web site: www.unhcr.ch/

**United Nations Industrial
Development Organization
(UNIDO)**
Vienna International Centre
P.O. Box 300
A – 1400 Vienna
Austria
Tel: + 43 1 260 26 0
Fax: + 43 1 269 2669
Web site: www.unido.org

**United Nations Interim
Administration in Kosovo
(UNMIK)**
Pristina, Kosovo, Serbia and
Montenegro
Tel: +381 38 504 604 + extension
Fax: +1 212 963 8113
Web site: www.unmikonline.org/

**United Nations Office on Drugs
and Crime (UNODC)**
Vienna International Centre
P.O. Box 500
A – 1400 Vienna
Austria
Tel: +43 1 260 60 0
Fax: +43 1 260 60 5866
Web site: www.unodc.org

Western European Union (WEU)
15 rue de l'Association
B – 1000 Brussels
Belgium
Tel: + 32 2 500 44 12
Fax: + 32 2 500 44 70
Web site: www.weu.int

World Customs Organization (WCO)
30, rue du Marché
B – 1210 Brussels
Belgium
Tel: + 32 2 209 92 11
Fax: + 32 2 209 92 92
Web site: www.wcoomd.org

World Food Programme (WFP)
Via Cesare Giulio Viola, 68
Parco dei Medici
00148 Rome
Italy
Tel: + 39 06 65131
Fax: + 39 06 6513 2840
Web site: www.wfp.org

World Health Organization (WHO)
20 avenue Appia
CH – 1211 Geneva 27
Switzerland
Tel: + 41 22 791 2111
Fax: + 41 22 791 3111/733 5428/ 791 0746
Web site: www.who.int

World Intellectual Property Organization (WIPO)
34 Chemin des Colombettes
PO Box 18
CH – 1211 Geneva 20
Switzerland
Tel: + 41 22 338 9111 / 733 5428
Fax: + 41 22 733 5428
Web site: www.wipo.int or www.ompi.int

World Meteorological Organization (WMO)
7bis Avenue de la Paix – CP 2300
CH – 1211 Geneva 2
Switzerland
Tel: + 41 22 730 8111 / 8220 (SG)
Fax: + 41 22 730 8181
Web site: www.wmo.ch

World Tourism Organization (WTO)
Capitan Haya 42
E – 28020 Madrid
Spain
Tel: + 34 91 567 81 00
Fax: + 34 91 571 37 33
Web site: www.world-tourism.org

World Trade Organization (WTO)
Centre William Rappard
154 rue de Lausanne
CH – 1211 Geneva 2
Switzerland
Tel: + 41 22 739 5111
Fax: + 41 22 739 4206
Web site: www.wto.org

Appendix 4

International Federation of Journalists

Declaration of Principles on the Conduct of Journalists

This international Declaration is proclaimed as a standard of professional conduct for journalists engaged in gathering, transmitting, disseminating and commenting on news and information in describing events.

1. Respect for truth and for the right of the public to truth is the first duty of the journalist.
2. In pursuance of this duty, the journalist shall at all times defend the principles of freedom in the honest collection and publication of news, and of the right of fair comment and criticism.
3. The journalist shall report only in accordance with facts of which he/she knows the origin. The journalist shall not suppress essential information or falsify documents.
4. The journalist shall use only fair methods to obtain news, photographs and documents.
5. The journalist shall do the utmost to rectify any published information which is found to be harmfully inaccurate.
6. The journalist shall observe professional secrecy regarding the source of information obtained in confidence.

7. The journalist shall be aware of the danger of discrimination being furthered by the media, and shall do the utmost to avoid facilitating such discrimination based on, among other things, race, sex, sexual orientation, language, religion, political or other opinions, and national or social origins.

8. The journalist shall regard as grave professional offences the following:
   - plagiarism;
   - malicious misrepresentation;
   - calumny, slander, libel, unfounded accusations;
   - acceptance of a bribe in any form in consideration of either publication or suppression.

9. Journalists worthy of the name shall deem it their duty to observe faithfully the principles stated above. Within the general law of each country the journalist shall recognise in professional matters the jurisdiction of colleagues only, to the exclusion of every kind of interference by governments or others.

(Adopted by 1954 World Congress of the IFJ. Amended by the 1986 World Congress.)

Code of Conduct for Journalism and Media in Brussels

The expansion of news outlets in Brussels is recognition of the importance of the city as a hub for information on political, corporate and civil society affairs and further enhances the role of Brussels as one of the world's main news centres. This expansion, including new electronic media, provides flexible and versatile ways of providing information services in the public interest.

The growth of new media services also provides a welcome opportunity to restate and reaffirm the values of independent journalism in a city where lobbying interests and political policymakers compete for influence.

All journalists groups and media working from and based in Brussels should declare:

- their commitment to maintaining the highest standards of journalism, freedom of the press and pluralism;
- that all issues relating to the ethics of journalism should be a matter for journalists and media professionals alone;
- that the credibility of news and information depends on the highest ethical standards in the gathering, presentation and circulation of news material.

With these principles in mind, journalists' groups and news media organizations working in Brussels may consider adopting the following guidelines to promote editorial quality and internal and external transparency over media activity.
Media should:

1. define and publish, where appropriate, an editorial mission statement;

2. establish an internal editorial charter, in line with international standards, that secures the editorial independence of journalists and respects the norms of ethical practice (concerning, for example, right to act according to conscience, policy on receipt of inducements, gifts and facilities provided by public and private interests, dealing with complaints, etc);

3. develop and publish a code of editorial conduct regarding content quality (concerning, for example, respect for the truth, the need for clearly attributed sources, respect for non-discrimination and tolerance, the objective of doing no harm, protection of sources, etc);

4. ensure clear separation of advertising material and paid for space from editorial content in all publications, whatever the mode of dissemination;

5. implement internal standards for monitoring the personal interests of employees and owners that may compromise editorial independence and which must be made known to the Editor in Chief;

6. make available information on the external interests and ownership profile of the organization;

7. make available information regarding any benefits providing a pecuniary advantage provided by public authorities, including information on engagement in projects or activities funded by international organizations;

8. provide employment conditions and/or working relations that reflect adherence to national and international labour standards;

9. set up and publish details of a mechanism for dealing with complaints and making corrections where errors of fact have been made;

10. appoint or designate a member of the staff to act as an ombudsman or contact person to whom concerns and problems of an ethical and professional nature can be addressed.

IFJ, 2004
www.ifj.org

Index

Also published by Kogan Page
in association with the Institute of Public Relations

Ethics in Public Relations: A Guide to Best Practice
by Patricia J Parsons

and

PR in Practice Series
Series Editor: Anne Gregory

Kogan Page has joined forces with the Institute of Public Relations to publish this unique series which is designed specifically to meet the needs of the increasing numbers of people seeking to enter the public relations profession and the large band of existing PR professionals. Taking a practical, action-oriented approach, the books in the series concentrate on the day-to-day issues of public relations practice and management rather than academic history. They provide ideal primers for all those on IPR, CAM and CIM courses or those taking NVQs in PR. For PR practitioners, they provide useful refreshers and ensure that their knowledge and skills are kept up to date.

Titles in the series:

Creativity in Public Relations by Andy Green
Effective Media Relations by Michael Bland, Alison Theaker and David Wragg
Effective Writing Skills for Public Relations by John Foster
Managing Activism by Denise Deegan
Online Public Relations by David Phillips
Planning and Managing Public Relations Campaigns by Anne Gregory
Public Relations: A practical guide to the basics by Philip Henslowe
Public Relations in Practice edited by Anne Gregory
Public Relations Strategy by Sandra Oliver
Risk Issues and Crisis Management in Public Relations by Michael Regester and Judy Larkin
Running a Public Relations Department by Mike Beard

The above titles are available from all good bookshops. To obtain further information, please contact the publishers at the address below:

Kogan Page Limited
120 Pentonville Road
London N1 9JN
Tel: 020 7278 0433
Fax: 020 7837 6348
www.kogan-page.co.uk